Adobe® Acrobat® 4.0

Classroom in a Book

D1370199

Adobe

Contents

Getting Started

Welcome to the Adobe® Acrobat® application—the essential tool for universal document exchange. You can use Acrobat to publish virtually any document in Portable Document Format (PDF). Documents in PDF preserve the exact look and content of the originals, complete with fonts and graphics. Distribute your document by e-mail or store it on the World Wide Web, an intranet, a file system, or a CD. Other users can view your work on the Microsoft® Windows®, Mac® OS, and UNIX® platforms. A variety of tools and features let you add interactive elements to your document, from custom hyperlinks and media clips, to form fields and buttons. Also use Acrobat to create a searchable electronic library of files, and place security locks on sensitive files.

About Classroom in a Book

Adobe Acrobat 4.0 Classroom in a Book® is part of the official training series for Adobe graphics and publishing software developed by experts at Adobe Systems. The lessons are designed to help you learn at your own pace. If you're new to Adobe Acrobat, you'll understand the fundamental concepts and features you'll need to master the program. If you've been using Acrobat for a while, you'll find Classroom in a Book teaches many advanced features, including tips and techniques for using this latest version.

Although each lesson provides step-by-step instructions for creating a specific project, there's room for exploration and experimentation. You can follow the book from start to finish, or do only the lessons that correspond to your interests and needs. Each lesson concludes with a review section summarizing what you've covered.

Prerequisites

Before beginning to use *Adobe Acrobat 4.0 Classroom in a Book*, you should have a working knowledge of your computer and its operating system. Make sure you know how to use the mouse and standard menus and commands and also how to open, save, and close files. If you need to review these techniques, see the printed or online documentation included with your system. You must also have the Adobe Acrobat 4.0 application installed on your computer. Acrobat 4.0 is not included in this package. To read Web-based documents, you need a browser compatible with Netscape® Navigator® 3.0 or later, or one compatible with Internet Explorer® 3.0 or later.

Checking system requirements

Before you begin using *Adobe Acrobat 4.0 Classroom in a Book*, make sure that your system is set up correctly. To use Adobe Acrobat, you need the following hardware and software:

Windows

• An Intel® i486™ or Pentium® processor-based personal computer (Pentium recommended).

• Microsoft Windows 95, Windows 98, or Windows NT® 4.0 with Service Pack 3.

• 16 MB of RAM for Acrobat on Windows 95 and Windows 98, 24 MB of RAM for Acrobat on Windows NT (32 MB recommended).

• 16 MB of RAM for Acrobat Reader®.

• 32 MB of RAM for the Paper Capture plug-in (64 MB recommended).

• A hard drive with at least 75 MB of available space.

• A CD-ROM drive.

Mac OS

• An Apple Power Macintosh® computer.

• Apple System Software version 7.5.3 or later for Acrobat.

• Apple System Software version 7.1.2 or later for Acrobat Reader.

• 6 MB of RAM for Acrobat (12 MB recommended).

• 16 MB of RAM for Distiller® or the Paper Capture plug-in (32 MB recommended).

• A hard drive with at least 60 MB of available space.

• A CD-ROM drive.

Playing movies and sounds

If you're using Acrobat on a Windows or Macintosh system, you can play movies and sounds that have been added to a PDF document. To play movies or sounds, you need the following hardware and software:

• In Windows you need to have the appropriate sound and video boards installed in your computer, and Apple QuickTime® 2.0 or later software.

• On the Macintosh you need Apple QuickTime 2.0 or later.

QuickTime software is included as an installation option in the Acrobat 4.0 installer.

More RAM, faster processors, and large, fast hard drives will improve Acrobat's perfor-mance. For the latest system requirements, see the ReadMe file in the Adobe Acrobat 4.0 folder.

For information on technical support and troubleshooting, see the Troubleshooting appendix in the online Adobe Acrobat User Guide.

Installing the program

You must purchase the Adobe Acrobat software separately. For complete instructions on installing the software, see the Introduction to the *Adobe Acrobat 4.0 User Guide*. Be sure to follow the instructions for installing ATM®/fonts and other software as described for your platform.

Install the Classroom in a Book fonts

To ensure that the lesson files appear on your system with the correct fonts, you may need to install the Classroom in a Book font files. The lessons use Myriad® Condensed Semi-bold, and Adobe Garamond®. These fonts are located in the Fonts folder on the Acrobat Classroom in a Book CD. If you already have these on your system, you do not need to install them. If you have ATM, see its documentation on how to install fonts. If you do not have ATM, installing it from the CIB CD will automatically install the necessary fonts.

Copying the Classroom in a Book files

The Classroom in a Book CD includes folders containing all the electronic files for the lessons. Each lesson has its own folder, and you must copy the folders to your hard drive to do the lessons. To save room on your drive, you can install only the necessary folder for each lesson as you need it, and remove it when you're done.

To install the Classroom in a Book files for Windows:

1 Insert the Adobe Acrobat Classroom in a Book CD into your CD-ROM drive.

2 Create a subdirectory/folder on your hard drive and name it **AA4_CIB**.

3 Do one of the following:

• Drag the Lessons folder from the CD into the AA4_CIB folder.

• Copy only the single lesson folder you need.

To install the Classroom in a Book folders for Mac OS:

1 Insert the Adobe Acrobat Classroom in a Book CD into your CD-ROM drive.

2 Create a folder on your hard drive and name it **AA4_CIB**.

3 Do one of the following:

• Drag the Lessons folder from the CD into the AA4_CIB folder.

• Copy only the single lesson folder you need.

Additional resources

Adobe Acrobat 4.0 Classroom in a Book is not meant to replace documentation provided with the program. Only the commands and options used in the lessons are explained in this book. For comprehensive information about program features, refer to these resources:

• The online User Guide included with the Adobe Acrobat software. This guide contains a complete description of all features.

• The Adobe Web site, which you can view by choosing File > Adobe Online if you have a connection to the World Wide Web.

Adobe certification

The Adobe Training and Certification Programs are designed to help Adobe customers improve and promote their product proficiency skills. The Adobe Certified Expert (ACE) program is designed to recognize the high-level skills of expert users. Adobe Certified Training Providers (ACTP) use only Adobe Certified Experts to teach Adobe software classes. Available in either ACTP classrooms or on site, the ACE program is the best way to master Adobe products. For Adobe Certified Training Programs information, visit the Partnering with Adobe website at partners.adobe.com.

A Quick Tour of Adobe Acrobat

This interactive tour of Adobe Acrobat provides an overview of the key features of Acrobat in approximately 45 minutes. For detailed instructions on using the features introduced in this tour, see the online Adobe Acrobat User Guide installed with the Acrobat product.

In this tour, you'll prepare a PDF document for online distribution and review over a company's internal Web, or intranet. You'll work with the following documents:

• An online dining guide, originally created with Adobe PageMaker® and converted to PDF with Acrobat Distiller. To prepare this guide for review, you'll attach pages and add interactive features to it.

• A review memo, created with a word-processing application. You'll convert this memo to PDF with PDF Writer and attach it to the guide.

• An image saved as a TIFF file. You'll import this image and append it to the guide.

• An online order form, based on a document that was converted to PDF. You'll add an interactive field to this form and attach the form to the guide.

If needed, copy the Tour folder onto your hard drive.

Converting a document to PDF

Acrobat provides a variety of ways for converting documents to Portable Document Format, or PDF. You use PDF Writer to convert simple documents, such as those created with word-processing or spreadsheet applications. You use Acrobat Distiller to convert more complex documents, such as those created with page-layout, drawing, or photo-editing applications. You use the Import Image command in Acrobat to import and convert image files. And you use the Import Scan command in Acrobat to create a PDF file from a paper document.

If you are using Acrobat for Windows, you also use the Open Web Page command in Acrobat to download HTML pages from the World Wide Web and convert them to PDF.

To begin this tour, you'll convert a word-processing document to PDF with PDF Writer. You can "print" to PDF with PDF Writer in the same way you print to paper—using the Print command of the application you used to create the document.

1 Start your word-processing application.

2 Open the Memo.doc file in the Tour folder, located inside the Lessons folder within the AA4_CIB folder on your hard drive.

Note: If you have problems opening or converting the Memo.doc file, you can complete this tour by using the preprocessed copy of the file. If you choose to use the preprocessed file, skip to "Navigating a PDF document" on page 8.

3 To print the review memo to PDF, follow the instructions for your computer platform:

In Windows:

• Choose File > Print.

• From the Printer Name menu, choose Acrobat PDFWriter, and click OK.

• Name the file **Memo.pdf**, select the Tour folder as the destination, and select Edit Document Info.

• Enter your name in the Author text box, and click OK.

• Click Save.

• Exit your word-processing application.

In Mac OS:

• Hold down Control, and choose File > Print. (You can also select Acrobat PDFWriter as your printer driver in the Chooser, and choose File > Print.)

• Select Prompt for Document Info, and click OK.

• Enter your name in the Author text box, and click OK.

- Name the file **Memo.pdf**, select the Tour folder as the destination, and click Save.

- Quit your word-processing application.

Now that you have converted the memo to PDF, you can add it to another PDF document. (Later in this tour, you'll add the memo to an online dining guide.)

Navigating a PDF document

In addition to converting documents to PDF, you use Acrobat to navigate existing PDF documents. You can turn pages as in a traditional book, change the magnification of the page that you are viewing, and return easily to previous page views. You'll navigate an online dining guide.

1 Start Acrobat.

2 Choose File > Open. Select Guide.pdf in the Tour folder, located inside the Lessons folder within the AA4_CIB folder on your hard drive, and click Open. Then choose File > Save As, rename the file **Guide1.pdf**, and save it in the Tour folder.

Notice that the first page of the guide appears at actual size in the Acrobat window. (The status bar at the bottom of the window indicates 100% magnification.)

3 Choose Window > Show Bookmarks to display bookmarks.

Bookmarks appear in the navigation pane to the left of the document pane. They are special types of links that can serve as a table of contents.

4 To see a bookmark in action, select the hand tool (✋) in the tool bar, and click the Introduction bookmark to jump to page 2 of the guide.

Click Introduction bookmark.   *Result*

5 Select the zoom-in tool (🔍) in the tool bar, and drag a rectangle around the map on page 2 to zoom in.

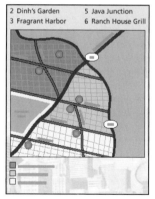

Drag rectangle around map to   *Result*
zoom in.

6 Hold down Ctrl (Windows) or Option (Mac OS), and click in the document to zoom out.

7 Click the Actual Size button (🔲) to return to a 100% view.

The guide contains a number of links to other pages in the document.

8 Select the hand tool, and move the pointer over the Chez Maison text. Notice that the hand pointer changes to a pointing finger when positioned over a link.

Click Chez Maison text to follow link.   *Result*

9 Click the Chez Maison text to jump to the link destination—a magnified view of page 3.

You can also view thumbnails in the navigation pane. Thumbnails are miniature previews of each page in the document. You can use thumbnails to navigate and edit PDF documents.

10 Click the Thumbnails tab to bring the Thumbnails palette to the front.

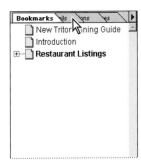

Click Thumbnails tab to   *Result*
bring palette to front.

11 If needed, use the scroll bar to bring the thumbnail for page 4 into view. Then double-click it to go to page 4 of the guide.

You can keep palettes docked inside the navigation pane, or you can float them over the desktop.

12 To float the Thumbnails palette over the Acrobat window, drag the Thumbnails tab to the document pane.

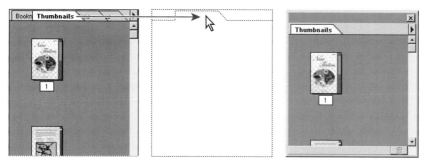

Drag Thumbnails tab to document pane.   *Result*

13 To dock the Thumbnails palette, drag the Thumbnails tab to the navigation pane.

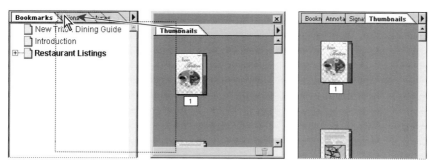

Drag Thumbnails tab to navigation pane.   *Result*

You can also navigate documents using the navigation buttons on the command bar.

14 Click the Go to Previous View button (◆) several times. Then click the Go to Next View button (◆) several times. These buttons let you retrace your viewing path through pages and magnification levels.

15 Click the First Page button (◄), and choose 100% magnification from the magnification pop-up menu in the status bar.

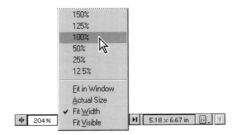

Editing a PDF document

You can use Acrobat to make final edits and modifications to PDF documents. You can correct typos, insert pages from other PDF documents, change the order of pages, and change how Acrobat numbers pages.

Editing text

You use the touchup text tool in Acrobat to make small changes to text. In addition to replacing characters, you can make adjustments in font size, color, and alignment. You'll update the year displayed on the first page of the guide.

1 Select the touchup text tool (𝕋) in the tool bar, and drag the I-beam to select the text to be replaced in the year 1998.

Drag I-beam to select text to be replaced.   Type new text.

2 Replace the original text by typing the current year.

3 Select the hand tool (✍), and click in the blank space beneath the current year to deselect the text.

Inserting pages

Now you'll add the memo to the guide.

1 Choose Document > Insert Pages.

2 Select Memo.pdf, and click Open (Windows) or Select (Mac OS).

Note: If you did not create the Memo.pdf file, select the preprocessed file named Memo1.pdf, located inside the Tour folder.

3 Choose Before from the Location menu. For Page, select the first page. Click OK. A copy of the memo is inserted as the first page of the guide.

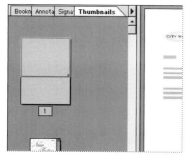

Memo inserted as first page of guide

Now you'll import an alternate image for Dinh's Garden and append it to the guide. (Later in this tour, you'll create a note instructing reviewers to compare the alternate image with the current image in the guide.)

4 Choose File > Import > Image.

5 Select Image.tif, located inside the Tour folder. Click Open (Windows), or click Add and Done (Mac OS).

6 Select Current Document, and click OK. A copy of the alternate image for Dinh's Garden is inserted as the last page of the guide.

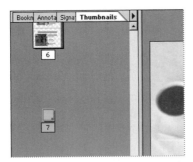

Image imported and appended to guide

Reordering pages

In addition to providing convenient previews of your pages, thumbnails let you change the placement of pages by dragging. You'll use thumbnails to move the alternate image for Dinh's Garden from the last page of the guide to page 2.

1 To create thumbnail images for the inserted pages, hold down the mouse button on the triangle in the upper right corner of the Thumbnails palette to display the Thumbnails palette menu, and choose Create All Thumbnails.

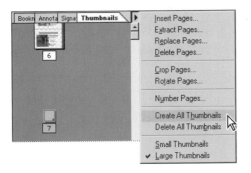

2 Drag the right border of the navigation pane to enlarge it. Resize the navigation pane so that you can view the thumbnails in two or more columns.

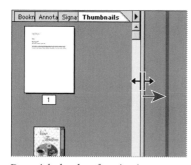 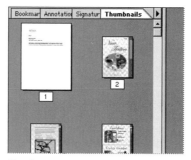

Drag right border of navigation pane to enlarge it. *Result*

3 Click the alternate image's thumbnail to select it. A rectangle outlines the thumbnail, indicating that you can move it.

4 Drag the thumbnail upward in the navigation pane to move it. Drag upward until the insertion bar appears to the right of the page 1 thumbnail, and release the mouse.

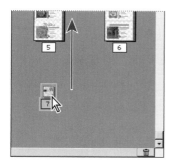 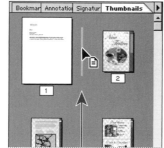

Drag thumbnail upward to move it. *When insertion bar appears to right of page 1 thumbnail, release mouse.*

The alternate image is repositioned in the guide as page 2, and the remaining page numbers change accordingly.

Renumbering pages

By default, Acrobat sets page numbers in a PDF document to arabic numerals starting with page 1. You can renumber pages in a variety of ways, including specifying a different numbering style for groups of pages.

1 Choose Document > Go to Page.

2 Enter **4**, and click OK.

Notice that the page numbers on the original pages of the guide no longer match the page numbers that appear in the status bar. You'll specify a different numbering style for the front matter that you have added to the guide.

Page numbers no longer match

3 Choose Document > Number Pages.

4 For the page range, enter pages from **1** to **2**. For the page numbering, select Begin New Section, choose "i, ii, iii" from the Style menu, and enter **1** in the Start text box. Click OK.

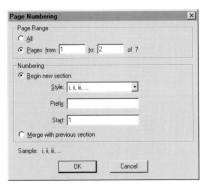

Specify new numbering style for pages 1 and 2.   *Result*

The page numbers on the original pages of the guide now match the page numbers that appear in the status bar.

5 Choose File > Save to save the Guide1.pdf file.

Customizing PDF navigation

You can use Acrobat to add bookmarks and links to PDF documents.

You can also generate bookmarks and links automatically from several desktop-publishing applications, including Adobe FrameMaker®, Adobe PageMaker, and Microsoft Word for Windows. Automatic linking is especially useful for large documents with a table of contents and index.

[?] For information on generating bookmarks and links automatically, see "Working with bookmarks" in Chapter 6 of the online Adobe Acrobat User Guide.

Now you'll create a bookmark to direct reviewers to the memo in the guide.

1 Click the First Page button (◄) to go to page i of the guide.

2 Click the Bookmarks tab to bring the Bookmarks palette to the front.

3 Select the text select tool (T) in the tool bar, and drag the I-beam to select the Memo header text at the upper left of the page.

Drag I-beam to select Memo header text.

4 Hold down the mouse button on the triangle in the upper right corner of the Bookmarks palette to display the Bookmarks palette menu, and choose New Bookmark. A bookmark with the title Memo appears at the bottom of the bookmark list.

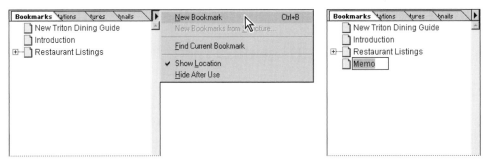

Choose New Bookmark from Bookmarks palette menu.   *Memo bookmark*

5 Click in the blank space beneath the bookmark list to deselect the bookmark text.

6 Click the Last Page button (▶|) to move away from page i so that you can test the new bookmark.

7 Select the hand tool (🖑), and test the Memo bookmark by clicking it.

Now you'll create a link to direct reviewers from the alternate image for Dinh's Garden to the current image on page 3.

8 Click the Next Page button (▶) to go to page ii of the guide.

9 Select the link tool (🖐) in the tool bar, and drag a rectangle around the alternate image. The Create Link dialog box appears.

10 Under Appearance, for Type, choose Invisible Rectangle.

11 Choose Go to View from the Action Type menu. Go to View tells Acrobat that you want the link to jump to the page view that you specify.

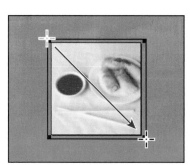

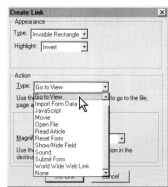

Drag rectangle around alternate image.

Specify properties in Create Link dialog box.

Notice the variety of other actions that you can assign to links, such as playing a movie, opening a file, or connecting to a Web site.

12 Without closing the Create Link dialog box, choose Document > Go to Page. Then enter **3** and click OK.

13 Choose Fit View from the Magnification menu, and click Set Link. This establishes the link and returns you to the page that contains it.

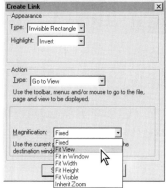

Without closing Create Link dialog box, go to page 3.

Choose Fit View from Magnification menu.

14 Select the hand tool, and test the new link by clicking the alternate image for Dinh's Garden.

15 Choose File > Save to save the Guide1.pdf file.

Annotating a PDF document

You can use Acrobat to add annotations to PDF documents in a variety of formats, including notes, text, audio, stamps, files, graphic markups, and text markups. You can review annotations using the Annotations palette or a summary of all annotations.

Reviewing annotations

Annotations from two reviewers have already been added to the guide. You'll review these annotations using the Annotations palette.

1 Click the Annotations tab to bring the Annotations palette to the front.

2 Click the Start Annotation Scan button (🖺) at the bottom of the Annotations palette. A list of annotations associated with the open document appears. By default, the list is sorted by author. You can also sort the list by type, page number, and date.

3 Double-click the first annotation listed under Reviewer 1 to jump to the page that contains it.

The green note is highlighted, indicating it is the annotation that you selected from the Annotations palette.

Double-click first annotation listed   *Result*
under Reviewer 1.

4 Double-click the green note to read it.

5 Click the close box at the top of the note window when you have finished reading the note.

Adding a note

Now you'll add your own note to page ii of the guide.

1 Click the Previous Page button (◄) to go to page ii of the guide.

2 Choose File > Preferences > Annotations.

3 Enter your name in the Author text box, and click OK.

4 Select the notes tool (⊞) in the tool bar, and click the upper left corner of the document pane. An empty note window appears.

5 Type the note text as desired. We used the following: "Let me know if you'd like to use this alternate image for Dinh's Garden. Click the alternate image to go to the location of the current image in the guide."

6 Choose Edit > Properties.

7 Select the Text Note icon to represent your type of note. Click the color button to select a color for the note. Then click OK.

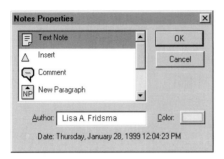

8 Close the note.

9 Select the hand tool ( ), and double-click the note that you have just created to view the message.

Because the note contains instructions for reviewers, you'll leave the note window open. If needed, you can easily adjust the size and position of the note so that it does not obstruct the alternate image. To resize the note, drag the resize button in the lower right corner of the note window. To reposition the note, drag its title bar.

Marking up text

You can also use Acrobat to mark up text in a document and add a note associated with the marked-up text. You'll highlight text on page 4 of the guide, and then add a note associated with the highlighted text.

You'll use the page box in the status bar to switch directly to page 4.

1 Move the pointer over the page box until it changes to an I-beam, and double-click to highlight the current page number. Be sure to highlight the entire page number "ii (2 of 7)."

2 Type **4** to replace the current page number, and press Enter or Return.

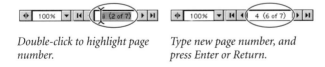

Double-click to highlight page number.   *Type new page number, and press Enter or Return.*

3 Select the highlight text tool ( ) in the tool bar. Move the I-beam to the area of the page describing the Fragrant Harbor restaurant, and drag to highlight the phrase Reservations: No.

Drag I-beam to highlight "Reservations: No."

Result

4 To associate a note with the highlighted text, move the pointer over the highlighted text until it changes to an arrow ( ), and double-click to create a note window.

5 Type the note text as desired. We used the following: "The Fragrant Harbor restaurant now accepts reservations." Then close the note.

6 Select the hand tool ( ), and double-click the highlighted text. The note associated with the highlighted text opens.

Notice that you opened the note by double-clicking the highlighted text rather than a note icon.

7 Close the note when you have finished viewing it.

Besides marking up text, you can use Acrobat to mark up a document with a graphic, such as a rectangle, ellipse, or line. Then you can add a note associated with the graphic.

Applying stamps

You can also use Acrobat to apply a stamp to a document in much the same way you would use a rubber stamp on a paper document. You'll apply a stamp to the cover page of the guide.

1 Move the pointer over the page box until it changes to an I-beam, and double-click to highlight the current page number.

2 Type **1** to replace the current page number, and press Enter or Return.

3 Hold down the mouse button on the notes tool (▤) to display a set of hidden tools, and drag to select the stamp tool (⬚).

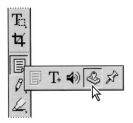

Drag to select stamp tool from set of hidden tools.

4 Click the upper left corner of the page. By default, the Approved stamp appears.

You'll select a different stamp from the Acrobat stamp library.

5 Choose Edit > Properties.

6 Choose Standard from the Category menu, select Draft from the list in the left pane of the dialog box, and click OK.

Click upper left corner of page.

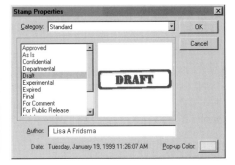

Specify properties in Stamp Properties dialog box.

7 Select the hand tool (✋), and click inside the document pane to deselect the stamp.

In addition to using stamps from the Acrobat stamp library, you can create your own custom stamps and use them as annotations.

8 Choose File > Save to save the Guide1.pdf file.

If you are using Acrobat for Windows, you can also add digital signatures to PDF documents. You might sign a document to show that you have read it or approved it, or to certify it is ready for others to review.

For information on adding digital signatures, see "Signing documents" in Chapter 14 of the online Adobe Acrobat User Guide.

Summarizing annotations

Now you'll generate a summary of all annotations in the guide.

1 Choose Tools > Annotations > Summarize Annotations. The text from all the annotations is copied into a new document.

Notice that the annotations are numbered sequentially in the annotations summary. You can set preferences in Acrobat to display these numbers with the annotations in the document, so that you can easily locate annotations while reviewing the summary.

2 To save the summary, choose File > Save As, rename the file, and save it in the Tour folder.

3 Choose File > Close to close the summary.

Creating a PDF form

You can use Acrobat to create interactive forms for other Acrobat users to fill in. Users can simply print the forms, or they can submit them over the World Wide Web. Submitted form data is imported and exported independently of the forms themselves, allowing for efficient transmitting and archiving.

1 Choose File > Open, select Form.pdf in the Tour folder, and click Open.

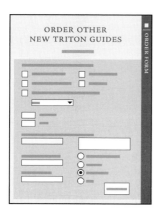

2 Select the form tool ( ) in the tool bar.

Notice that all the form fields but one have been created for you. They include check boxes for selecting guides to order, a text field for entering an address, radio buttons for selecting a credit card type, and a button for sending the form data to a server or Web site. You'll add the one field missing, a text field for entering a name.

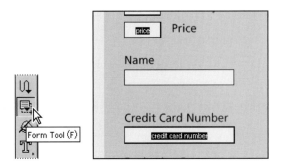

3 Drag around the rectangle below the word Name to create a form field for names.

4 In the Field Properties dialog box, type **Name** in the Name text box (to label the field "Name"). Choose Text from the Type menu.

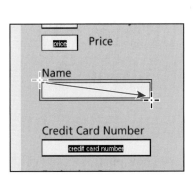

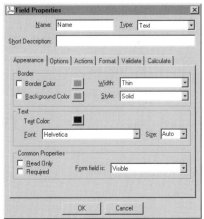

Drag around rectangle below "Name" to create form field.

Specify properties in Field Properties dialog box.

5 Click the Appearance tab.

6 Under Border, select Border Color and Background Color. Click the appropriate color box to access the system palette and set the Border Color to black and the Background Color to white. For Width, choose Thin, and for Style, choose Solid.

7 Under Text, for Font, choose a font (we used Helvetica*). For Size, choose 12. Click OK.

8 Select the hand tool (✋), and test the form by clicking in the text fields and typing. Notice that the Address field, which contains multiple lines, accepts carriage returns whereas the other fields do not.

Now you'll attach this form to the guide using thumbnails. Thumbnails allow you to copy pages between PDF documents.

9 Choose Window > Tile > Vertically so the windows for both the form and guide are visible.

10 In the guide window, click the Thumbnails tab to bring the Thumbnails palette to the front.

11 In the form window, choose Window > Show Thumbnails to display thumbnails. Then click the form's thumbnail to select it.

12 Drag the form's thumbnail to the guide's thumbnail list, and drop it after the last thumbnail page. (A bar indicates the insertion point as you drag.)

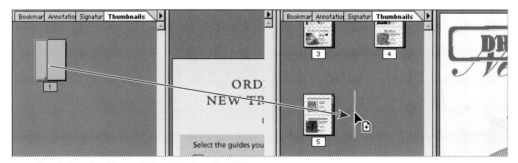

Drag form's thumbnail to end of guide's thumbnail list.

The form is copied and becomes the last page of the guide.

13 Because you have made a copy of the form, you can now put the original away. Choose File > Close to close the Form.pdf file. Click No (Windows) or Don't Save (Mac OS) to confirm closing the file without saving changes.

14 Resize the guide window.

Distributing PDF files

Converting your electronic or paper publications to PDF lets you distribute them via e-mail, on the World Wide Web, or on a CD. You can optimize PDF files to reduce their file size significantly. When you distribute PDF files that have been optimized, you cut down on transmission time and save disk space. Now you'll optimize the guide.

1 Choose File > Save As, make sure that Optimize is selected, and save Guide1.pdf in the Tour folder. Click Yes (Windows) or Replace (Mac OS) to confirm replacing the file. The Save As command lets you save a smaller, optimized version of your finished file.

2 Choose File > Close to close the guide. The guide is now ready for online distribution.

If you want to publish a collection of PDF documents, such as a set of conference papers or chapters in a large technical manual, you can use Acrobat Catalog to index them. Acrobat users can then quickly search the collection using the index.

For information on indexing document collections, see "Preparing PDF document collections for indexing" in Chapter 11 of the online Adobe Acrobat User Guide.

Users can view PDF documents with the free Acrobat Reader, which comes in versions for Windows, Mac OS, OS/2®, and UNIX. You can copy any version of Reader from the Acrobat Reader CD and distribute it freely. Users can also download Acrobat Reader from the Adobe Web site at http://www.adobe.com.

Congratulations! You have finished the Acrobat tour. For more information on Adobe Acrobat, see the online Adobe Acrobat User Guide.

Lesson 1

Introducing Adobe Acrobat

Quality publishing tools are within reach of more people than ever before, and easy access to the Internet and to CD-ROM recorders enables wider distribution of electronic publications. Adobe Acrobat can help you create those electronic documents quickly and easily—and Acrobat Reader can provide your audience free access to them.

In this lesson, you'll do the following:

• Learn about the Adobe Acrobat set of programs.

• Understand the different uses of electronic documents designed for printing or online viewing.

• Identify the types of formatting and design decisions you need to make when creating an electronic publication.

This lesson will take about 20 minutes to complete.

If needed, copy the Lesson01 folder onto your hard drive.

About Adobe Acrobat

Adobe Acrobat is a set of programs used to create, enhance, and read Portable Document Format (PDF) documents.

• You create PDF documents by converting electronic documents or scanned printed documents using Acrobat Distiller or PDF Writer. PDF documents maintain the look and layout of the originals.

• You enhance PDF documents by adding interactivity such as links, forms, and movies using Adobe Acrobat. You can also provide full-text indexes for PDF document collections using Acrobat Catalog.

• You read PDF documents using Acrobat Reader, Adobe Acrobat, or Web browsers. You can publish documents on network and Web servers, CDs, and disks.

The Adobe Acrobat 4.0 program set can be divided into three categories as shown in the following table.

Producers	Viewers	Indexers
PDF Writer	Adobe Acrobat	Acrobat Catalog
Acrobat Distiller	Acrobat Reader	
Adobe Acrobat		

User workflow and document type determine which producer you should use to create a PDF file as well as which viewer to view it.

• PDF Writer lets you convert simple documents, such as those created with word-processing or spreadsheet programs, to PDF documents. For information on using PDF Writer, see Lesson 3, "Creating PDF from Authoring Programs."

• Acrobat Distiller lets you convert more complex documents to PDF, such as those created with drawing, page-layout, or image-editing programs. Lesson 3, "Creating PDF from Authoring Programs," provides step-by-step instructions for creating PDF documents with Acrobat Distiller. Lesson 12, "Customizing PDF Output Quality," provides more details on advanced Distiller options.

• Adobe Acrobat lets you produce, modify, and view PDF documents, giving them state-of-the-art electronic document features such as password protection, hypertext links, electronic bookmarks, media clips, and interactive forms. You can also convert scanned paper documents into portable, searchable PDF pages. You'll be using Adobe Acrobat in most of the lessons in this book.

• Acrobat Reader lets you view PDF documents. You can download this viewer free of charge for all platforms from the Adobe Web site at www.adobe.com. If you need to read a PDF document and have not purchased Adobe Acrobat 4.0, you would use Acrobat Reader to do so. Acrobat Reader can be used to view, navigate, and print a PDF document. You cannot make any changes to a PDF document with Acrobat Reader.

• Acrobat Catalog lets you create a full-text index of a collection of PDF documents. You can then use this index to search the document collection using the search query tool in Adobe Acrobat or Acrobat Reader. You'll use Acrobat Catalog to build a searchable PDF library in Lesson 11, "Building a Searchable PDF Library and Catalog."

Publishing on the World Wide Web

The World Wide Web has greatly expanded the possibilities of delivering electronic documents to a wide and varied audience. Because Web browsers can be configured to run other applications inside the browser window, you can post PDF files as part of a Web site. Your users can then download or view these files inside the browser window using Acrobat Reader.

[?] For information on how to view PDF files inside a browser window, see "Configuring Web browsers for viewing PDF" in the online Adobe Acrobat User Guide.

Based on the PostScript® programming language, PDF is a flexible, cross-platform file format that is transportable and viewable on Windows, Mac OS, or UNIX computer systems. Users need a viewer such as Acrobat Reader or Adobe Acrobat 4.0 to view a PDF document. When including a PDF file as part of your Web page, you should direct your users to the Adobe Web site, so the first time they look at a PDF document, they can download Reader free of charge. Properties of PDF documents include the following:

• PDF preserves the exact layout, fonts, and text formatting of electronic documents, regardless of the computer system or platform used to view these documents. As a result, publishing a Web page in PDF ensures that the page always appears in its original format and design.

• PDF documents can contain multiple languages, such as Japanese and English, on the same page.

• PDF documents can be viewed one page at a time and printed from the Web. With page-at-a-time downloading, the Web server sends only the requested page to the user, thus decreasing downloading time. In addition, the user can easily print selected pages or all pages from the document. PDF is a suitable format for publishing long electronic documents on the Web.

• PDF documents print predictably with proper margins and page breaks.

• You can use security passwords to lock your PDF documents from undesired changes or printing, or to limit access to important documents. Password protection provides you with an extra measure of security when publishing over the Web. Lesson 7, "Using Acrobat in a Document Review Cycle," covers document security in detail.

• Users can change the view magnification of a PDF page using controls in Adobe Acrobat or Acrobat Reader. This feature can be especially useful for zooming in on graphics or diagrams containing intricate details.

• You can use a Web search engine to index PDF documents for rapid searching on the Web.

About viewing PDF documents on the Web

Here are four possible scenarios for viewing PDF on the Web:

• *The browser supports PDF viewing, the PDF file is optimized, and the Web server supports page-at-a time downloading (byte-serving)—so the PDF file downloads a page at a time and displays in the Web browser window. This is the fastest scenario possible for viewing PDF documents on the Web.*

• *The browser supports PDF viewing, but the PDF file is not optimized or the server does not support byte-serving—so the entire PDF file downloads to the machine with the browser and then appears within the browser window.*

• *The browser supports PDF viewing, and PDF files are embedded in an HTML page—allowing the PDF document to appear in a frame rather than in a full window. An ActiveX® browser such as Internet Explorer supports navigating through the document in the frame. Netscape Navigator-compatible browsers can display the PDF document within an HTML page, but require a link to a full-window view for navigation.*

• *Adobe Acrobat or Acrobat Reader is configured as a helper application for the browser—which does or does not support PDF viewing within the browser window. The entire PDF file downloads to the machine with the browser, and the Acrobat viewer launches as a separate application and displays the PDF document.*

–From the online Adobe Acrobat User Guide, Chapter 5

Looking at some examples

Publishing your document electronically is a flexible way to distribute information. Using PDF, you can create documents for printing, for multimedia presentations, or for distribution on a CD or over a network. In this lesson, you'll take a look at some electronic document examples designed for printing on paper and for online reading.

1 Start Acrobat.

2 Choose File > Open. Select Introduc.pdf in the Lesson01 folder, located inside the Lessons folder within the AA4_CIB folder on your hard drive, and click Open. If necessary, use the scroll bars to bring the bottom part of the page into view.

The previews in this document are links to the corresponding electronic documents. The top three previews link to documents designed to be both distributed and viewed electronically; the bottom three previews link to documents intended to be distributed online, but printed out for viewing purposes.

3 Click the Schedule preview in the bottom row to open the corresponding PDF file.

This document is a work schedule that has been converted to PDF for easy electronic distribution.

4 Look at the status bar at the bottom of the document window. Notice that the page size is a standard 8-1/2-by-11 inches, a suitable size for printing on a desktop printer.

You might glance at the schedule online, but you'd also want to print out a hard-copy version for handy reference.

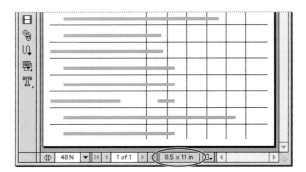

5 Click the Go to Previous View button (◀) in the command bar to return to the previews in the Introduc.pdf document.

Another example of a publication designed for printing is the Documentation file. This text-intensive document is much easier to read in printed format rather than online.

6 Click the Documentation preview in the bottom row to look at the file, and then click the Go to Previous View button to return to the previews.

7 Click the Slide Show preview in the top row to open that document.

This document is a marketing presentation designed to be shown and viewed exclusively on-screen. Notice that the presentation opens in Full Screen mode to occupy all available space on the monitor.

8 Press Enter or Return several times to page through the presentation. Notice that the colorful graphics, large type size, and horizontal page layout have been designed for optimal display on a monitor.

The Full Screen preference settings let you control how pages display in this mode. For example, you can have a full-screen document with each page displayed automatically after a certain number of seconds. Lesson 15, "Enhancing a Multimedia Project," covers how to set up a document for automatic full-screen display.

9 Press the Escape key to exit Full Screen mode.

10 Click the Go to Previous View button until you return to the previews in the Introduc.pdf document.

An online help publication or an electronic catalog are further examples of documents for which on-screen viewing is suitable and even preferred. Electronic publishing offers intuitive navigational features, such as hypertext links, which are well suited for publications meant to be browsed or used as quick reference guides.

Designing documents for online viewing

Once you have identified the final format for your publication, you can begin to make the design and production decisions that will help make the publication attractive and easy to use. If you're simply converting an existing paper document to electronic format, you'll inevitably weigh the benefits of reworking the design against the time and cost required to do so. If your publication will be viewed on-screen and on paper, you may have to make the design accommodate the different requirements of both.

First you'll take a look at a document designed to be browsed online but printed out for closer viewing.

1 In the Introduc.pdf file, click the Brochure preview at the bottom of the page to open the corresponding document.

This document is a printed brochure that was converted exactly as it was to electronic format. Converting the document to PDF is a good way to distribute it cheaply and easily. It also enables you to use features such as hypertext links to make navigation of the online brochure both easy and intuitive.

2 If necessary, click the Fit in Window button (▣) to view the entire page. Click the Next Page button (▶) in the command bar a few times to page through the brochure.

Notice, however, that while the online brochure is useful for quick browsing and printing selected pages, it is not designed to be read on-screen. The long and narrow pages are inconveniently shaped for the screen, and the small image and type sizes make reading a strain for the user.

Now you'll look at the same brochure redesigned and optimized for online reading. The topics in the brochure have been redesigned as a series of nested, linked topic screens that lead the reader through the document.

3 Click the Go to Previous View button (◆) until you return to the Introduc.pdf file, and click the Park Kiosk preview at the top of the page to open that document.

4 If necessary, click the Fit in Window button to view the entire page.

Notice that the horizontal page orientation is well suited for display on a monitor.

5 Click About the Park to activate that link.

The About the Park topic screen appears, with its own list of subtopics. Notice how the larger image and type sizes make this document easier to view than the online brochure.

Notice also the use of sans serif fonts in the publication. Sans serif fonts have simpler and cleaner shapes than serif fonts, making them easier to read on-screen.

M ount Rainier was established on March 2, 1899 as the country's fifth national park. The park encompasses 378 square miles (980 square kilometers). Elevation ranges from 880 feet (282 meters) at the Carbon River rainforest to 14,411 feet (4,612 meters) at the summit of the glacier-covered peak. Approximately two million people visit the park each year.

6 Click Flora & Fauna to jump to that topic screen. Then click Lowland Forest to view a specific information screen about the Olympic Elk in this region.

Notice that the pages of the original brochure have been redesigned to accommodate a navigational structure based on self-contained, screen-sized units.

The formatting considerations of on-screen publications—fonts, page size, layout, color, and resolution—are the same as those of other kinds of publications; however, each element must be reevaluated in the context of on-screen viewing. Decisions about issues such as color and resolution, which in traditional publishing may require a trade-off between quality and cost, may require a parallel trade-off between quality and file size in electronic publishing. Once you have determined the page elements that are important to you, you need to choose the publishing tools and format that will best maintain the desired elements.

7 Click the Go to Previous View button until you return to the Introduc.pdf file.

8 Click the Online Booklet preview to see another example of a PDF document designed for online viewing.

9 Choose File > Close to close the Online Booklet.

In this lesson, you have examined a variety of electronic documents designed in different file formats for different purposes. Later on in this book, you'll get some hands-on practice in creating and tailoring your own electronic documents.

Review questions

1 Describe the Adobe Acrobat 4.0 set of programs.

2 How do electronic documents designed for printing differ from documents optimized for online use?

3 What hardware and software do you need to view PDF documents?

4 What kinds of media can you use to distribute PDF documents?

5 What kinds of typefaces and type sizes are best suited for on-screen display?

Review answers

1 Adobe Acrobat 4.0 includes Adobe Acrobat, Acrobat Reader, PDF Writer, Acrobat Distiller, and Acrobat Catalog. Acrobat is used for producing, modifying, and viewing PDF documents. Acrobat Reader, available on the Adobe Web site without charge, is used for viewing PDF documents. PDF Writer and Acrobat Distiller are used for converting simple and complex (respectively) documents into PDF documents. Acrobat Catalog is used for creating indexes.

2 Electronic documents designed for paper output tend to be longer, text-intensive documents. Optimized online documents have been redesigned for optimal display on a monitor and may contain more graphics and screen-based navigational features.

3 You can view PDF documents on Windows, Mac OS, or UNIX computer systems. In addition to a computer, you need Acrobat Reader or Adobe Acrobat to view PDF documents.

4 You can distribute PDF documents via floppy disk, CD, electronic mail, corporate intranet, or the World Wide Web. You can also print PDF documents and distribute them as printed documents.

5 Large typefaces with simple, clean shapes display most clearly on the screen. Sans serif fonts are more suitable than serif fonts, which contain embellishments more suitable for the printed page.

Lesson 2

Getting to Know the Work Area

In this lesson, you'll learn how to navigate through a PDF document. You'll page through an online magazine using controls built into Adobe Acrobat, and create your own custom navigational controls to link from one section of the magazine to another.

In this lesson, you'll learn how to do the following:

• Work with Acrobat tools and palettes.

• Page through a PDF document using Acrobat's built-in navigational controls.

• Change how a PDF document scrolls and displays in the document window.

• Change the magnification of a view.

• Create and edit links to different views within a document.

• Retrace your viewing path through a document.

• Create a link to a site on the World Wide Web.

• Use the online Adobe Acrobat User Guide.

This lesson will take about 30 minutes to complete.

If needed, remove the previous lesson folder from your hard drive and copy the Lesson02 folder onto it.

Opening the work file

You'll practice navigating through a fictional online magazine called *Digital Arts*. *Digital Arts* is a glossy, tabloid-style magazine that contains the hottest news in the computer world. In addition to buying the printed magazine from newsstands, readers can view and download the electronic version.

Digital Arts was created using Adobe PageMaker and then converted to PDF.

1 Start Acrobat.

2 Choose File > Open. Select Digarts.pdf in the Lesson02 folder, located inside the Lessons folder within the AA4_CIB folder on your hard drive, and click Open. Then choose File > Save As, rename the file **Digarts1.pdf**, and save it in the Lesson02 folder.

Using the work area

The Acrobat work area includes a window with a document pane for viewing PDF documents and a navigation pane with bookmarks, thumbnails, annotations, and so on related to the current document. A menu bar, command bar, tool bar, and status bar around the outside of the window provide everything you need to work with documents.

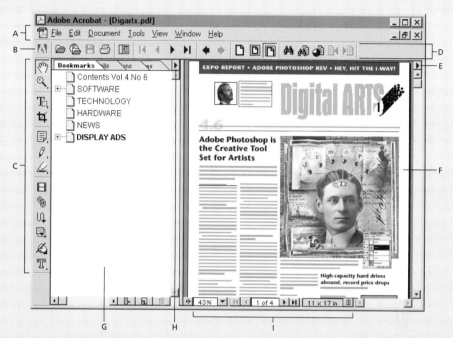

A. *Menu bar* **B.** *Adobe Online button* **C.** *Tool bar* **D.** *Command bar* **E.** *Document pane menu* **F.** *Document pane* **G.** *Navigation pane* **H.** *Palette menu* **I.** *Status bar*

The buttons and menus in the status bar provide quick ways to change your on-screen display and to navigate through documents.

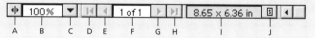

A. *Navigation Pane button* **B.** *Magnification level* **C.** *Magnification pop-up menu* **D.** *First Page button* **E.** *Previous Page button* **F.** *Current page* **G.** *Next Page button* **H.** *Last Page button* **I.** *Page size* **J.** *Page layout pop-up menu*

Using Acrobat tools

The tool bar contains tools for scrolling, zooming, changing the appearance of text, cropping pages, adding annotations, and making other changes to the current PDF document. This section introduces the tool bar and shows you how to select tools. As you work through the lessons, you'll learn more about each tool's specific function.

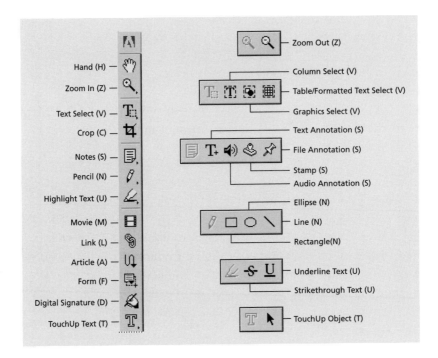

1 To select a tool, you can either click the tool in the tool bar or press the tool's keyboard shortcut. For example, you can press Z to select the zoom-in tool from the keyboard. Selected tools remain active until you select a different tool.

2 If you don't know the keyboard shortcut for a tool, position the mouse over the tool until its name and shortcut are displayed.

3 Some of the tools in the tool bar display a small triangle at the bottom right corner, indicating the presence of additional hidden tools. Select hidden tools in any of the following ways:

• Hold down the mouse button on a tool that has additional hidden tools, and drag to select the desired tool.

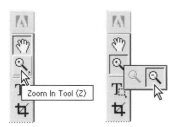

Drag to select desired tool.

• Press Shift + the tool's keyboard shortcut repeatedly until the tool that you want is selected. For example, press Shift+Z to select the zoom-in tool ($\mathbb{Q}$).

Using Acrobat palettes

Acrobat provides palettes to help you organize and keep track of a document's bookmarks, thumbnails, annotations, signatures, articles, and destinations. Palettes can be docked inside the navigation pane or floated in windows over the work area. They can also be grouped with other palettes. This section introduces the navigation pane and shows you how to display palettes. As you work through the lessons, you'll learn more about each palette's specific function.

Displaying palettes

You can display palettes in a variety of ways. Experiment with several techniques:

• To show or hide the navigation pane as you work, click the Show/Hide Navigation Pane button (⊞) in the command bar, the Navigation Pane button (◀▶) in the status bar, or the left border of the document pane.

• To show or hide a palette, choose the palette's Show or Hide command from the Window menu. The palette appears in the navigation pane or in a floating window.

Changing the palette display

You can change the palette display in a variety of ways. Experiment with several techniques:

- To change the width of the navigation pane while it's visible, drag its right border.

- To bring a palette to the front of its group, click the palette's tab.

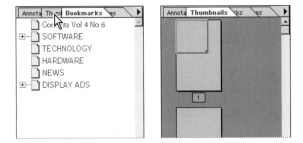

- To move a palette to its own floating window, drag the palette's tab to the document pane.

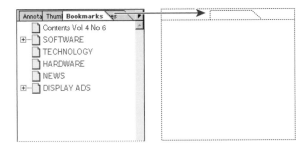

- To move a palette to another group, drag the palette's tab to the other group.

• To display a palette menu, hold down the mouse button on the triangle in the upper right corner of the palette. To hide a palette menu without making a selection, click in the blank space in the navigation pane.

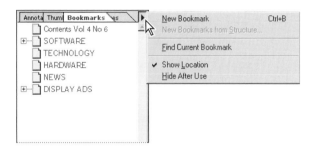

About navigation

Acrobat and Reader contain built-in navigational controls in the menu, command, tool, status, and scroll bars that let you browse a PDF document page by page, or quickly jump to a specific page of the document. Using these controls, you can view a PDF document in much the same way as you would view a printed book, while taking advantage of the greater speed and efficiency of electronic navigation.

In addition to these built-in controls, Acrobat lets you create custom navigational controls in your document. These controls include links, bookmarks, thumbnails, articles, and buttons. Bookmarks, thumbnails, and articles are discussed in Lesson 4, "Creating Navigational Structures," while buttons are discussed in Lesson 9, "Adding Buttons".

About on-screen display

Take a look at the status bar, located at the bottom of the document window. Notice that the magazine is tabloid size (11-by-17 inches) and currently appears at 100% magnification on-screen.

The magnification shown in the status bar does not refer to the printed size of the page, but rather to how the page is displayed on-screen. Acrobat determines the on-screen display of a page by treating the page as a 72 ppi (pixels-per-inch) image. For example, if your page has a print size of 2-by-2 inches, Acrobat treats the page as if it were 144 pixels wide and 144 pixels high (72 x 2 = 144). At 100% view, each pixel in the page is represented by 1 screen pixel on your monitor.

How large the page actually appears on-screen depends on your monitor size and your monitor resolution setting. For example, when you increase the resolution of your monitor, you increase the number of screen pixels within the same monitor area. This results in smaller screen pixels and a smaller displayed page, since the number of pixels in the page itself stays constant. The following illustration shows the variation among 100% displays of the same page on different monitors.

Pixel dimensions and monitor resolution

Regardless of the print size specified for an image, the size of an image on-screen is determined by the pixel dimensions of the image and the monitor size and setting. A large monitor set to 640-by-480 pixels uses larger pixels than a small monitor with the same setting. In most cases, default PC monitor settings display 96 pixels per inch, and default Macintosh monitor settings display approximately 72 pixels per inch.

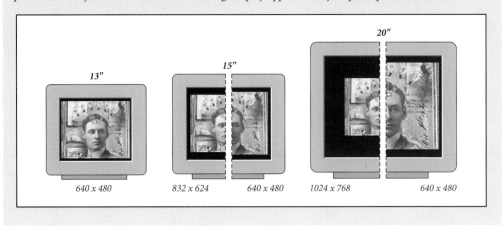

Navigating the magazine

Acrobat provides a variety of ways for you to move through and adjust the magnification of a PDF document. For example, you can scroll through the magazine using the scroll bar at the right side of the window, or you can turn pages as in a traditional book using the browse buttons in the command bar. You can also jump to a specific page using the status bar at the bottom of the window.

Browsing the document

1 If needed, click the Show/Hide Navigation Pane button (▥) to hide the navigation pane. In addition, if you have a palette displayed in a floating window, choose the palette's Hide command from the Window menu.

2 Select the hand tool (🖐) in the tool bar, move your pointer over the document, and hold down the mouse button.

The hand pointer changes to a closed hand when you hold down the mouse.

3 Drag the closed hand in the window to move the page around on the screen. This is similar to moving a piece of paper around on a desktop.

Drag with hand tool to move page.   *Result*

4 Press Enter or Return to display the next part of the page. You can press Enter or Return repeatedly to view the document from start to finish in screen-sized sections.

5 Click the Fit in Window button (▣) to display the entire page in the window. If needed, click the First Page button (◀) to go to page 1.

6 Place the pointer over the Down arrow in the scroll bar, and click once.

The document scrolls automatically to display all of page 2. You can control how PDF pages scroll and display in the document window.

7 Click the page layout pop-up menu in the status bar to display the page layout options. Notice that the Single Page option is currently chosen.

8 Choose Continuous from the pop-up menu. Then use the scroll bar to scroll to page 3.

The Continuous option displays pages end to end like frames in a filmstrip.

Click Down arrow in scroll bar.   *Choose Continuous from pop-up menu.*

9 Now choose Continuous - Facing from the pop-up menu to display page spreads, with left- and right-hand pages facing each other, as on a layout board.

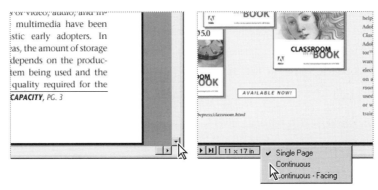

Continuous option   *Continuous - Facing option*

10 Click the First Page button to go to page 1.

In keeping with the conventions of printed books, a PDF document always begins with a right-hand page.

11 Reset the layout to Single Page.

You can use the page box in the status bar to switch directly to a specific page.

12 Move the pointer over the page box until it changes to an I-beam, and double-click to highlight the current page number.

13 Type **4** to replace the current page number, and press Enter or Return.

You should now be viewing page 4 of *Digital Arts.*

The scroll bar also lets you navigate to a specific page.

14 Begin dragging the scroll box upward in the scroll bar. As you drag, a page status box appears. When page 1 appears in the status box, release the mouse.

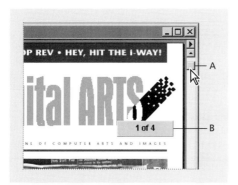

A. *Scroll box* **B.** *Page status box*

You should now be back at the beginning of *Digital Arts.*

Changing the view magnification

You can change the magnification of the page view using controls in the command and status bars, or by clicking or dragging in the page with the zoom-in or zoom-out tool.

1 Click the Fit Width button ( ). This control adjusts the magnification to spread the page across the whole width of your screen. Notice that a new magnification appears in the status bar.

2 Click the Next Page button ( ) to advance to page 2. Notice that the magnification remains the same.

3 Click the Actual Size button ( ) to return the page to a 100% view.

4 Click the magnification pop-up menu in the status bar to display the preset magnification options. Drag to choose 200% for the magnification.

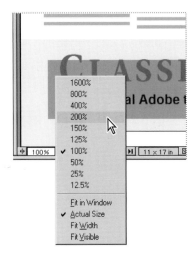

You can also enter a specific value for the magnification.

5 Move the pointer over the magnification box in the status bar until it changes to an I-beam, and double-click to highlight the current magnification.

6 Type **75** to replace the current magnification, and press Enter or Return.

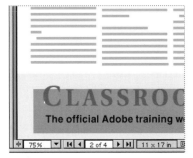

Double-click to highlight magnification.   *Type new magnification, and press Enter or Return.*

7 Now click the Fit in Window button ( ) to display the entire page in the window.

Next you'll use the zoom-in tool to magnify a specific portion of a page.

8 Enter **3** in the page box to go to page 3. Then select the zoom-in tool ( ) in the tool bar.

9 Click in the top right section of the page to increase the magnification. Notice that the view centers around the point you clicked. Click in the top right section of the page once more to increase the magnification again.

10 Now press Ctrl (Windows) or Option (Mac OS). Notice that the zoom pointer now appears with a minus sign, indicating that the zoom-out tool is active.

11 With Ctrl or Option pressed, click in the document to decrease the magnification. Ctrl- or Option-click once more to decrease the magnification again. Then release Ctrl or Option.

The entire page should fit on your screen again.

Now you'll drag the zoom-in tool to magnify the Contents area.

12 Place the pointer near the top left of the Contents, and drag over the text as shown in the following illustration.

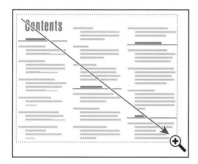

Marquee-zooming

The view zooms in on the area you enclosed. This is called *marquee-zooming.*

Using and creating links

In a PDF document, you don't always have to view pages in sequence. You can jump immediately from one section of a document to another using custom navigational aids such as links.

One benefit of placing *Digital Arts* online is that you can convert traditional cross-references into links, which users can use to jump directly to the referenced section or file. For example, you can make each item under the contents list of *Digital Arts* into a link that jumps to its corresponding section. You can also use links to add interactivity to traditional book elements such as glossaries and indexes.

Following a link

You'll try out an existing link before creating your own. You should be viewing the Contents at the bottom of page 3.

1 Select the hand tool (). Move the pointer over the Trapping Pitfalls listing in the Contents so that the pointing finger appears, and click to follow the link.

This item links to the Trapping Pitfalls section at the bottom of the first page.

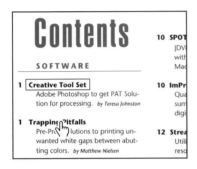

2 Click the Go to Previous View button (◀) to return to your previous view of the Contents.

You can click the Go to Previous View button at any time to retrace your viewing path through a document. The Go to Next View button (▶) lets you reverse the action of your last Go to Previous View.

Creating a link

Now you'll create a link between the PIFL: Imaging Technology listing in the Contents and the corresponding article in the magazine.

You use the link tool to create new links in a document. To specify an activation area for the link, you drag over the desired area with the link tool. Then you set the destination view for the link.

1 Select the link tool (🔗) in the tool bar.

The link tool appears as a cross-hair pointer when you move it into the document. When you select the link tool, all the existing links in the document appear temporarily as black rectangles.

2 Place the cross hair above and to the left of the PIFL: Imaging Technology listing, and drag to create a marquee that encloses the entire text block.

The Create Link dialog box appears. This dialog box lets you specify the appearance of the activation area as well as the link action.

3 Under Appearance, for Type, choose Invisible Rectangle.

4 Under Action, for Type, choose Go to View.

The Go to View option lets you specify a page view as the destination for the link. The Go to View action is just one among many actions that you can assign to your link.

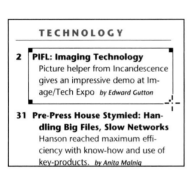 

For information on the different action types, see "Using actions for special effects" in Chapter 10 of the online Adobe Acrobat User Guide.

5 With the Create Link dialog box still open, click the Previous Page button (◀) to go to page 2 of *Digital Arts.* The PIFL section is at the top of this page.

6 In the Create Link dialog box, for Magnification, choose Fit Width.

 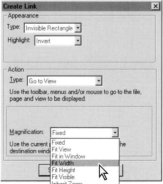

7 Click Set Link. The page view returns to the Contents.

You have now created a link from the Contents to page 2. The view will fill the width of the screen when the link is activated.

8 Select the hand tool (✋), and move the pointer over the PIFL: Imaging Technology listing in the Contents. Notice that the pointing finger indicates the activation area that you have just created.

9 Click the activation area to test your link. You should jump to the PIFL section with a Fit Width magnification view.

10 Click the Go to Previous View button (◀) to return to the Contents.

11 Choose File > Save to save the Digarts1.pdf file.

Next, you'll edit an existing link in the Contents.

Editing a link

You can edit a link at any time by changing its activation area, appearance, or link action.

1 Using the hand tool, click the Creative Tool Set listing to follow its link.

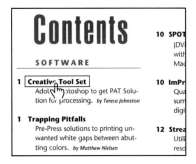 

Notice that the link does not link to the correct section. You'll edit the destination of this link and make the link appearance invisible.

2 Click the Go to Previous View button (◀) to return to the Contents.

3 Select the link tool (), and double-click inside the black rectangle surrounding the Creative Tool Set listing to open the Link Properties dialog box.

This dialog box lets you edit the appearance and destination of the selected link.

4 Under Appearance, for Type, choose Invisible Rectangle.

5 Click Edit Destination.

6 Click the First Page button (◀) to navigate to the beginning of *Digital Arts,* where the section entitled "Adobe Photoshop is the Creative Tool Set for Artists" appears.

7 Click the Fit in Window button (▣). If needed, move the Link Properties dialog box out of the way by dragging its title bar.

8 Select the zoom-in tool (⊕), and marquee-zoom around the story to enlarge it, as shown in the following illustration.

9 In the Link Properties dialog box, for Magnification, choose Fixed.

The Fixed option sets the link destination at the current magnification displayed on your screen.

10 Click Set Link.

11 Select the hand tool (), and click the Creative Tool Set listing to test your revised link.

You should jump to the enlarged view of the correct story on page 1.

12 Click the Go to Previous View button to return to the Contents.

Now you'll expand the activation area around the Creative Tool Set listing so that it encompasses the entire text block.

13 Select the link tool, and click inside the rectangle surrounding the Creative Tool Set listing.

Handles appear at the corners of the rectangle, indicating that the link is selected.

14 Move the pointer over the bottom right handle so that the double-headed arrow appears. Then drag down to stretch the rectangle around the text block below the title.

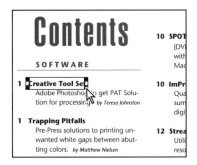
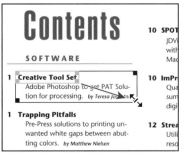

15 Select the hand tool, and move the pointer over the Creative Tool Set listing.

Notice that the activation area includes the entire text block below the title.

16 Click the activation area to test your link.

Creating a link to a Web site

Earlier you created a link from one area of *Digital Arts* to another. Now you'll add a link that leads to a page on the World Wide Web.

1 Click the Fit in Window ([■]) button.

2 Click the Next Page button (▶) to advance to page 2.

3 Select the zoom-in tool (⌕), and click in the cream-colored area at the bottom of the page to enlarge it.

This area of the page contains an advertisement for the Classroom in a Book series by Adobe Press. You'll create a link from an image in the ad to Adobe Systems Web page, which describes the book series in greater detail.

4 Select the link tool (🔗), and drag to create a marquee around the center image of the *Adobe Acrobat 4.0 Classroom in a Book*.

The Create Link dialog box appears.

5 Under Appearance, for Type, choose Visible Rectangle.

6 For Width, choose Medium. For Color, choose Red. For Style, choose Solid.

Now you'll assign the action to link to the World Wide Web. First you'll copy the target URL from the advertisement.

7 Select the text select tool (T₁) in the tool bar. Drag to highlight the URL at the bottom of the ad. Then press Ctrl+C (Windows) or Command+C (Mac OS) to copy the text to the Clipboard.

8 In the Create Link dialog box, under Action, for Type, choose World Wide Web Link. Click Edit URL.

9 Press Ctrl+V (Windows) or Command+V (Mac OS) to paste the URL that you just copied, and click OK.

10 Click Set Link.

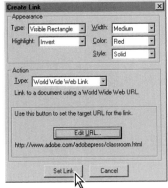

If you have a Web browser and a connection to the World Wide Web, you can go on to the next step and try out your newly created link. First you'll specify a Web browser to use when opening Weblinks. Once you establish your browser preference, Acrobat automatically uses that browser to open all Weblinks.

11 Choose File > Preferences > Weblink. Then click Browse (Windows) or Select (Mac OS).

12 Select your browser application, and click Open. Then click OK to return to the document.

13 Select the hand tool ($\mathcal{E}^{m}$), and try out your Weblink.

If you are using Acrobat for Windows, the Specify Weblink Behavior dialog box appears. Select the option to open the Weblink in the Web browser, and click OK. Opening Weblinks in Acrobat is discussed in Lesson 10, "Creating PDF Documents from Paper and the Web."

The link opens the Adobe Systems Web site using the browser that you have just specified. The site opens to the page describing the Classroom in a Book series.

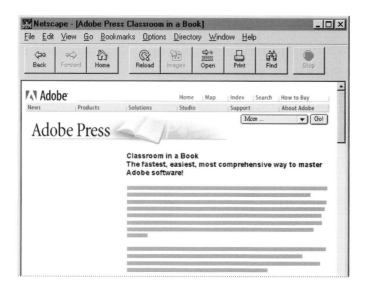

14 Close the browser window when you have finished viewing the Web site, and return to Acrobat.

15 Choose File > Save As, make sure that Optimized is selected, and save Digarts1.pdf in the Lesson02 folder. Click Yes (Windows) or Replace (Mac OS) to confirm replacing the file. The Save As command lets you save a smaller, optimized version of your finished file.

16 Choose File > Close to close the Digarts1.pdf file.

Using the online Adobe Acrobat User Guide

For complete information on using tools and palettes, you can use the online Adobe Acrobat User Guide. The user guide is easy to use because you can look for topics in several ways:

• Scanning a table of contents.

• Searching for keywords.

• Using an index.

To open the user guide, choose Acrobat Guide from the Acrobat Help menu.

The user guide contains a table of contents with links that you can click to go to particular chapters and sections in the guide. If you can't find the topic that you are interested in by scanning the table of contents, then you can try searching using a keyword. You can also search using the index. For information on how to use and print the guide, click the "?" button at the top of any page in the guide.

In this lesson, you have learned how to page through a PDF document, change the magnification and page layout mode, and create and edit links. In later lessons, you'll learn how to create and use other navigational features, such as bookmarks, thumbnails, and articles.

Review questions

1 Name three ways in which you can switch to a different page.

2 Name three ways in which you can change the view magnification.

3 To what kinds of destinations can a link jump?

4 How do you control the view magnification of a link destination?

5 How do you edit an existing link?

Review answers

1 You can switch pages by clicking the Previous Page or Next Page button in the command bar, dragging the scroll box in the scroll bar, double-clicking the page box in the status bar and entering a page number, clicking a bookmark or link that jumps to a different page, or clicking the thumbnail for a different page.

2 You can change the view magnification by clicking the Actual Size, Fit in Window, or Fit Width button in the command bar; marquee-zooming with the zoom-in or zoom-out tool; choosing a preset magnification from the magnification menu in the status bar; or double-clicking the magnification box and entering a specific percentage.

3 A link can jump to a different view within the same or different PDF document, or to a page on the World Wide Web. A link can also jump to other application files and be used to trigger actions such as playing a sound or executing a menu command.

4 You can set the view magnification of a link destination by choosing a preset level from the Magnification menu in the Create Link dialog box, or choosing Fixed from the Magnification menu and adjusting the magnification of the destination page as desired.

5 To edit a link, select the link tool and double-click inside the link to open the Link Properties dialog box. After you have changed the desired properties, click Set Link.

Lesson 3

Creating PDF from Authoring Programs

Acrobat provides several ways for you to create PDF documents quickly and easily from existing electronic files. The PDFWriter and Distiller methods offer different advantages depending on the content and layout of the original document.

In this lesson, you'll learn how to do the following:

• Use PDFWriter to create a PDF document.

• Use Distiller to create a PDF document.

• Compare the output between PDF documents created with Distiller and PDFWriter.

This lesson will take about 30 minutes to complete.

If needed, remove the previous lesson folder from your hard drive, and copy the Lesson03 folder onto it.

Creating PDF documents

The content of a PDF document must be created in a program other than Acrobat. You can use any of your favorite word-processing, page-layout, graphic, or business programs to create content and then convert those documents to PDF at the time you would normally print to paper. You can think of PDF files as the electronic paper version of your original documents.

Creating PDF files is as easy as printing from your application. You have two "printing" choices, PDFWriter and Distiller. Both are installed as part of the default Acrobat installation process. But when should you use one and when the other?

PDFWriter or Acrobat Distiller?

Your workflow process, document type, and document content determine which Acrobat producer—PDFWriter or Acrobat Distiller—you should use to create your PDF document.

• Use PDFWriter for quick conversion of simple business documents to PDF. If you do not obtain satisfactory results with PDFWriter, convert the document to PDF with Distiller.

• Use Distiller for documents containing Encapsulated PostScript (EPS) graphics, documents containing bitmap images for which you need to choose specific resampling and compression methods, or documents produced from desktop publishing applications, such as Adobe FrameMaker, Adobe PageMaker, and QuarkXPress®, that have been optimized to print to PostScript. Also use Distiller for batch processing on your hard drive.

The following table provides general guidelines to help you determine which method to select for specific types of documents.

Use Distiller if you:	Use PDFWriter if you:
Have desktop publishing documents such as those created with PageMaker, FrameMaker, QuarkXPress, Illustrator, or FreeHand®	Have simple business documents such as those created with Microsoft Word or Excel™
Have documents containing EPS graphics	Have documents that do not contain EPS graphics
Have documents containing images in which you need precise control over compression and down-sampling options	Want to add a Create PDF macro to applications that use macros
Have documents containing PostScript features that you need to maintain in the PDF document such as OPI comments	Do not want to install a PostScript printer driver on your system (PostScript printer drivers are required to use Distiller)
Send documents to prepress or service bureaus for high-end publishing	Have limited amounts of RAM
Have documents you would like to batch process	Want to produce PDF documents more quickly than you can with Distiller
Obtain unsatisfactory results from PDFWriter	

Using fonts with this lesson

In this lesson, you'll work with several source files that contain specific fonts. If you receive a message indicating that the necessary fonts are not installed, see the introduction, "Getting Started" and install the fonts from the Classroom in a Book CD.

Creating a PDF file with PDFWriter

PDFWriter is best used with simple business documents that contain mostly text. The process of using PDFWriter to create a PDF file is often faster than using Distiller. But for some documents, especially those containing placed EPS images, PDFWriter may not produce satisfactory results. In those cases, use Distiller to process the files.

In this section, you'll use PDFWriter to create a PDF file from a word-processing document that contains a simple graphic. We have supplied a Microsoft Word document. If your word processor cannot open Microsoft Word documents, skip to "Viewing the PDF contract" on page 75, and use the PDF document that has been supplied.

Opening the contract file

1 Start your word processor.

2 Choose File > Open. Select Contract.doc in the Lesson03 folder, located inside the Lessons folder within the AA4_CIB folder on your hard drive, and click Open.

Take a minute to look at the contract document. Notice that the document contains a simple graphic logo at the top of the page.

Creating the PDF file

Creating a PDF file is as easy as selecting PDFWriter and printing. This section has been organized by platform. Find your platform and follow the steps in that section.

In Windows:

1 Choose File > Print.

2 Choose Acrobat PDFWriter from the Name menu in the Printer section, and click OK. In some applications, you may need to click Setup in the Print dialog box to get access to the Name menu.

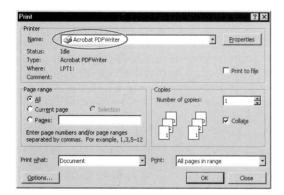

3 In the Save PDF File As dialog box, click Edit Document Info.

The Acrobat PDFWriter Document Information dialog box appears. Document information fields are used by search engines to help you categorize documents and provide a descriptive title for Search Results lists. Searching and Search Results lists are explained and used in Lesson 11, "Building a Searchable PDF Library and Catalog." (By default, the filename appears in the Title field, and the registered user of the authoring application appears in the Author field. However, this information is not always an adequate description of the PDF document.)

4 Enter the following information for Document Info, clicking OK when you are done:

• For Title, enter **Sales Agency Agreement**.

• For Subject, enter **Sales**.

• For Author, enter **Legal department**.

• For Keywords, enter **sales, payment, agreement**. (Be sure to enter a comma and space between each keyword.)

5 Name the PDF document **Contract1.pdf**, and save it in the Lesson03 folder.

6 Exit your word processor.

In Mac OS:

1 Hold down the shortcut key (the Control key by default) and choose File > Print. The shortcut allows you to access PDFWriter even if a different item is selected in the Chooser.

Note: *To change the shortcut key for PDFWriter, use the PDFWriter Shortcut control panel located in the Control Panels folder inside the System Folder.*

2 Select All as the page range, deselect View PDF File, select Prompt for Document Info, and click OK.

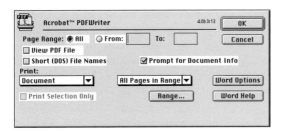

The Acrobat PDFWriter Document Information dialog box appears. Document information fields are used by search engines to help you categorize documents and provide a descriptive title for search results lists. Searching and search results lists are explained and used in Lesson 11.

3 Enter the following information for Document information, clicking OK when you are done:

- For Title, enter **Sales Agency Agreement**.

- For Subject, enter **Sales**.

- For Author, enter **Legal department**.

- For Keywords, enter **sales, payment, agreement**. (Be sure to enter a comma and space between each keyword.)

4 Name the PDF document **Contract1.pdf**, and save it in the Lesson03 folder.

5 Quit your word processor.

Converting files to PDF from Microsoft applications (Windows)

The default Acrobat installation in Windows includes macros that allow you to create PDF files quickly and easily from Microsoft Office applications. A macro called PDFMaker works with Microsoft Word 97 and PowerPoint 97®; a PDFWriter macro works with Microsoft Word 95 and Excel 97 and 95. These macros are installed automatically with Acrobat if you have the appropriate Microsoft application on your system.

When you create a PDF file directly from Microsoft Word, you can set options that control the appearance and other aspects of the PDF file. The PDFMaker macro (with Word 97) can create PDF using either PDF-Writer or Distiller, and it supports Acrobat 4.0 features such as structured bookmarks. The PDFWriter macro (with Word 95) is a more basic utility that uses PDFWriter to create PDF.

To convert a file to PDF from a Microsoft application (Windows):

Do one of the following:

• *In Microsoft Word 97, choose File > Create PDF File, or click the Adobe Acrobat icon on the Microsoft application tool bar. Select PDFWriter or Distiller, set other options if necessary, and click Create. You can click the Help button in this dialog box to open a document with more information.*

• *In Microsoft Word 95, choose File > Create Adobe PDF > Print, or click the Adobe Acrobat PDF icon on the Microsoft application tool bar.*

• *In PowerPoint, click the Adobe Acrobat icon on the Microsoft application tool bar.*

• *In Excel, choose File > Create Adobe PDF, or click the Adobe Acrobat icon on the Microsoft application tool bar.*

–From the online Adobe Acrobat User Guide, Chapter 2

Viewing the PDF contract

1 Start Acrobat.

2 Choose File > Open. Select Contract1.pdf in the Lesson03 folder, and click Open.

Note: If you need to use the supplied PDF document, locate and open the Supply folder inside the Lesson03 folder, select Contract.pdf from the list of files, and click Open.

Take a moment to look at the document. Notice that PDFWriter has re-created the original document maintaining the format, fonts, and layout.

3 Minimize or hide Acrobat.

Creating a PDF file with Acrobat Distiller

Acrobat Distiller creates a PDF file that maintains all the formatting, graphics, and photographic images in the original document. In general, Distiller provides higher output quality than PDFWriter. In this part of the lesson, you'll convert a sample flyer document directly to PDF using preset Distiller options.

Opening the flyer document

Saved in Adobe PageMaker format, the flyer document contains general information about a fictitious company that repairs and restores antique automobiles. If you do not have PageMaker, proceed to "Viewing and comparing the PDF files" on page 77 and open the PDF file that has been supplied.

1 Start PageMaker.

2 Choose File > Open. Select Flyerpc.p65 (Windows) or Flyermc.p65 (Mac OS) in the Lesson03 folder, located inside the Lessons folder within the AA4_CIB folder on your hard drive, and click Open (Windows) or OK (Mac OS).

Take a minute to look at the flyer document. Notice that the flyer contains a number of photographic and graphic elements.

Choosing a Distiller job option setting

Distiller provides three default job option settings that control the quality of the resulting PDF document for different output needs:

• The ScreenOptimized job options create PDF files appropriate for display on the World Wide Web or an intranet, or for distribution through an e-mail system for on-screen viewing. This option set produces a PDF file that is as small as possible.

• The PrintOptimized job options create PDF files that are intended for printers, digital copiers, publishing on a CD-ROM, or distribution as a publishing proof. This option set compresses the PDF file size while striving to preserve the color, image quality, and font attributes of the original document.

• The PressOptimized job options create PDF files that are intended for high-quality printed output. This option set produces the largest file size, but preserves the maximum amount of information about the original document.

For the purposes of the informational flyer, you'll instruct Distiller to create a PDF document suitable for output on a color desktop printer.

1 Start Acrobat Distiller.

2 For Job Options, choose PrintOptimized.

3 Exit or quit Distiller.

In general, the default Distiller options produce good results. However, you may want to set custom options to control the appearance of converted pages and to fine-tune the quality and compression of images. For added control over the PDF creation process, you may want to convert your document first to a PostScript language file, and then convert the PostScript file to PDF using Distiller. For information on using these advanced Distiller features, see Lesson 12, "Customizing PDF Output Quality."

Creating the PDF file

Now that you've specified a Distiller job option setting, you can convert the flyer directly to PDF from PageMaker. You'll use a special PageMaker feature that exports a PDF file using Distiller.

1 Return to the PageMaker flyer document, and choose File > Export > Adobe PDF.

2 Deselect Override Distiller's Options. Accept the remaining settings, and click Export.

3 Name the PDF file **Flyer1.pdf**, and save it in the Lesson03 folder. Distiller will open, and you can see the progress of the conversion.

4 Exit or quit Distiller.

5 Exit or quit PageMaker. You don't need to save any changes to the PageMaker flyer document.

Many applications also let you use the Print command to create PDF files with Distiller. For more information, see "Creating PDF files with Distiller" in Chapter 2 of the online Adobe Acrobat User Guide.

Viewing and comparing the PDF files

Now you'll compare the two PDF documents you created.

1 Maximize or show Acrobat.

2 If needed, choose File > Open, select Flyer1.pdf in the Lesson03 folder, and click Open.

3 Choose View > Fit in Window to view the entire document.

Note: If you need to use the supplied PDF document, open the Flyer.pdf file located in the Supply folder inside the Lesson03 folder.

As you can see, Distiller created an exact duplicate of the original file. Take particular notice of the car logo at the top of the page. This was a placed Encapsulated PostScript (EPS) image in the PageMaker document. You'll now compare it with the PDF document you created with PDFWriter that contains the same logo.

4 If you closed Contract1.pdf earlier, open it again.

Note: If you need to use the supplied PDF document, open the Contract.pdf file located in the Supply folder inside the Lesson03 folder.

5 Choose Window > Tile > Vertically to view the two documents side by side.

6 Select the zoom-in tool (🔍) and marquee-zoom around the car logo at the top of the page in each document to magnify the view of the logo.

Notice that the PDF file produced by Distiller (the flyer) displays a cleaner logo than the logo displayed in the PDFWriter document (the contract). Because PDFWriter does not understand the PostScript language, it supplies a bitmap image of placed EPS files in the PDF documents it creates. In contrast, Acrobat Distiller maintains the resolution independence of the placed EPS graphic because it understands the PostScript information that describes it, and passes that along in the PDF file.

PDFWriter

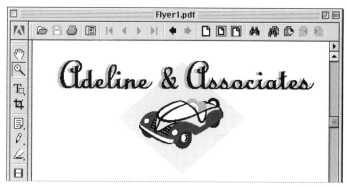

Distiller

7 Now scroll to view the text in each document.

Notice that the text in each document is smooth and easy to read. You can use either Distiller or PDFWriter to get acceptable results from text-based documents.

8 When you have finished viewing the documents, choose Window > Close All to close the documents, and exit or quit Acrobat.

In this lesson, you learned how to create PDF files from electronic documents with Acrobat Distiller and PDFWriter. In the following lessons, you'll learn more about electronic publishing and how to enhance your PDF documents to make them interactive and easier to navigate.

Exploring on your own (Windows)

If you are using Windows, you can open a document from another application in Acrobat and convert it automatically to PDF, using the currently selected set of Distiller job options. Distiller does not have to be running to convert the file.

You can open a document from Adobe FrameMaker, Corel WordPerfect®, or Microsoft Word, Excel, or PowerPoint; an HTML or text file; or an image file of type GIF, JPEG, TIFF, PCX, PNG, or BMP.

1 In Acrobat, choose File > Open.

2 Locate and open the source file you want to convert, and click Open. If you don't see your source file, choose All Files (*.*) from the Files of Type menu.

The source file is converted to PDF and opened in Acrobat.

Review questions

1 If your documents contain placed EPS images, which PDF creator should you use to create a PDF file?

2 What are the advantages of using Distiller to create PDF files instead of PDFWriter?

3 What are the advantages of using PDFWriter to create PDF files instead of Distiller?

4 Why is it important to enter information in the Document Info fields?

Review answers

1 If your documents contain placed EPS images and you want to retain the scalability of the image, you should use Acrobat Distiller to create a PDF file.

2 Distiller:

• Retains image resolution of placed EPS images.

• Provides precise control of image compression and downsampling.

• Retains PostScript features such as OPI comments in PDF documents.

• Provides batch processing options.

3 PDFWriter:

• Maintains searchable text in documents created with embedded TrueType™ fonts from Windows.

• Can be used in a macro to create PDF documents.

• Can be faster to create a PDF document than Distiller.

4 It is important to enter information in the Document Info fields because these fields are used by search engines to help you categorize documents and to provide descriptive information about them in a search results list.

Lesson 4

Creating Navigational Structures

Acrobat includes several features that let you organize and navigate a document from an overview perspective. Bookmarks represent headings that link to their corresponding sections in the document, thumbnails let you preview the contents of and navigate each page, and articles let you follow a thread of information that spans more than one column on a page or across pages.

In this lesson, you'll learn how to do the following:

- Create bookmarks that link to specific views in a document.
- Use thumbnails to navigate through a document.
- Use thumbnails to change the magnification level and viewed area.
- Create a link that jumps to a different PDF document.
- Replace a page with another page from a different PDF document.
- Follow an article thread.

This lesson will take about 35 minutes to complete.

If needed, remove the previous lesson folder from your hard drive, and copy the Lesson04 folder onto it.

Opening the work file

You'll start by opening an online newsletter published by a fictitious company called Juggler Toys.

1 Start Acrobat.

2 Choose File > Open. Select News.pdf in the Lesson04 folder, located inside the Lessons folder within the AA4_CIB folder on your hard drive, and click Open. Then choose File > Save As, rename the file **News1.pdf**, and save it in the Lesson04 folder.

Using bookmarks

A bookmark is a link represented by text in the Bookmarks palette. Instead of creating an activation area on the document page, you create a text list in the Bookmarks palette that is linked to different views or pages in the document.

You can use electronic bookmarks as you would paper bookmarks—to mark a place in a document that you want to recall or return to later. You can also use bookmarks to create a brief custom outline of a document or to open other documents.

Working with bookmarks

Acrobat generates bookmarks automatically from the table of contents of documents created by most desktop publishing applications. The creator (or sometimes the user) of a PDF document can also set up additional bookmarks in an existing PDF document to link to another PDF document or to a Web page. In addition to the bookmarks Acrobat generates automatically from a table of contents and index, Acrobat can create structured bookmarks from Web pages (HTML) and Microsoft Word documents converted to PDF using PDFMaker.

–From the online Adobe Acrobat User Guide, Chapter 6

Looking at existing bookmarks

When bookmarks are displayed, they appear in the Bookmarks palette, which is docked in the navigation pane to the left of the document pane. To maximize the screen area used for display, the Juggler Toys newsletter is set to open with the navigation pane closed. You use the Show/Hide Navigation Pane button in the command bar to display the navigation pane.

1 Click the Show/Hide Navigation Pane button ( ) in the command bar. If needed, click the Bookmarks tab to bring the Bookmarks palette to the front.

A list of bookmarks representing stories in the newsletter appears. You may not be able to read all of the bookmark text on your screen. You'll resize the navigation pane to display the bookmarks completely.

2 Adjust the width of the navigation pane by dragging its right border.

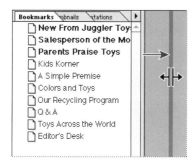

Drag right border of navigation pane.   *Result*

Notice that the text for some bookmarks is bold. Bookmarks with bold text have destinations that are located on the current page of the document. If desired, you can hide the location indicators of bookmark destinations. To do so, hold down the mouse button on the triangle in the upper right corner of the Bookmarks palette to display the Bookmarks palette menu, and choose Show Location. (A check mark appears next to the command name when this feature is enabled.)

3 Select the hand tool (✋) in the tool bar, and click the Q & A bookmark to go to the page where the corresponding topic appears.

You should be viewing the Q & A topic on page 3.

Click Q & A bookmark.   *Result*

Adding bookmarks

The current bookmark list lacks a few needed entries. You'll add some of the missing bookmarks to the list.

1 Click the Kids Korner bookmark to go to the corresponding topic on page 2.

2 If needed, scroll up to bring the "Family Night Focus" topic into view.

Notice that the "Family Night Focus" topic does not have a corresponding bookmark in the Bookmarks palette. You'll add a bookmark for this topic to the list.

3 Select the text select tool (T̪) in the tool bar.

4 Move the I-beam into the page, and drag to highlight the title "Family Night Focus."

Family Night Focus

The Theme of October's Family Night will be "Flyi
jects." Three teams will present their prototypes
to the Juggler Toys community. Here are a few hir
what's in store: flying saucers, self-propelling crea
other airborne objects. (Okay, now *you* guess.)

As always, we encourage you to bring your ch
They're always our best critics. Dining will begin a
Show-and-Test will begin around 8 ᴾᴹ. Wear comf
clothes and bring a dish to share. Beverages and c
be provided. We'll look forward to seeing you the

If you have trouble highlighting the title, hold down Ctrl (Windows) or Option (Mac OS) and drag a marquee around the title.

5 Choose New Bookmark from the Bookmarks palette menu. A new bookmark appears with the highlighted text as its title.

The Family Night Focus bookmark appears at the bottom of the bookmark list. If no bookmarks are selected when you create a new bookmark, the new bookmark appears at the bottom of the list.

By default, the new bookmark links to the current page view displayed on your screen.

6 Click in the blank space beneath the bookmark list to deselect the bookmark text. Then click the First Page button (◄) to go to the start of the newsletter.

7 Select the hand tool ( ), and click the Family Night Focus bookmark to jump to the corresponding topic.

Moving a bookmark

After creating a bookmark, you can move it to its proper place in the list. You reorder bookmarks by dragging them.

1 Drag the Family Night Focus bookmark upward until a bar appears under the page icon for the Parents Praise Toys bookmark. (Make sure the bar appears under the page icon, not the bookmark text.) The bar indicates the new location for the selected bookmark.

2 Release the mouse button to reorder the bookmark. Then click OK to confirm moving the selected bookmark.

Position pointer over bookmark. *Drag bookmark upward until bar appears.* *Release mouse.*

3 Click in the blank space beneath the bookmark list to deselect the bookmark.

Setting bookmark destinations

Bookmark destinations default to the view that you are looking at when you create a bookmark. Although you can set bookmark destinations as you create each bookmark, it is sometimes easier to create a group of bookmarks, and set the destinations later. For example, if you are creating a table of contents, you can create the bookmark list first, and then page through the document to set the destinations.

In this section, you'll add the bookmarks for the pictures and advertisements in this newsletter. You'll add three bookmarks and then set their destinations.

1 Click the New From Juggler Toys bookmark to select it.

2 Choose New Bookmark from the Bookmarks palette menu. A new untitled bookmark appears below the previously selected bookmark.

3 Type **Pictures and Ads** as the bookmark title. Then click in the blank space beneath the bookmark list to deselect the bookmark text.

New untitled bookmark

Type title, and click in blank space to deselect text.

4 Click the Pictures and Ads bookmark to select it.

5 Choose New Bookmark from the Bookmarks palette menu to create another untitled bookmark, and type **Guy Galaxy** as the bookmark title. Then click in the blank space beneath the bookmark list to deselect the bookmark text.

6 Click the Guy Galaxy bookmark to select it.

7 Choose New Bookmark from the Bookmarks palette menu again, and type **Retro Toys Ad** as the bookmark title. Then click in the blank space beneath the bookmark list to deselect the bookmark text.

8 Use the hand tool to try out your new bookmarks.

Notice that by default all the bookmarks link to the current page view. Next, you'll reset the destinations for the Guy Galaxy and Retro Toys Ad bookmarks.

9 Click the Guy Galaxy bookmark to select it.

10 Click the Fit in Window button (🗖) to view page 1 in its entirety.

11 Select the zoom-in tool (🔍) in the tool bar, and marquee-zoom around the Guy Galaxy picture.

Marquee-zoom around picture.

Result

12 Choose Set Bookmark Destination from the Bookmarks palette menu to reset the destination to the view currently displayed on-screen. Click Yes to confirm resetting the bookmark destination.

13 Click the Retro Toys Ad bookmark to select it.

14 Choose Document > Go to Page. Then enter **3** and click OK.

15 Click the Fit in Window button, and use the zoom-in tool to marquee-zoom around the Retro Toys advertisement at the bottom of the page.

Marquee-zoom around picture.

Result

16 Choose Set Bookmark Destination from the Bookmarks palette menu, and click Yes to the message.

Instead of assigning a view destination for the Pictures and Ads bookmark, you'll make the bookmark into a heading for the Guy Galaxy and Retro Toys Ad bookmarks.

17 Click the Pictures and Ads bookmark, and choose Bookmark Properties from the Bookmarks palette menu.

18 For Type, choose None, and click Set Action.

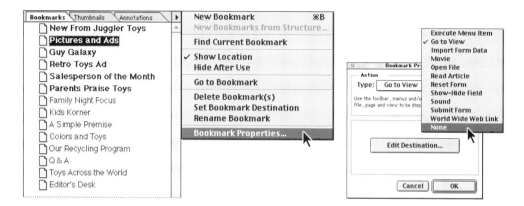

The default bookmark action is to link to a page view. Choosing None as the action type for the Pictures and Ads bookmark means that the bookmark does not link to any destination and acts solely as a heading.

19 Click in the blank space beneath the bookmark list to deselect the bookmark.

20 Select the hand tool (🖑), and try out your bookmarks. Notice that the Pictures and Ads bookmark does not change the page view.

Nesting bookmarks

Bookmarks can be used to create a hierarchical outline of a document, with several bookmarks nested under a common heading. In this section, you'll nest the Guy Galaxy and Retro Toys Ad bookmarks under the Pictures and Ads bookmark.

1 Click the Guy Galaxy bookmark to select it.

2 Hold down Shift, and click the Retro Toys Ad bookmark to add it to the selection. Then release Shift.

3 Position the pointer over the Retro Toys Ad bookmark.

4 Drag upward until a bar appears under the "P" in Pictures and Ads.

5 Release the mouse button. Then click OK to confirm moving the selected bookmarks.

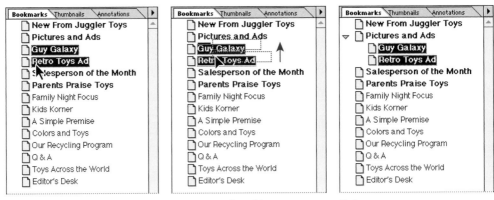

Position pointer over Retro Toys Ad bookmark.   *Drag upward until bar appears.*   *Release mouse.*

The selected bookmarks appear as sub-bookmarks under the Pictures and Ads bookmark.

You have just learned how to create, move, and assign actions to bookmarks. In later lessons, you'll learn how to create bookmarks that play other actions such as movies and sounds.

6 Choose File > Save to save the News1.pdf file.

Using thumbnails

Thumbnails are miniature previews of your document pages. When thumbnails are displayed, they appear in the Thumbnails palette, which is docked in the navigation pane to the left of the document pane.

In this part of the lesson, you'll use thumbnails to navigate and change the view of pages in the newsletter. In Lesson 5, "Modifying PDF Documents," you'll learn how to use thumbnails to reorder pages in a document.

1 If needed, click the First Page button (◀) to return to the start of the newsletter. Click the Actual Size button (⬜) to view the page at 100% magnification.

2 Click the Thumbnails tab to bring the Thumbnails palette to the front.

Notice that gray thumbnail placeholders appear for each page in the document. Because thumbnails take up extra file space (about 3K per thumbnail), they are not automatically created with a document. You'll generate the actual thumbnails in the next step.

3 Hold down the mouse button on the triangle in the upper right corner of the Thumbnails palette to display the Thumbnails palette menu, and choose Create All Thumbnails.

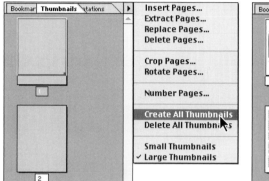 

Choose Create All Thumbnails from Thumbnails palette menu. *Result*

Thumbnails for every page in the document are created. You can cancel thumbnail generation at any time by clicking Cancel (Windows) or pressing Command-period (Mac OS). The thumbnails created before you canceled will appear in the navigation pane.

4 If all the thumbnails are not visible in the navigation pane, use the scroll bar to scroll through them.

Notice that the thumbnails represent both the content and page orientation of the pages in the newsletter. Page-number boxes appear beneath each thumbnail.

5 Double-click the page 3 thumbnail to go to page 3.

The page number for the thumbnail is highlighted, and a 100% view of page 3 appears in the document window, centered on the point that you clicked.

Take a look at the page 3 thumbnail. The rectangle inside the thumbnail, called the page-view box, represents the area displayed in the current page view. You can use the page-view box to adjust the area and magnification being viewed.

6 Position the pointer over the lower right corner of the page-view box. Notice that the pointer turns into a double-headed arrow.

7 Drag upward to shrink the page-view box and release the mouse button. Take a look at the status bar and notice that the magnification level has increased to accommodate the smaller area being viewed.

> A Simple Premise
>
> We asked Juggler Toys CEO Jane Dean to put down her candy cigar for a few moments to talk about the good old-fashioned principles and basic values that have helped her company rise to the top of the international toy market.
>
> Currency, tradition, and simplicity, says Dean, form the basis of the Juggler Toys philosophy. Balancing capricious trends with tried and true classics of the toy industry has proven to be one of the greatest challenges for Dean. "Fads may come and go, but a few stick around long enough to become new classics for a whole generation. The trick is figuring out which new ideas will leave lasting impressions on the youngsters of today."
>
> For example, the latest crop of toy automobiles from the Retro Toys collection combines sensible wind-up technology with a nineties sensibility. Girls and

Double-click page 3 thumbnail.   *Drag lower right corner of page-view box upward.*   *Result*

8 Now position the pointer over the bottom border of the page-view box. Notice that the pointer changes to a hand.

9 Drag the page-view box within the thumbnail, and watch the view change in the document window when you release the mouse button.

10 Drag the page-view box down to focus your view on the ad at the bottom of the page.

Thumbnails provide a convenient way to monitor and adjust your page view in a document.

11 Click the Show/Hide Navigation Pane button (🗔) to hide the navigation pane.

Creating a cross-document link

In Lesson 2, "Getting to Know the Work Area," you learned how to create links to different page views and Web sites. Now you'll learn how to create a link that jumps to a different PDF document.

In addition to the toy newsletter, Juggler Toys publishes a variety of documents to help advertise, catalog, and sell its products. You'll create a link from the Retro Toys ad in this newsletter to an online brochure detailing the Retro Toys collection.

1 Click the Fit in Window button (🗎).

2 Select the link tool (🔗) in the tool bar, and drag a marquee around the Retro Toys ad.

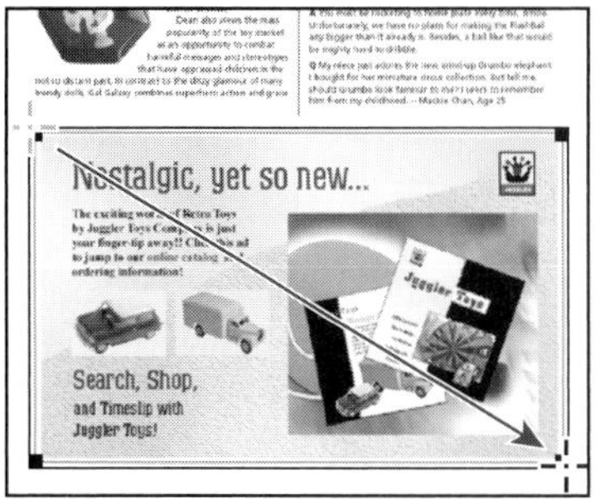

3 Under Appearance, for Type, choose Invisible Rectangle.

In addition to setting the appearance of a link's border, you can also specify the highlight appearance of a link when it is clicked.

4 For Highlight, choose Outline.

The Outline option displays the link as a black rectangle when clicked. The following illustration shows the different highlight appearances available in Acrobat.

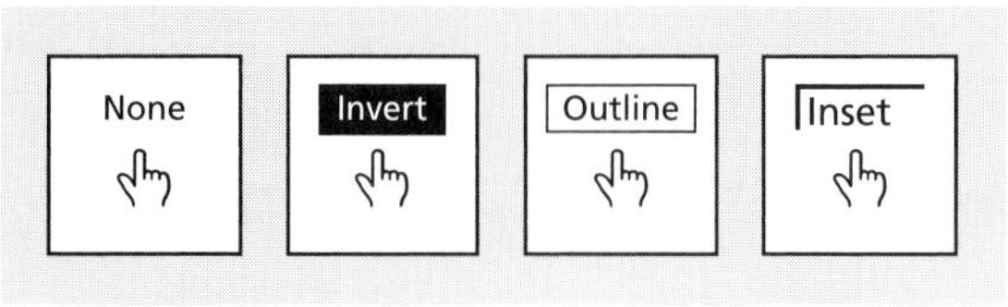

5 Under Action, for Type, choose Go to View.

In Acrobat, a view consists of a specific PDF page and magnification. The page can be part of the current document or an entirely different PDF document.

6 From the menu bar, choose File > Open. Select Brochure.pdf, located inside the Lesson04 folder, and click Open.

7 In the Create Link dialog box, for Magnification, choose Fit in Window to display the full brochure page when the link is activated.

8 Click Set Link.

Online Juggler Toys brochure

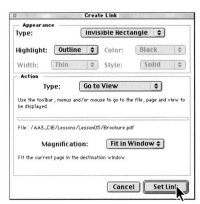

Click Set Link.

9 Select the hand tool (🖑), and try out the link that you have just created.

10 Click the Go to Previous View button (◄) to retrace the link back to the original document and view.

Setting magnification options

You can specify a bookmark's or link's destination to be a particular view of a page. To do so, you set the magnification for the bookmark's or link's destination page. You can choose from the following magnification options:

Fixed Displays the destination at the magnification level and page position in effect when you create the bookmark or link. Use the zoom-in or zoom-out tool, the view buttons in the command or status bar, or the scroll bar to adjust the view before accepting this setting.

Fit View Displays the visible portion of the current page as the destination. The magnification level and window size vary with monitor resolution.

Fit in Window Displays the current page in the destination window.

Fit Width Displays the width of the current page in the destination window.

Fit Height Displays the height of the current page in the destination window.

Fit Visible Displays the width of the visible contents of the current page in the destination window.

Inherit Zoom Displays the destination window at the magnification level the readers are using when they click the bookmark or link.

–From the online Adobe Acrobat User Guide, Chapter 6

Replacing a page

Sometimes you may want to replace an entire PDF page with another PDF page. For example, if you want to change the design or layout of a PDF page, you can revise the source page in your original design application, convert the modified page to PDF, and use it to replace the old PDF page. When you replace a page, only the text and graphics on the original page are replaced. The replacement does not affect any interactive elements associated with the original page, such as bookmarks or links.

In this part of the lesson, you'll replace page 3 of the newsletter with a page that contains a new version of the Retro Toys ad and observe what happens to the link that you just created around the ad.

1 Choose Document > Replace Pages.

2 Select Newspage.pdf, located in the Lesson04 folder, and click Open (Windows) or Select (Mac OS).

3 In the Replace Pages dialog box, make sure that you are replacing page 3 to 3 of News1.pdf with page 1 to 1 of Newspage.pdf, and click OK.

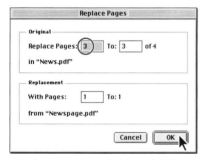

Specify pages to be replaced, and click OK.   *Result*

Acrobat replaces the page with the revised page from the Newspage.pdf document. Notice the different graphics used in the new ad.

Now you'll verify that the original ad link is still in place.

4 Using the hand tool, click the ad to jump to the brochure.

5 Click the Go to Previous View button (◀) to return to the newsletter.

6 Choose File > Save to save the News1.pdf file.

You can think of PDF links as existing in their own layer on top of pages in a document. Links are not inherently tied to graphic or text elements in a document. When you replace pages from a document, the links remain unaffected and maintain their relative positions and sizes in their link layer.

Because the Retro Toys ad in your replacement page has the same size and position as the ad in the original page, the cross-document link you created still references the correct part of the new page. However, if your replacement page contains shifted graphics and text blocks, you may have to move your links to correct their positions.

Using articles

Although the Juggler Toys newsletter has been converted to an online format, it still uses a layout associated with printed newsletters. The restrictions of the screen can make the reading of some documents quite difficult. For example, documents created in a column format can be particularly difficult to follow.

Acrobat's article feature lets you guide users through material that lies in columns or across a series of nonconsecutive pages. You use the article tool to create a series of linked rectangles that connect the separate sections of the material and follow the flow of text. You can also generate article threads automatically from a page layout file when you convert the file to PDF using Acrobat Distiller.

In this part of the lesson, you'll examine an article that has already been created. In Lesson 6, you'll learn how to create an article thread.

1 Choose Window > Show Articles to display articles. By default, the Articles palette floats on the desktop and is grouped with the Destinations palette.

2 Double-click the Colors and Toys article.

The beginning of the "Colors and Toys" article on page 2 appears. You may not be able to view the article on your screen because of the position of the palette group. If needed, move the palette group out of the way by dragging its title bar. Move your pointer on top of the article. The downward pointing arrow inside the hand pointer indicates that you are following an article thread.

3 Click to advance to the next section of the article that will fit on your screen.

4 Hold down Shift.

Notice that the arrow in the hand pointer now points upward. You hold down Shift to reverse your direction in an article.

Colors and Toys

Even superheroes can use a fashion lift sometimes. "I stumbled through the universe with the same flash sky boots and aquamarine torpedo pack for I don't know how many eons," says Gal Galaxy, the crime-busting heroine and beloved space icon. "Baby blu cramping my style. I needed a change." Well, thanks to world-renowned color specialists at Juggler Toys Company, Gal Galaxy can wash her blues away. This fall season finds our intrepid interstellar cadet decked out in brand new acid-washed rocket overalls available in a variety of colors, including Asteroid Belt Sunrise, Cosmic Marine, Martian Rust, and Plutonium Peach. Exclaims the seasonal action figure, "My awesome new threads have put a spring in my step and a wallop in my rocket booster.

Click to advance to next section of article.

ists at Juggler Toys Company, Gal Galaxy can wash her blues away. This fall season finds our intrepid interstellar cadet decked out in brand new acid-washed rocket overalls available in a variety of colors, including Asteroid Belt Sunrise, Cosmic Marine, Martian Rust, and Plutonium Peach. Exclaims the seasonal action figure, "My awesome new threads have put a spring in my step and op in my rocket booster. I've mopped up three toxic s rounded up four runaway satellites, and reversed the greenhouse effect on two planets already. And that's just today."

With her newly expanded wardrobe, Gal Galaxy can look forward to a fresh change of costume after every adventure. *(Continued on p4)*

Shift-click to move back one section of article.

5 While holding down Shift, click inside the article. Then release Shift.

You are moved back one view along the article thread.

6 If needed, scroll down the article until you reach the text that reads "Continued on p4."

Look at the status bar and notice that you are currently on page 2.

7 Click inside the article.

Look at the page number in the status bar. You have advanced from page 2 to page 4 to follow the article.

You can exit an article at any time by choosing any navigational method not associated with articles.

8 Click the Fit in Window button (▢) to exit the article.

9 Select the zoom-in tool (⊕), and marquee-zoom around the text under the elephant image in the left column.

10 Select the hand tool (🖐), and move the pointer over the parenthetical text that reads "Colors and Toys continued." A downward-pointing arrow with a bar above it appears inside the hand pointer, indicating the text beneath is part of an article thread.

Marquee-zoom around text in left column.

Select hand tool, and position pointer over parenthetical text.

11 Click the text to enter the article thread. Notice that you enter the article at the section you clicked.

You can return to the beginning of an article at any time.

12 Hold down Ctrl (Windows) or Option (Mac OS) so that an upward-pointing arrow with a bar above it appears in the hand pointer. Click inside the article to go to the start of the article.

Here, you first entered the article at its middle section and then used the Ctrl or Option key to jump to the start of the article. You can also go directly to the start of an article by holding down Ctrl or Option and clicking any section of the article.

13 Click inside the article to advance through the article. When you reach the end of the article, a bar appears below the arrow in the hand pointer.

14 Click the Actual Size button (🗔) to exit the article.

15 Choose Window > Hide Articles to hide the Articles palette.

16 Choose File > Save As, make sure that Optimized is selected, and save News1.pdf in the Lesson04 folder. Click Yes (Windows) or Replace (Mac OS) to confirm replacing the file. The Save As command lets you save a smaller, optimized version of your finished file.

17 Close all documents.

Using destinations

A destination is a link represented by text in the Destinations palette. You use destinations in conjunction with the link tool to navigate from one PDF document to another. You create a link in a source document to a destination in a target document. Creating a link to a destination, rather than a specific page, is recommended when creating a link across documents. Unlike a link to a page, a link to a destination is not affected by the addition or deletion of pages within the target document.

–From the online Adobe Acrobat User Guide, Chapter 6

In this lesson, you have learned how to use bookmarks and thumbnails to make navigation of your document easier. In later lessons, you'll learn how to assign actions to bookmarks and change page order using thumbnails.

Review questions

1 What does it mean when the text of a bookmark is bold in the Bookmarks palette menu?

2 How do you create a bookmark?

3 Why are thumbnails not automatically created with a document?

4 Using thumbnails, how do you change the area that you are viewing? How do you change the magnification?

5 If you replace a page with links on it, what happens to the links after the replacement?

6 Name two ways by which you can enter an article thread.

Review answers

1 If a bookmark's text is bold in the Bookmarks palette menu, the bookmark's destination is located on the current page of the document. To hide the location indicators of bookmark destinations, choose Show Location from the Bookmarks palette menu. (A check mark appears next to the command name when this feature is enabled.)

2 You can create a bookmark by navigating in the document to the desired destination, choosing New Bookmark from the Bookmarks palette menu, and entering text for the bookmark's title.

3 Thumbnails are not automatically created with a document because they take up extra file space (about 3K per thumbnail).

4 To adjust the area that you are viewing, drag a border of the page-view box inside the thumbnail. To adjust the magnification, drag the lower right corner of the page-view box to resize it.

5 Because links reside on a different layer from the content of a page, they are not affected when the page content is replaced. Your links will still jump to the correct destination or activate the correct action after the replacement.

6 You can enter an article thread by choosing Window > Show Articles and selecting the desired article, or by using the hand tool to click inside a section of an article. When the hand tool is positioned over an article, a downward pointing arrow with a bar above it appears inside the hand pointer.

Lesson 5

Modifying PDF Documents

Once you have converted your document to PDF, you can use Acrobat to make final edits and modifications. In addition to adding links and bookmarks to a document, you can edit text and images, and insert, reorder, and extract pages.

In this lesson, you'll learn how to do the following:

- Import a TIFF image file.

- Rotate and crop pages.

- Use thumbnails to rearrange pages in a document.

- Insert and extract pages from a document.

- Renumber pages.

- Edit the placement and contents of images in a document.

- Create links and bookmarks that play actions.

This lesson will take about 45 minutes to complete.

If needed, remove the previous lesson folder from your hard drive, and copy the Lesson05 folder onto it.

Opening and examining the work file

You'll work with an edition of *Aesop's Fables* that has been designed for online viewing and converted to PDF. Because this online book has passed through multiple designers and review cycles, it contains a number of mistakes. In this lesson you'll use Acrobat to correct the problems in this PDF document and optimize *Aesop's Fables* for the next generation of wise youngsters.

1 Start Acrobat.

2 Choose File > Open. Select Afables.pdf, located in the Lesson05 folder, located inside the Lessons folder within the AA4_CIB folder on your hard drive, and click Open. Then choose File > Save As, rename the file **Afables1.pdf**, and save it in the Lesson05 folder.

Notice that bookmarks for the individual fables in this document have already been created.

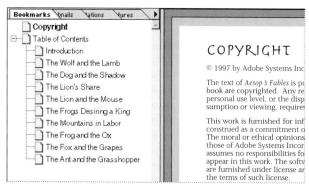

Bookmarks for Aesop's Fables

3 Select the hand tool, and click the Table of Contents bookmark to go to the table of contents.

4 Move the pointer into the document. Notice that the titles in the list have already been linked.

Move pointer into document.

This example of *Aesop's Fables* was originally designed using Adobe PageMaker. When the PageMaker file was converted to PDF, the entries in the formatted table of contents were converted to PDF bookmarks and links automatically.

Certain page-layout and book-publishing programs, such as PageMaker or Adobe FrameMaker, work in conjunction with Acrobat to automate the creation of links and bookmarks during the conversion to PDF. In Windows, you can preserve links created in Microsoft Word 95 or 97 by using the Create Adobe PDF command.

5 Click The Fox and the Grapes to follow its link.

6 Click the Go to Previous View button (◆) to return to the table of contents. You'll continue exploring this edition of *Aesop's Fables*.

Editing pages

Take a few moments and page through *Aesop's Fables*. Go to the first page of the document and notice that the book has no title page. We've created a separate title page for you by scanning a printed image into a computer and saving the image as a TIFF file.

Converting image files to PDF

You can import BMP, GIF, JPEG, PCX, PICT (Mac OS only), PNG, or TIFF image files into Acrobat. If you have a digital camera with a TWAIN scanner driver connected to your computer, you can also import a JPEG image from the camera into Acrobat. An imported image is automatically converted to the PDF Image Only format. The maximum image size you can import is 45inches by 45 inches.

In the PDF Image Only format, images and text are bitmaps, and therefore text cannot be edited. If your converted image has text, you may want to "capture" the image to change the bitmap text to regular PDF text that can be edited and searched in Acrobat.

An imported image can be in a new PDF file or appended to an existing file.

–From the online Adobe Acrobat User Guide, Chapter 2

Importing an image

To add a title page to the document, you'll import the TIFF image we created and edit the page to fit the rest of the book.

1 Choose File > Import > Image.

2 Select the image to be imported:

• In Windows, select Cover.tif in the Lesson05 folder, located inside the Lessons folder within the AA4_CIB folder on your hard drive, and click Open.

• In Mac OS, select Cover.tif in the Lesson05 folder, located inside the Lessons folder within the AA4_CIB folder on your hard drive, and click Add to add Cover.tif to the Select Files to Import message box. Then click Done.

The Import Image dialog box appears.

3 Select Current Document for Destination, and click OK.

The cover image is appended to the end of the document. The imported page is converted to PDF Image Only mode, meaning that only the image objects (not the text) in the page can be edited in Acrobat.

For information on importing different image formats into Acrobat, see "Converting image files to PDF" in Chapter 2 of the online Adobe Acrobat User Guide.

Rotating a page

Now that you have imported the new title page, you'll rotate it to the correct orientation.

1 Click the Fit in Window button ( ) to view the whole page you imported. Notice that the page orientation is incorrect—a problem that commonly occurs when scanning an image.

2 Choose Document > Rotate Pages.

The Rotate Pages dialog box lets you rotate one or more pages by 90° in a specified direction.

3 For Direction, select Counterclockwise. For Pages, make sure that you are rotating just page 17 of the document.

4 Click OK. When the confirmation message appears, click OK to rotate the page.

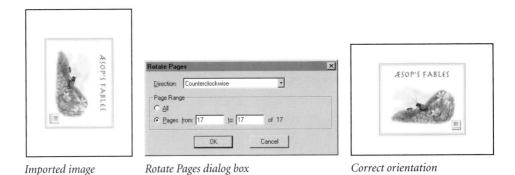

Imported image · *Rotate Pages dialog box* · *Correct orientation*

5 Select the Thumbnails tab in the navigation pane, and scroll down in the Thumbnails palette to view the last thumbnail for the page you just rotated.

Although the thumbnail is gray, you can see that this page is larger than the other pages in the book. You'll crop the imported page to make it exactly the same size as the other pages.

Cropping a page

You'll use the Crop Pages dialog box to enter dimensions for the imported page that match the other pages in the document.

1 Choose Document > Crop Pages.

The Crop Pages dialog box appears, which lets you specify the margins.

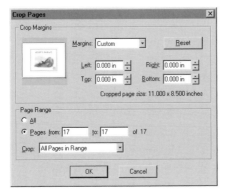

2 For Left, enter **2.15** and press Tab. A line representing the crop location appears both in the preview in the dialog box and in the document.

You may need to drag the Crop Pages dialog box out of the way to view the crop line in the document.

3 Use the arrows for Left in the Crop Pages dialog box to fine-tune the location of the crop line so that it aligns with the left edge of the title border.

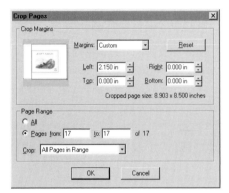

Fine-tuning location of left cropmark   *Crop line on left edge of title border*

4 For Top, enter **1.55** and press Tab. Use the arrows to align the crop line with the top edge of the title border.

5 Enter the following values for the remaining crop text boxes: **2.15** for Right and **1.60** for Bottom. Then use the arrows to fine-tune the crop lines.

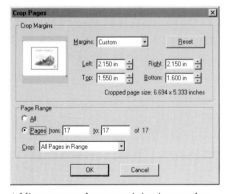
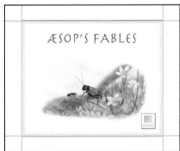

Adding crop marks to remaining image edges   *Result*

6 For Page Range, make sure that you are cropping just page 17 of the document, and click OK.

7 Choose File > Save to save the Afables1.pdf file.

Moving a page

Now that you have corrected the size and page orientation of the cover, you'll move it to the front of the book. You rearrange pages in a PDF document by using thumbnails.

1 Hold down the mouse button on the triangle in the upper right hand corner of the Thumbnails palette to display the Thumbnails palette menu, and choose Create All Thumbnails. This command updates all the thumbnails in the document, including the thumbnail for the imported page.

2 Drag the double-headed arrow at the bottom right corner of the navigation pane to enlarge the pane. Resize the navigation pane so that you can view the thumbnails in two columns.

 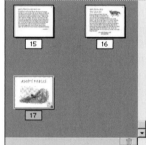

Drag to resize navigation pane.   *Result*

Thumbnails offer convenient previews of your pages, and you can drag them to alter the pagination.

3 If needed, scroll to view the page 17 thumbnail, and click to select it. A solid border outlines the thumbnail, indicating that you can move it.

4 Drag the selected thumbnail upward in the Thumbnails palette (the palette scrolls automatically). Drag upward until the insertion bar appears to the left of the page 1 thumbnail, and release the mouse button.

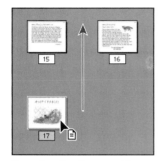
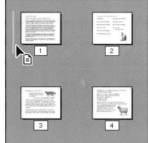

Drag thumbnail to reposition page.   *Insertion bar indicates new location.*

The cover page is repositioned in the document as page 1, and the remaining page numbers change accordingly.

Moving multiple pages

Next, you'll move two pages of a fable that we placed in the wrong section of the book.

1 Double-click the page 3 thumbnail to go to the table of contents.

2 Click the Fit Width button ( ) to display all of the contents.

3 Using the hand tool, click "The Ant and the Grasshopper" to jump to that fable. Although listed last in the contents, it is not the last fable in the book.

4 Click the page 13 thumbnail to select it. Hold down Shift and click the page 14 thumbnail to select it as well. Release Shift.

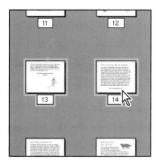

The technique of holding down Shift as you click thumbnails lets you select multiple thumbnails.

5 Begin dragging the page 13 thumbnail down until the insertion bar appears to the right of the page 17 thumbnail. Because the page 14 thumbnail is part of the selection, you're also moving that thumbnail.

6 Release the mouse button to insert the thumbnails into their new position.

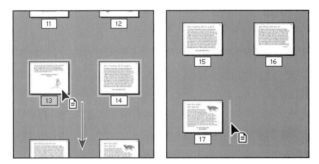

Drag thumbnail to set new insertion point.

Inserting a single page

Next you'll insert a page from a different file to complete a fable in this book. You use thumbnails to insert a single page into a document.

1 Resize the navigation pane to view the thumbnails in a single column.

2 Double-click the thumbnail for page 14. Then click the Fit in Window button (▣).

You are viewing "The Frog and the Ox." Notice that this fable is continued on another page.

3 Click the Next Page button (▶).

Unfortunately, you can't read the end of the fable because it isn't there. You'll open the PDF document that contains the missing page and insert the page into this file.

4 Choose File > Open. Select Frog_ox.pdf in the Lesson05 folder, located inside the Lessons folder within the AA4_CIB folder on your hard drive, and click Open.

5 Choose Window > Tile > Vertically to arrange the two document windows side by side.

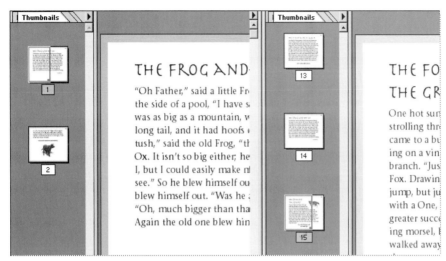

Displaying two document windows side-by-side with Tile Vertically

You can insert pages by dragging thumbnails between document windows.

6 Select the page 2 Frog_ox.pdf thumbnail.

7 Drag the selected thumbnail into the Thumbnails palette for Afables1.pdf. When the insertion bar appears between the page 14 and page 15 thumbnails, release the mouse button.

Dragging thumbnail between documents

The second page of the Frog_ox.pdf file becomes page 15 in the book.

8 Close Frog_ox.pdf, and resize the Afables1.pdf window to fill your desktop.

9 Double-click the page 15 thumbnail to view your newly inserted page.

Inserting an entire file

In Acrobat, you can insert a page, a specified range of pages, or all pages from one PDF document into another. In the previous section, you used thumbnails to insert a page from one PDF document into another. Now you'll add a fable to the Afables1.pdf file by inserting all the pages of another file. You can insert an entire file easily by using the Insert Pages command.

1 Click the Bookmarks tab in the navigation pane to display the bookmarks. If needed, resize the navigation pane to view the entire bookmark text.

Although the Lion's Share bookmark appears in the list, the corresponding fable is missing from the book. You'll insert the missing fable from another document.

2 Drag the scroll box in the scroll bar to go to page 9.

3 Choose Document > Insert Pages. Select Lions.pdf in the Lesson05 folder, located inside the Lessons folder within the AA4_CIB folder on your hard drive, and click Open (Windows) or Select (Mac OS).

The Insert dialog box appears.

4 For Location, choose Before.

5 Select Page Number (Windows) or Page (Mac OS), enter **9** in the page text box, and then click OK.

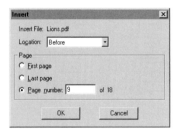

The fable entitled "The Lion's Share" is inserted where it belongs.

6 Page through the document to verify that the fable has been inserted in the correct location. "The Lion's Share" should appear after "The Dog and the Shadow" and before "The Lion and the Mouse."

Updating a bookmark destination

Now that you have inserted the "Lion's Share" fable in the book, you'll update its bookmark link.

1 Go to page 9 of the document.

2 Click The Lion's Share bookmark to select it. Then choose Set Bookmark Destination from the Bookmarks palette menu, and click Yes to the confirmation message to update the bookmark destination.

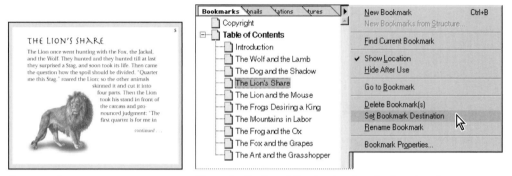

Go to page 9.   *Choose Set Bookmark Destination from Bookmarks palette menu.*

3 Choose File > Save to save the Afables1.pdf file.

Extracting a page

Now you'll remove an unnecessary page from the document and save it as a separate PDF file.

1 Go to page 6, and notice that this page functions as a second title page.

Although a second title page might be appropriate for a printed book, it seems repetitive and unnecessary in an online document, in which readers will probably not flip through the pages in order.

2 Choose Document > Extract Pages.

3 Make sure that you are extracting from page 6 to 6 of the document, and select Delete Pages After Extracting. Click OK. When the confirmation message appears, click OK again.

Go to page 6.   *Extract Pages dialog box*

The title page is deleted from the Afables1.pdf file and opened as a new one-page document.

4 Choose File > Save As. Name the document **Title.pdf**, and save it in the Lesson05 folder.

5 Close Title.pdf.

Notice that the extra title page has been deleted from the fables book.

Renumbering pages

You may have noticed that the page numbers on the document pages do not always match the page numbers that appear below the thumbnails and in the status bar. An Acrobat viewer automatically numbers pages with arabic numerals, starting with page 1 for the first page in the document, and so on.

1 Click the Thumbnails tab in the navigation pane to display the thumbnails.

2 Double-click the page 3 thumbnail to go to the table of contents.

The first three pages of the document contain front matter such as the cover, copyright page, and table of contents. You'll renumber these pages using lowercase roman numerals.

3 Choose Document > Number Pages.

4 For the page range, enter pages from **1** to **3**. For the page numbering, select Begin New Section, choose "i, ii, iii" from the Style pop-up menu, and enter **1** in the Start text box. Click OK.

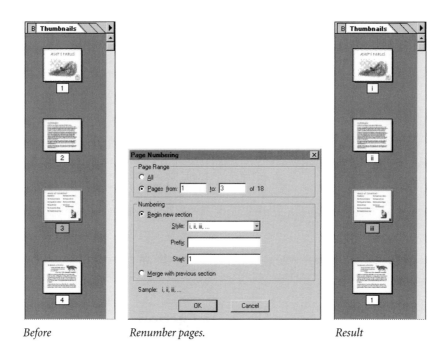

Before   *Renumber pages.*   *Result*

5 Choose Document > Go to Page, enter **1**, and click OK.

Notice that the number 1 is now assigned to the first page of the body, the Introduction, and matches the page number appearing at the top right of the page.

Editing text and images

You use the touchup text tool to make last-minute corrections to text in a PDF document. The touchup text tool lets you edit text, one line at a time, and change text attributes such as spacing, point size, and color. For information on using the touchup text tool, see "A Quick Tour of Adobe Acrobat" in this book.

You use the touchup object tool to make last-minute corrections to images in a PDF document. The touchup object tool lets you modify the placement of images and layout elements on the page. You can also launch Photoshop from within Acrobat to edit the composition of a PDF image.

In this part of the lesson, you'll reposition the dog image on the page.

1 Make sure that you are viewing page 4 of the document.

2 Select the touchup object tool ( ), located under the touchup text tool in the tool bar.

3 Click the dog image at the bottom of the page. A rectangular border indicates that the image is selected.

4 Drag the dog to its new location just to the right of the moral.

 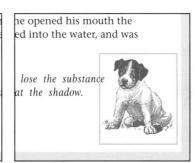

Select touchup   *Click dog image and drag to its new*   *Result*
object tool.   *location.*

Using links and bookmarks to play actions

In most cases, you use links and bookmarks to jump to different views of a document. However, you can also use links and bookmarks to execute commands from the menus and to play movies, sound clips, or perform other actions.

Creating a link that executes a menu item

You'll add a link to the title page that can perform an action.

1 Go to page i (the first page) of the book and click the Fit in Window button ( ).

2 Select the hand tool and move the hand over the button labeled "Full Screen" at the bottom right corner of the page.

Notice that the button is not currently linked. You'll create a link so that users can click the button to display the book in Full Screen mode.

Full Screen mode maximizes the page display area by hiding the menu bar, command bar, and tool bar.

3 Select the link tool ( ), and drag a marquee around the Full Screen button.

4 Under Appearance, for Type, choose Invisible Rectangle; for Highlight, choose Invert. Under Action, for Type, choose Execute Menu Item.

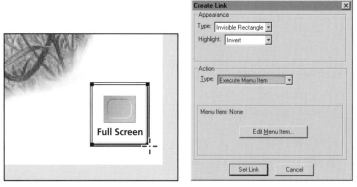

Drag with link tool and then define link's appearance and action.

5 Click Edit Menu Item. In the Menu Item Selection window that appears, choose View > Full Screen, and click OK.

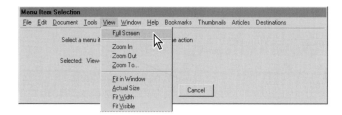

Notice that the command name now appears in the Create Link dialog box.

6 Click Set Link.

7 Select the hand tool and test the link that you have created. In Full Screen mode, use Enter or Return to turn pages.

8 Press Esc to exit Full Screen mode.

Creating a bookmark that plays a sound

For the final task in this lesson, you'll create a bookmark that plays sound. You'll be able to hear the sound if your computer has the proper audio hardware installed.

1 Click the Show/Hide Navigation Pane button (▤) to show the navigation pane.

2 In the navigation pane, click the Bookmarks tab to view the bookmark list.

3 Click The Lion and the Mouse bookmark text to jump to that fable.

You'll create a bookmark that will play the moral of this story aloud.

4 With The Lion and the Mouse bookmark selected, click the Create New Bookmark button (◫) at the bottom of the Bookmarks palette, or choose New Bookmark from the Bookmarks palette menu, and name the new bookmark **Mouse Moral**.

5 Drag the page icon for the Mouse Moral bookmark up and to the right until the insertion bar appears under the "T" in The Lion and the Mouse bookmark.

6 Release the mouse. Click OK to confirm the placement of the bookmark.

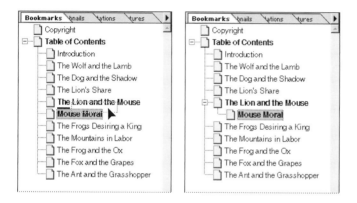

7 Click this new bookmark, and choose Edit > Properties.

8 For Type, choose Sound. Then click Select Sound.

9 Select Mouse.wav (Windows) or Mouse.aif (Mac OS) from the Lesson05 folder, and click Open.

This sound file was created using a sound-editing program and then saved in a file format recognized by Acrobat.

10 Click Set Action.

11 Click in the blank area in the Bookmarks palette to deselect all bookmarks.

12 Use the hand tool to test your new bookmark.

You'll hear the moral if you have the proper audio hardware installed on your computer.

🔋 For more information on sound system requirements and the types of sound file formats you can use with Acrobat, see "Using actions for special effects" in Chapter 10 of the online Adobe Acrobat User Guide.

13 Choose File > Save As, make sure that Optimize is selected, and save Afables1.pdf in the Lesson05 folder. Click Yes (Windows) or Replace (Mac OS) to confirm replacing the file. The Save As command lets you save a smaller, optimized version of your finished file.

14 Choose File > Close to close the fables book.

In this lesson, you have practiced making editorial changes to the pages in a PDF document. You have learned how to use thumbnails to reorder pages and created a bookmark that plays a sound. Later in this book, you'll learn how to add more multimedia features to your PDF documents.

Exploring on your own

Now that you have finished this lesson on modifying PDF documents, you can explore other document-editing features in Acrobat. In addition to adjusting the position of a PDF image, you can edit its contents by launching Adobe Photoshop® 5.0 from within Acrobat. You can then save the edited image in Photoshop to update and replace the original image in the PDF document. To complete these steps, you must have Photoshop installed and configured correctly on your computer.

🔋 For more information about installing Photoshop and Illustrator, see "Getting Started" in the online Adobe Acrobat User Guide, or refer to the printed Getting Started Guide.

1 Select Afables1.pdf in the Lesson05 folder, located inside the Lessons folder within the AA4_CIB folder on your hard drive, and click Open.

2 Navigate to page 4, where the "Dog and the Shadow" fable appears.

3 Select the touchup object tool (➤).

4 Hold down Ctrl (Windows) or Option (Mac OS), and double-click the dog image. Adobe Photoshop is launched.

Hold down Ctrl or Option, and double-click image.   *Result*

5 Make the desired changes in Photoshop, and then flatten the image by choosing Layer > Flatten Image.

Flattening an image merges all visible layers into the background, discards all hidden layers, and fills the remaining transparent areas with white.

6 Choose File > Save.

7 Close the image file and exit or quit Photoshop. Return to Acrobat to view the change to the image.

Review questions

1 How do you change the order of pages in a document?

2 What kinds of text attributes can you change from within Acrobat?

3 How do you select multiple thumbnails?

4 How do you insert an entire PDF file into another PDF file?

5 How do you insert one page, or a range of pages, from one PDF file into another?

6 What types of actions can you assign to links and bookmarks?

Review answers

1 You change the page order by selecting the thumbnails corresponding to the pages you want to move, and dragging them to their new locations.

2 You can use the touchup text tool to change text formatting—font, size, color, and alignment—or to change the text itself.

3 To select more than one thumbnail, click the first thumbnail. Hold down Shift and click additional ones to add them to the selection.

4 To insert all the pages from a PDF file into another PDF file, choose Document > Insert Pages and select the file you wish to insert.

5 To insert a selection of pages from one PDF file into another, open both files with their thumbnails visible. Select the thumbnails for the pages you wish to insert, and drag the thumbnails to the desired location in the Thumbnails palette of the other document.

6 You can assign these actions to links and bookmarks: Execute Menu Item, Go to View, Import Form Data, Movie, Open File, Read Article, Reset Form, Show-Hide Field, Sound, Submit Form, World Wide Web link, and None.

Lesson 6

Creating an Online Version of a Book

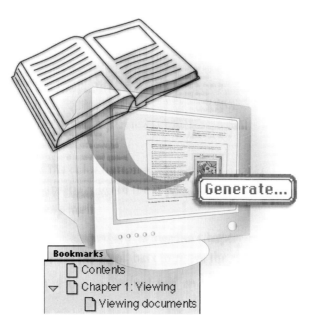

This lesson guides you through the process of converting a printed book to online format. You'll start with a PDF document from the electronic files of the original book layout, and add a variety of hyperlink features to enhance your electronic publication. In the course of this project, you'll review many of the concepts and techniques that were introduced in previous lessons.

In this lesson, you'll review and learn how to do the following:

- Create custom bookmarks.
- Create an article thread.
- Replace a page of a PDF file.
- Compare the design differences between online and print publications.

This lesson will take about 35 minutes to complete.

If needed, remove the previous lesson folder from your hard drive, and copy the Lesson06 folder onto it.

About this lesson

In this lesson, you'll work with a reference manual about Adobe Illustrator. You'll create an electronic print-on-demand version of it without altering the content or design of the original book. Then you'll compare your print-on-demand document with another electronic version that has been redesigned and optimized for online viewing.

Viewing the converted PDF file

You'll start by opening a PDF version of the Adobe Illustrator manual.

We created this version from the original Adobe FrameMaker file by first making a PostScript file and then using Acrobat Distiller to convert it to PDF. For information on using this technique to create a PDF, see Lesson 3, "Creating PDF from Authoring Programs," and Lesson 12, "Customizing PDF Output Quality."

1 Start Acrobat.

2 Choose File > Open. Select Ai.pdf in the Lesson06 folder, located inside the Lessons folder within the AA4_CIB folder, and click Open. Choose File > Save As, rename the file **Ai1.pdf**, and save it in the Lesson06 folder.

The PDF file contains two chapters, a table of contents, and an index, just as in the original FrameMaker file. The table of contents entries, cross-references, index entries, and text flows in the FrameMaker file have been converted to bookmarks, links, and articles in the PDF file.

You can automatically generate PDF links from files that have been properly formatted in an application that supports this automation capability, such as Adobe FrameMaker or Adobe PageMaker.

3 If needed, drag the right border of the Bookmarks palette (a double-headed arrow appears) to resize the Bookmarks palette so that you can see the complete bookmark text.

4 Select the hand tool (✋), and click the Contents bookmark to view the table of contents. If needed, adjust the view magnification to display the entire page on your screen.

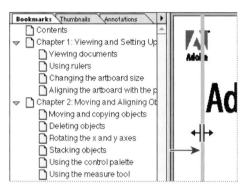

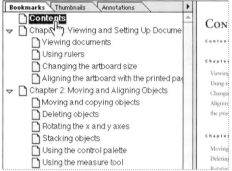

Drag double-headed arrow to resize palette.   *Click to view Contents.*

5 Move the pointer over the contents list and notice that the pointing finger appears over each linked entry.

6 Click the text of a contents entry to jump to its corresponding section of information. Then move your pointer over a column of text and notice the downward pointing arrow inside the hand pointer that indicates an article thread.

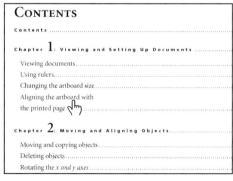

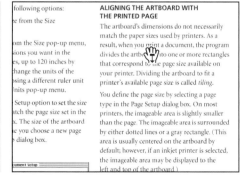

Click the text of a contents entry.   *A downward arrow indicates an article thread.*

7 Click once to enter the article. Press Enter or Return several times to follow the article thread.

8 Click the Index bookmark to view the index listings. Each page number listing links to the appropriate reference in the text.

9 Position your pointer over the number next to the "artboard" entry so that the pointing finger appears. Click to jump to the section about the Illustrator artboard.

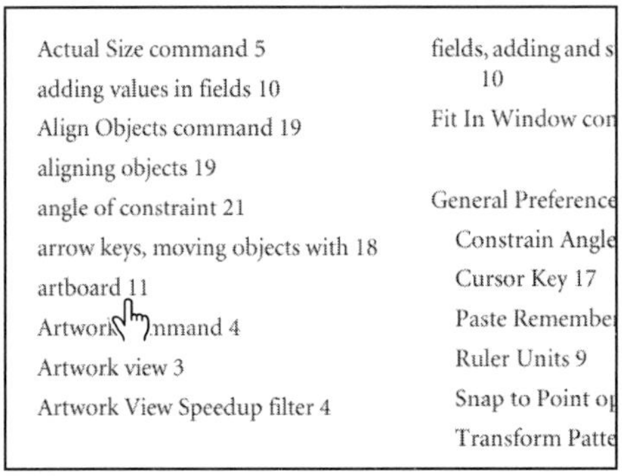

Actual Size command 5	fields, adding and s
adding values in fields 10	10
Align Objects command 19	Fit In Window cor
aligning objects 19	
angle of constraint 21	General Preference
arrow keys, moving objects with 18	Constrain Angle
artboard 11	Cursor Key 17
Artwork command 4	Paste Remember
Artwork view 3	Ruler Units 9
Artwork View Speedup filter 4	Snap to Point o
	Transform Patte

Click the artboard entry

10 Choose File > Save As, make sure that Optimize is selected, and save Ai1.pdf in the Lesson06 folder. Click Yes (Windows) or Replace (Mac OS) to confirm replacing the file. The Save As command lets you save a smaller, optimized version of your finished file.

The index for this user guide was originally created in Adobe FrameMaker and then converted automatically to a linked PDF index during the Distiller conversion process. The following chart outlines the procedure for generating a PDF index from a FrameMaker file.

Index creation from a FrameMaker book file

You can convert an index generated in FrameMaker to an interactive PDF index whose entries link to the referenced document pages.

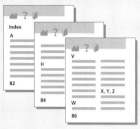

1. Add index markers to FrameMaker documents.

2. Name documents exactly as you want PDF filenames to appear. For example, rename "Exchange.fm" to "Exchange." Then create the book file for these documents.

3. Generate index.

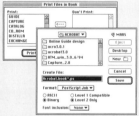

4. In Windows Explorer or the Finder, rename generated index to final PDF name.

5. In book file, redirect index path to renamed index.

6. Print book file to PostScript. Enter * (asterisk) as book filename to preserve original document filenames and create links.

Adding bookmarks

Although the basic bookmarks and links for the book have already been generated, you can still add your own custom bookmarks and links using the tools in Acrobat. In this part of the lesson, you'll add some new bookmarks that link just to the charts, or sidebars, in the book.

Creating bookmarks

You'll create three new bookmarks under the Index bookmark.

1 Click the Index bookmark or its page icon to select the bookmark. Any bookmarks you create appear below the selected bookmark.

2 Click the Create New Bookmark button (⬚) at the bottom of the Bookmarks palette. Or hold down the mouse button on the triangle in the upper right corner of the Bookmarks palette to display the Bookmarks palette menu, and choose New Bookmark. A new bookmark appears beneath the Index bookmark and is selected.

3 Type **Sidebars** to name the bookmark.

You'll create the remaining two bookmarks using the keyboard shortcut for the New Bookmarks command. Many Acrobat commands can be executed using keyboard shortcuts, which appear next to the command names in the menus.

4 Press Ctrl+B (Windows) or Command+B (Mac OS) to create a new bookmark, and name it **Work area**.

5 Press Ctrl+B (Windows) or Command+B (Mac OS), and name the new bookmark **Control palette**.

Now you'll nest the Work area and Control palette bookmarks under the Sidebars bookmark.

6 Hold down Shift and click the Work area and Control palette bookmarks to select them both, and then release Shift.

7 Position the pointer on one of the selected bookmarks, hold down the mouse button, and drag the bookmarks up and to the right. When the black bar appears under the "S" in the Sidebars bookmark, release the mouse. Click OK at the prompt.

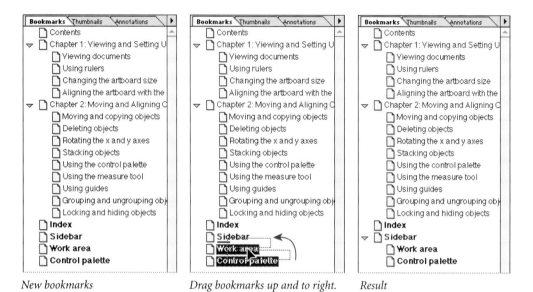

New bookmarks   *Drag bookmarks up and to right.*   *Result*

8 Click in the blank area of the Bookmarks palette to deselect the bookmarks.

9 Choose File > Save to save your work.

Resetting bookmark destinations

Remember from Lesson 5 that bookmark destinations are set automatically to the current document view that your screen displays. Now you'll assign a correct destination or action to each of the new bookmarks that you have created.

1 Click the Work area bookmark to select it.

2 Go to page 11 by dragging in the scroll bar or by choosing Document > Go to Page, entering **11**, and clicking OK.

3 If needed, click the Fit in Window button (🔲) to display the whole page. Then use the zoom-in tool (🔍) to magnify the sidebar. (A sidebar is a text insert, with or without graphics, that is formatted differently from the rest of a document.)

4 Choose Set Bookmark Destination from the Bookmarks palette menu. At the prompt, click Yes.

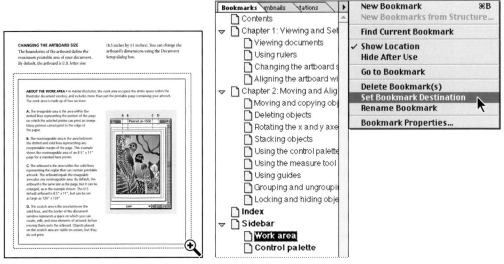

Using zoom-in tool to magnify sidebar   *Setting bookmark destination*

5 Click the Control palette bookmark to select it. Repeat steps 2 and 3, going to page 25, clicking the Fit in Window button, and then using the zoom-in tool to marquee-drag around the sidebar titled "Using the Control palette."

6 Choose Set Bookmark Destination from the Bookmarks palette menu. At the prompt, click Yes.

Next, you'll turn the Sidebars bookmark into a placeholder heading for its sub-bookmarks.

7 Click the icon to the left of the Sidebars bookmark to hide its nested sub-bookmarks.

8 Click the Sidebars bookmark or its page icon to select the bookmark.

9 Choose Edit > Properties. From the Type pop-up menu, choose None as the action type, and click Set Action.

10 In the Bookmarks palette, click in the blank area to deselect all bookmarks. Click the icon next to the Sidebars bookmark to display its nested sub-bookmarks.

11 Use the hand tool to test your new bookmarks. Notice that nothing happens when you click the Sidebars bookmark. This bookmark functions not as a link but as a hierarchical placeholder.

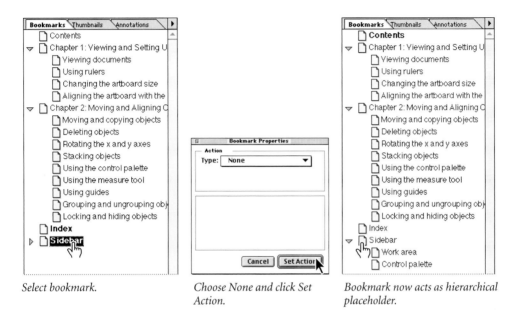

Select bookmark.

Choose None and click Set Action.

Bookmark now acts as hierarchical placeholder.

12 Click the Show/Hide Navigation Pane icon (▣) to close the Bookmarks palette.

Creating an article thread

At the beginning of this lesson, you followed an automatically generated article thread to follow text that spanned a number of nonconsecutive columns and pages. Now you'll define an article and edit the thread.

Defining the article

You use the article tool to define articles. You'll create your own thread to connect several short tip segments that appear throughout the user guide.

1 Use the scroll bar or choose Document > Go to Page to go to page 5. Click the Fit in Window button (▣) to view the entire page.

2 Select the zoom-in tool (🔍), and marquee-zoom to magnify the top left corner of the page, where a tip appears.

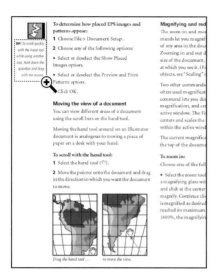

3 Select the article tool ( ). When you first use the article tool, it appears as a cross-hair pointer in the document window.

4 Drag a marquee around the tip text. An article box appears around the enclosed tip, and the pointer changes to the article pointer ( ).

The "2-1" label at the top of the article box indicates that this is the first section of the second article in the file. Now you'll add another article box to continue the thread.

5 Go to page 8 using the scroll bar or by choosing Document > Go to Page. If needed, use the scroll bars to bring the tip in the left margin of the page into view.

Note: Don't use the status bar to advance to another page, to avoid breaking the article thread.

6 Drag an article box around the tip on this page. You point with the top left corner of the article pointer.

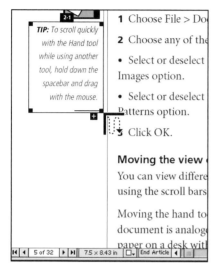

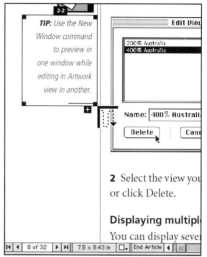

Use article tool to create first article.

Drag to create second article in article thread.

Note: *If you make a mistake and the label doesn't state "2-2," select the hand tool. Then reselect the article tool, select the incorrect thread, press Delete, and at the prompt, click Box. Then go back to the first article, click the plus sign, and repeat steps 5 and 6.*

7 Go to page 27 using the scroll bar or by choosing Document > Go to Page. Drag an article box around the tip on that page.

8 Click End Article in the status bar to end the article thread.

The display returns to the first article box you created, and the Article Properties dialog box appears.

Note: *You can also display the Article Properties dialog box by selecting an article with the article tool and choosing Edit > Properties.*

9 Do the following:

• For Title, enter **Tips**, and press Tab.

• For Subject, enter **Shortcuts and suggestions**.

• Leave the Author and Keywords fields blank, and click OK.

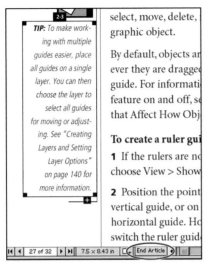

Click to end article thread.

Enter information about article.

Reading the article

You can move through an article in various ways.

1 Choose Window > Show Articles to display a palette listing available articles.

2 Drag the Articles palette so that the Ai1.pdf document remains visible on-screen.

3 Double-click Tips.

The contents of the first article box you created appears on-screen. You can control the magnification of article boxes by adjusting the Max "Fit Visible" Magnification preference, which you set in the General Preferences dialog box.

4 Click the Fit in Window button (⬚) to exit the article.

5 Choose File > Preferences > General to display the General Preferences dialog box.

6 For Max "Fit Visible" Magnification, choose 150, and click OK.

7 Move the hand pointer over the tip on the top left corner of the page, and click to enter the article. Look at the status bar and notice that the article box now appears at 150% magnification.

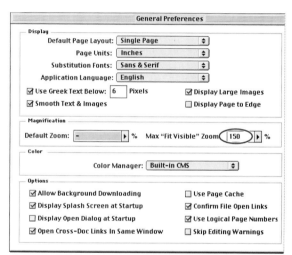

Set Max "Fit Visible" Magnification of 150%...   *...to constrain view to 150%.*

8 Move through the article using any of these techniques:

• To advance to the next article section, press Enter or Return.

• To move backward through the article, hold down Shift and press Enter or Return.

• To move to the beginning of the article, hold down Ctrl (Windows) or Option (Mac OS) and click inside the article.

9 Click the Fit in Window button to exit the article.

10 If desired, experiment with different Max "Fit Visible" Magnification settings and notice how they affect your article view.

Inserting an article box

You can edit an existing article thread using the article tool at any time. For example, you can delete an article box by clicking inside the box with the article tool and pressing Delete. In this part of the lesson, you'll insert another tip into the article thread you just created.

1 Navigate to page 5, and click the Fit in Window (▣) button.

2 Click the article tool to select it. Click inside the tip to select the article box. Handles appear at the corners of an article box when it is selected.

You'll insert a new article box after box 2-1.

3 Move your pointer over the plus sign at the bottom of box 2-1 so that the article pointer appears, and click. Click OK at the alert.

From now on, the pointer appears as the article pointer. In addition, "End Article" appears in the status bar, indicating that you are editing the article thread.

4 Click the Next Page button (▶) to go to page 6. Use the article pointer to drag a box around the tip in the left margin. Notice that this new article box is labeled "2-2."

5 Click End Article in the status bar.

6 Select the hand tool. In the Articles palette, double-click Tips to examine your edited article thread.

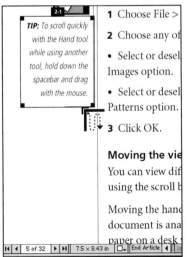

First article in thread

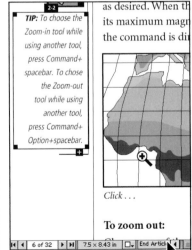

Second article in thread

Articles palette

7 Press Enter or Return to view the new article box you inserted. Click the Fit in Window button to exit the article when you have finished viewing it.

8 Close the Articles palette.

Replacing a page

The plain title page that currently opens the document represents the first page that appears in the printed version of the user guide. To make your PDF user guide look more like an actual book, you'll replace this title page with the full-color illustration that was used to create the front cover of the printed guide.

1 Click the First Page button to display the current title page, and click the Fit in Window button.

2 Choose Document > Replace Pages.

3 Select Cover.pdf in the Lesson06 folder, and click Open (Windows) or Select (Mac OS).

4 In the Replace Pages dialog box, make sure that you are replacing page 1 with 1, and click OK. The new cover illustration appears as page 1 of the document.

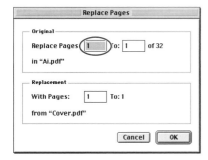

5 Choose File > Save to save the AI1.pdf file. Leave the file open.

Comparing different online versions of the same book

You may have noticed that you did not revise the content or layout of the user guide in creating the Ai1.pdf document. This print-on-demand document represents the quickest and least expensive option for converting a printed book to online. Now you'll open another PDF version of the user guide that has been redesigned and optimized for online use.

1 Choose File > Open, select Online.pdf in the Lesson06 folder, and click Open. Then choose File > Save As, rename the file **Online1.pdf**, and save it in the Lesson06 folder.

2 Choose Window > Tile > Vertically to view the two open documents side by side.

3 If needed, adjust the magnification to fit Online1.pdf on-screen. The tall and narrow page size has been designed for side-by-side viewing next to the Adobe Illustrator application window. This view lets users conveniently look up reference information without closing their illustration window.

Notice also that Online1.pdf contains a hypertext list of elements in the document. A few book elements have been created specially for the optimized online guide.

4 In the online guide artwork, click How to Use This Guide to jump to the section that explains basic navigational techniques to the user. Click the Go to Previous View button (◀) in the tool bar when you have finished viewing the instructions.

 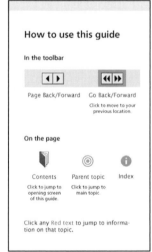

Jumping to How to Use This   *Result*
Guide instructions

5 Click "List of Topics" to view the text contents of the document.

Notice that you jump to a screen listing the main topic titles.

6 Click "Viewing and Setting up Documents" to display the subtopics under this topic.

7 Now click the Ai1.pdf document window to make it active, and go to page 2, the Contents page. Click the Actual Size button (▯) to display this page at 100%.

Compare the table of contents in Ai1.pdf (the print-on-demand guide) with the topic screens in Online1.pdf (the optimized online guide). Online1.pdf arranges its content listings in nested, hierarchical screens, while Ai1.pdf lists the main topics and their subtopics linearly on the page. Although the linear arrangement follows the conventional organization of a printed book, the hierarchical structure is better suited for an online environment where the most intuitive action involves clicking a link to follow a trail of information.

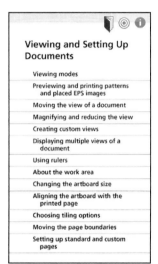

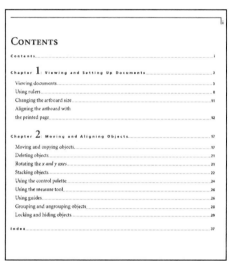

Contents of Online.pdf
online guide

Contents of Ai.pdf printed guide

8 Click "Using rulers" under the Chapter 1 heading to jump to that page of text. If needed, use the scroll bars to move the right column of the page into view.

9 Now return to Online1.pdf, and click "Using rulers" in the list of subtopics. If needed, click the Fit in Window button (![icon]) to view the entire page.

Notice that pages in the optimized online guide have been redesigned so that each topic has its own page. Related topic titles appear as red, linked text.

10 Now click the target icon at the top of the page to return to the parent list of subtopics, and then click "About the Work Area," about midway in the list.

This link jumps you to an overview text section that contains its own links to subtopics and art. Click the Jump to Art icon to view a diagram of the work area with all of its components labelled and linked.

11 Return to Ai1.pdf, and navigate to page 11 to view the linear equivalent of the "About the Work Area" section. If needed, adjust the magnification and use the scroll bar to view the entire section. Compare the text-intensive pages of Ai1.pdf with the more balanced text blocks in Online1.pdf.

By breaking longer topics into their subtopic components and placing these sections on separate pages, you minimize the amount of text shown on each page. As a result, you can display text in a larger, clearer typeface that users can read more easily. In addition, the smaller, self-contained pages reduce the need for scrolling and readjusting the page view. Ideally, a user of Online1.pdf should be able to navigate to any part of the document solely by clicking linked text and icons in the page.

12 Return to Online1.pdf, and click the book icon at the top of the page to return to the opening contents screen. Then click Index.

Like the index for the print-on-demand guide, the page-number listings in the online index link to their referenced section. However, the online index also includes an alphabet tab along the left of the page, which lets you jump to specific parts of the index quickly.

13 Choose File > Save As, make sure that Optimize is selected, and save the Online1.pdf file in the Lesson06 folder. Close the file. Repeat this step for the Ai1.pdf file. The Save As command lets you save a smaller, optimized version of your finished file.

This completes the lesson. For more practice in organizing and preparing documents for electronic distribution, see Lesson 13, "Distributing PDF Documents."

Exploring on your own (Windows)

Here's an idea you can try on your own to compare pages in two PDF documents. To identify content changes between documents more precisely, use the Compare Pages command, available for Windows only. This command compares every page in two documents, looking at PDF information that describes the pages precisely and can find even the most subtle differences between pages. You can use Compare Pages to identify both content changes between documents and changes that may not be visible.

This command is especially useful for comparing PDF documents that are nearly identical, such as document versions that have been digitally signed.

Compare Pages looks at the two most recently active PDF documents and produces a third document, a comparison file that shows every page that differs between the documents and highlights the differences on the pages.

1 Choose File > Open, select Ai.pdf in the Lesson06 folder, and click Open. Close the navigation pane.

2 Choose File > Open, select Ai1.pdf in the Lesson06 folder, and click Open. Close the navigation pane.

3 Make active the original Ai.pdf document; this document will be on the right in the comparison file. Then make active the Ai1.pdf document; this document will be on the left.

4 Choose Tools > Compare Pages. The two documents appear side by side in a read-only comparison file.

Each document in the comparison file begins with a summary page that gives the document's filename and describes how many pages were altered, added, moved, or deleted. The rest of the file shows the pages that differ between the documents. In the document on the left, the pages are listed in ascending order and are paired with pages from the document on the right.

Note: The pages on the right may not be in ascending order if any content or pages have been rearranged in the documents.

The differences are highlighted in magenta on the pages. Acrobat identifies differences in these ways:

• If any pixels differ on the two pages, the specific differences are highlighted on both pages. For example, a word may have been edited or deleted, or an annotation may have been added. The change may also be one that is barely noticeable, such as a slightly different tab stop or a small shift to one side of the page's content.

• If no pixels differ but the PDF information on the pages differs, both pages are entirely highlighted. For example, some PDF marking behind an opaque object may have changed, or the crop box may have changed without any additional cropping being obvious.

• If a page has been added, it is paired with a new blank page. If a page has been deleted, it is represented by a blank page and paired with its corresponding page in the other document.

The highlighted differences are stored as pencil annotations in the comparison file. You can use the Annotations palette to see a list of all the differences, and you can double-click a difference in the palette to go to that place on a page. To display the Annotations palette, click the Annotations tab. If the annotations do not appear in the palette, click the Start Annotation Scan button (🕮) at the bottom of the palette.

Each page in a comparison file is labeled in magenta with *A* (for pages on the left) or *B* (for pages on the right), plus the page's number in the actual PDF document. You can find this information on both lower corners of a page, surrounded by equal signs (for example, =A4=). The page number is helpful for matching these pages with those in the PDF document, especially when pages on the right side are not in ascending order.

Note: The side-by-side display of pages in comparison files is designed for two-up printing. If you are printing only one page, select Fit to Page in the Print dialog box to be sure you include all highlights and the page numbering in the printed copy.

Review questions

1 How do you generate a PDF index automatically when converting a FrameMaker file?

2 How do you create bookmarks in a document?

3 How can you control how a bookmark behaves?

4 How do you create an article thread?

5 How do you insert a new article box into an existing article thread?

6 How do you end an article thread?

7 How can the table of contents for a printed publication differ from the table of contents for a strictly online publication?

Review answers

1 Acrobat Distiller generates a linked PDF index automatically from the index markers inserted in a FrameMaker file.

2 To create a bookmark, click the Create New Bookmark button at the bottom of the Bookmarks palette or choose New Bookmark from the Bookmarks palette menu. Go to the page containing the information you want to bookmark. Then choose Set Bookmark Destination from the Bookmarks palette menu and verify the destination.

3 To control a bookmark's behavior, you select a bookmark, choose Edit > Properties, and specify the bookmark's action using the Type pop-up menu.

4 To create an article thread, you use the article tool and drag an article box. Then you go to the next desired page in the article using the scroll bar or the Document > Go To Page command, and drag another article box; you repeat this step for as many article boxes as desired. To end the article, you click End Article in the status bar.

5 To insert a new article box into an existing article thread, you select the article box using the article tool, move the pointer over the plus sign at the bottom of the article box, and click. Then you draw an article box around the new article that you want to include, and click End Article in the status bar when you have finished.

6 To end an article thread, you click End Article in the status bar.

7 The table of contents for a printed publication lists the main topics and their subtopics linearly on the page, whereas an online publication arranges its content listings in nested, hierarchical screens. Although the linear arrangement follows the conventional organization of a printed book, the hierarchical structure is better suited for an online environment where the most intuitive action involves clicking a link to follow a trail of information.

Lesson 7

Using Acrobat in a Document Review Cycle

Acrobat can play an effective role in a document review cycle, where a single document is distributed to an audience of reviewers. By circulating a PDF document, you can receive comments back in the form of annotations— notes, text, audio, stamps, files, graphic markups, and text markups attached to the file. You can then collate the annotations and compile them in a single file for easier viewing.

In this lesson, you'll learn how to do the following:

- Use and create annotations.

- Export, import, and summarize annotations.

- Specify security settings for a file.

- View security information for a document.

This lesson will take about 30 minutes to complete.

If needed, remove the previous lesson folder from your hard drive, and copy the Lesson07 folder onto it.

Opening the work file

In this lesson, you'll work with a marketing plan document for the Juggler Toys Company. This document is at an intermediate draft stage, and some of the marketing strategies are still being developed. You'll review existing comments in the document and add a variety of your own comments.

1 Start Acrobat.

2 Choose File > Open. Select Mktplan.pdf in the Lesson07 folder, located inside the Lessons folder within the AA4_CIB folder on your hard drive, and click Open. Then choose File > Save As, rename the file **Mktplan1.pdf**, and save it in the Lesson07 folder.

Working with annotations

Acrobat's annotation feature lets you attach comments to an existing document. These comments can be in the form of notes, text, audio, stamps, files, graphic markups, and text markups. With annotations, multiple reviewers can comment on and incorporate their comments into the same review version. Annotations from other document versions can also be collected and incorporated into the review version.

About annotations

The tool bar contains three types of tools for attaching comments to an existing document—annotation, graphic markup, and text markup. Each has a hidden tool menu.

- *The annotation tools—notes tool (📝), text annotation tool (T+), audio annotation tool (🔊), stamp tool (🏷️), and file annotation tool (📎)—allow you to attach comments to a PDF document in a variety of formats. The annotation tools are located below the crop tool on the tool bar.*

- *The graphic markup tools—pencil tool (✏️), rectangle tool (☐), ellipse tool (○), and line tool (＼)—allow you to visually mark an area of a PDF document with a graphic symbol and associate a note with the markup for additional comments. The graphic markup tools are located below the annotation tools on the tool bar.*

- *Text markup tools—highlight text tool (🖊️), strikethrough text tool (̶S̶), and underline text tool (U)—allow you to visually mark up text on a PDF document page and associate a note with the markup for additional comments. The text markup tools are located below the graphic markup tools on the tool bar.*

–From the online Adobe Acrobat User Guide, Chapter 8

Reviewing annotations

1 Choose Window > Show Annotations to display the Annotations palette.

2 Click the Start Annotation Scan button (🗂️) at the bottom of the Annotations palette to scan the document for annotations.

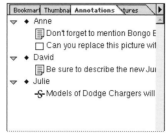

Click Start Annotation Scan button.   *Result*

A list of annotations associated with the open document appears. By default, the list is sorted by author. You can also sort the list by type, page number, and date.

3 Double-click the first annotation listed under Anne to jump to the page that contains it.

4 Click the Fit in Window button (🔳) to view the entire page. Notice the different colored annotations that appear on the page. The blue note is highlighted, indicating it is the annotation that you selected from the Annotations palette.

5 Select the hand tool (✋) in the tool bar, and double-click the blue note to read it.

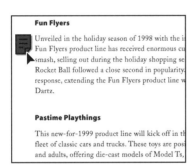
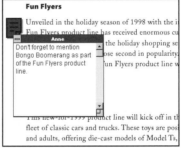

Double-click blue note to read it.   *Result*

6 Click the close box at the top of the note window when you have finished reading the note.

7 Double-click the yellow note to read it. Notice that the note's label is different from the previous note.

Annotations can be set to different colors to indicate that they were created by different reviewers.

8 Close the note when you have finished reading it.

Annotations in the form of stamps, graphic markups, and text markups can have notes associated with them. In these cases, double-clicking the annotation opens the note window.

9 Select the zoom-in tool (🔍) from the tool bar, and marquee-zoom around the Pastime Playthings section at the bottom of the page.

10 Select the hand tool, and double-click the green line that strikes through the phrase Dodge Chargers. A note associated with the text markup appears. Close the note when you have finished reading it.

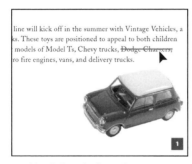

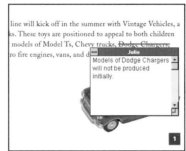

Double-click strikethrough text annotation.

Result

Except for text markups, annotations can be easily moved around on a page.

11 Click the Fit in Window button. Then drag the blue note to the right margin.

12 Double-click the blue note to read it. Notice that the note window is no longer aligned with the associated annotation.

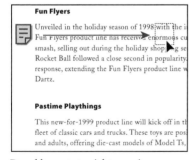

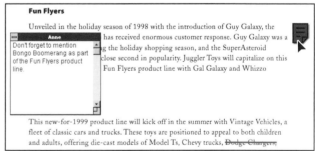

Drag blue note to right margin.

Notice that note window is no longer aligned with note.

You can easily reset the location of the note window.

13 Position the pointer over the blue note. Hold down the right mouse button (Windows) or Control-click (Mac OS). Choose Reset Note Window Location from the menu.

Position pointer over blue note.   *Choose Reset Note Window Location from menu.*

The note window realigns with the associated annotation.

14 Click the note window to select it, and close the note when you have finished viewing it.

You'll add a variety of your own annotations to this document. But first you'll customize your annotation style by setting preferences.

Setting annotation preferences

1 Choose File > Preferences > Annotations.

2 For Author, enter your name.

When you transfer an annotation between different files or systems, the author of the annotation is preserved.

You can also specify a font for displaying the note text. However, keep in mind that this font preference applies only to your system. Users viewing your note on other systems may see a different font, depending on their own preference settings.

3 Choose a font (we used Arial®). For Font Size, choose 12. Click OK.

Adding a note

You use the notes tool in Acrobat to create your own notes using the preferences that you have just specified. Although you can view notes and other annotations in a PDF file using Acrobat Reader, you can only create or edit annotations using Acrobat.

1 Click the First Page button (◀) to go to page i.

2 Select the notes tool (📄) in the tool bar, and click in the blank space beneath the title on the page.

An empty note window appears.

3 Type the note text as desired. We used the following: "Please provide the date this document was created."

4 Choose Edit > Properties.

💡 *To display an annotation's Properties dialog box, you can also position the pointer over the annotation, hold down the right mouse button (Windows) or Control-click (Mac OS), and choose Properties from the menu.*

5 Select the Text Note icon to represent your type of note.

6 Click the color button to select a color for the note.

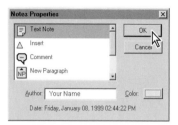

Notice that you can change the author name using the annotation's Properties dialog box. When you use the Properties dialog box to change the author name, the change only applies to the current annotation. To change the author name for all subsequent annotations, you must specify the change in the Annotation Preferences dialog box.

7 Click OK.

8 Close the note.

9 Select the hand tool ( ), and double-click the note that you have just created to view the message. Close the note when you have finished viewing it.

Adding a stamp

Acrobat's stamp tool lets you apply a stamp to a document in much the same way you would use a rubber stamp on a paper document. In addition to using stamps from the Acrobat stamp library, you can create your own custom stamps and use them as annotations. For information on creating your own custom stamps, see "Exploring on your own" on page 176.

1 Hold down the mouse button on the notes tool ( ) to display a set of hidden tools, and drag to select the stamp tool ( ).

Drag to select stamp tool.   Click in page to add stamp.

2 Click in the blank space at the top of the page. By default, the Approved stamp appears. You'll change the stamp using the Stamp Properties dialog box.

3 Choose Edit > Properties.

4 For Category, choose Standard. Select Confidential from the list in the left pane of the dialog box. A preview of the stamp that you have selected appears in the right pane of the dialog box.

Notice the color button in the bottom right corner of the dialog box. You use this button to specify the color of the note associated with the stamp. You cannot change the color of the stamp itself.

5 Click the color button to select a color for the note associated with the stamp. Then click OK.

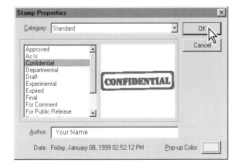

You'll add a note associated with the stamp.

6 Move the pointer over the stamp until it changes to an arrow. Then double-click to create a note window.

7 Type the note text as desired. We used the following: "Be sure to let reviewers know this document is for internal use only." Then close the note.

Double-click stamp to create note window.   *Type note text as desired.*

8 Select the hand tool ($\mathcal{E}$), and double-click the stamp to view the message. Close the note when you have finished viewing it.

Adding a file annotation

You use the file annotation tool in Acrobat to embed a file at a specified location in a document, so the reader can open it for viewing. You can attach any file type as a file annotation. However, to open it, your reader must have an application that can recognize the attachment.

1 Go to page 3.

As a reviewer of the document, you would like to see information added to the Worldwide Marketing Overview section, and the information you would like added is in a word-processing document called Update.doc. You'll attach the Update.doc file to the marketing plan.

2 Hold down the mouse button on the stamp tool ($\mathcal{S}$) to display the set of hidden tools, and drag to select the file annotation tool ($\mathcal{F}$).

3 Click in the blank space to the left of the Worldwide Marketing Overview heading.

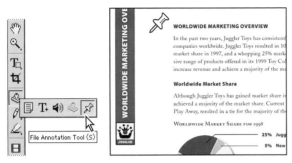

Drag to select file annotation tool.   Click in page to add a file annotation.

4 In the Select File to Attach dialog box, select Update.doc, located in the Lesson07 folder, and click Open (Windows) or Attach (Mac OS).

5 In the File Annotation Properties dialog box, select the Attach icon to represent this type of file annotation.

6 For Description, type the following: **Worldwide marketing update**.

7 Click the color button to select a color for the icon. Then click OK.

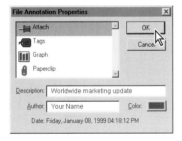

A pushpin appears on the page.

8 Select the hand tool (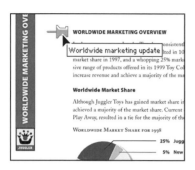), and move the pointer over the pushpin.

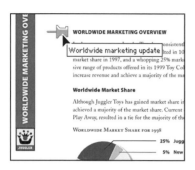

Notice that the description of the file appears below the pushpin.

If you have a word-processing application installed on your system, you can open the file that you have just attached.

9 If you have a word-processing application installed, double-click the pushpin to open the file. Click OK to confirm that you want to open the file. When you have finished viewing the file, exit or quit your word-processing application.

Marking up a document with graphic markup tools

Acrobat's graphic markup tools let you emphasize a specific area of a document, such as a graphic or table. The pencil tool creates a free-form line, the rectangle tool creates a rectangular boundary, the ellipse tool creates an elliptical boundary, and the line tool creates a straight line between two specified points. You can add a note associated with a graphic markup to comment on the area of the page being emphasized. Graphic markups are saved as annotations and appear in the Annotations palette.

You'll add a rectangle to the marketing plan, and then add a note associated with the rectangle.

1 Click the Next Page button (▶) to go to page 4.

2 Click the zoom-in tool (⌕), and marquee-zoom around the Production Schedules for the "Super Six" section at the bottom of the page.

3 Hold down the mouse button on the pencil tool (✐) to display a set of hidden tools, and drag to select the rectangle tool (▭).

4 Drag a rectangle around the table on the page.

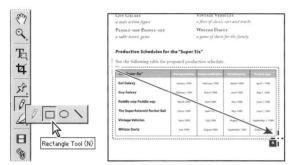

Drag to select rectangle tool.   *Drag to create rectangle around table.*

5 Choose Edit > Properties.

6 Choose a line width for the rectangle from the Thickness menu. Click the color button to select a color for the rectangle. Then click OK.

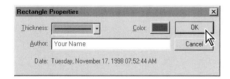

7 To associate a note with the rectangle, move the pointer inside the rectangle until it changes to an arrow, and double-click to create a note window. Type the note text as desired. We used the following: "Can you use a time line here instead of a table?" Then close the note.

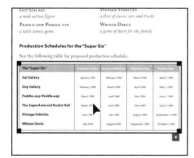 

Double-click inside rectangle to create note window.   *Type note text as desired.*

8 Select the hand tool (🖑), and double-click the border of the rectangle to view the message. (Be sure to double-click the border of the rectangle, not inside the rectangle.) Close the note when you have finished viewing it.

Marking up a document with text markup tools

You use the text markup tools in Acrobat to emphasize specific text in a document, such as a heading or entire paragraph. You can choose from the highlight text tool, the strikethrough text tool, and the underline text tool. You can add a note associated with a text markup to comment on the text being emphasized. Text markups are saved as annotations and appear in the Annotations palette.

You'll highlight text in the marketing plan, and then add a note associated with the highlighted text.

1 Select the highlight text tool (🖊) in the tool bar.

2 Drag the I-beam to highlight the word "schedule" in the last sentence on the page.

3 Choose Edit > Properties.

4 Click the color button to select a color for the highlighted text. Then click OK.

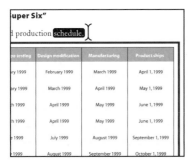

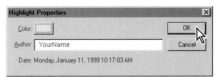

Drag to highlight "schedule."

Specify properties in Highlight Properties dialog box.

5 To associate a note with the highlighted text, move the pointer over the highlighted text until it changes to an arrow, and double-click to create a note window. Type the note text as desired. We used the following: "Make this word plural. Remember to check grammar before the final draft." Then close the note.

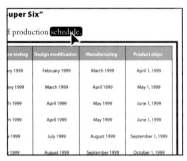
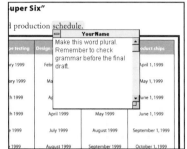

Double-click highlighted text to create note window.   *Type note text as desired.*

6 Select the hand tool (🖑), and double-click the highlighted text to view the message. Close the note when you have finished viewing it.

Deleting an annotation

You can easily delete unwanted annotations from a document.

1 Click the Fit in Window button (⊡).

2 Using the hand tool, click the border of the rectangle on page 4 to select it.

3 Press Delete, and click OK to confirm the deletion.

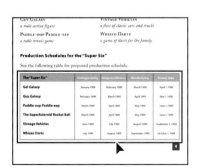
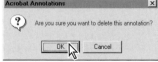

Click border of rectangle to select it, and press Delete.   *Click OK.*

4 Choose File > Save to save the Mktplan1.pdf file.

Exporting annotations

The marketing plan includes annotations from several different reviewers. However, another reviewer has placed his comments in a different copy of the marketing plan. You'll export just the annotations from this document copy and place them in a Forms Data Format (FDF) file. Because the file contains only the annotations, it is smaller in size than the original file and therefore more economical to distribute.

1 Choose File > Open. Select Review.pdf, located inside the Lesson07 folder, and click Open.

2 Choose File > Export > Annotations.

3 Name the file **Comments.fdf**, and save it in the Lesson07 folder.

4 Choose File > Close to close the Review.pdf file.

Now you'll import the annotations from the Comments.fdf file into the Mktplan1.pdf file, so that you can compile all the annotations in a single document.

Importing annotations

1 In the Mktplan1.pdf window, choose File > Import > Annotations.

2 Select Comments.fdf, located in the Lesson07 folder, and click Open (Windows) or Select (Mac OS).

The Annotations palette now lists annotations from Andrew, as well as those from other reviewers.

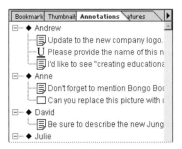

3 Page through the marketing plan and notice the new red annotations that have been imported. The imported annotations appear in their original locations on the pages.

4 Choose File > Save to save the Mktplan1.pdf file.

In addition to importing annotations from an FDF document, you can import annotations directly from one PDF document to another.

Summarizing annotations

At times you may want to display just the text of the notes so that you don't have to open each one individually to read it. By summarizing annotations, you can compile the text of all the notes into a new PDF document.

1 Choose Tools > Annotations > Summarize Annotations.

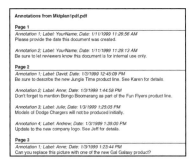

A new PDF file named "Annotations from Mktplan1.pdf" is created. This document lists each annotation that appears in the marketing plan, including the note label, the date and time the annotation was added to the file, and the full text of the note.

2 Choose File > Save As, rename the file **Summary.pdf**, and save it in the Lesson07 folder.

3 Close the Summary.pdf file when you have finished viewing it.

Now you'll append the annotations summary to the marketing plan.

4 In the Mktplan1.pdf window, choose Document > Insert Pages.

5 Select Summary.pdf, located in the Lesson07 folder, and click Open (Windows) or Select (Mac OS).

6 For Location, choose After. For Page, select the last page. Click OK to insert the annotations summary into the review version of the marketing plan.

7 Click the Actual Size button (□) to return the page to a 100% view.

Notice that the annotations are numbered in the annotations summary. These numbers show the order in which the annotations were created on each page. You can set preferences in Acrobat to display these numbers with the annotations in the document. Then you can easily locate annotations while reviewing the annotations summary.

8 Choose File > Preferences > Annotations.

9 Select Show sequence numbers in summarized notes, and click OK.

10 Click the First Page button (◀) to go to page i. Page through the marketing plan and notice the numbers that appear on the annotations. These numbers correspond to the numbers listed in the annotations summary.

11 Choose File > Save As, make sure that Optimize is selected, and save Mktplan1.pdf in the Lesson07 folder. Click Yes (Windows) or Replace (Mac OS) to confirm replacing the file. The Save As command lets you save a smaller, optimized version of your finished file.

Working with digital signatures (Windows)

You can add a digital signature to a document in Acrobat to attest to something about the document in its current state. For example, you might sign a document to show that you have read it or approved it, or to certify that it is ready for others to review. You can also see all the signatures that have been added to a document, check the validity of signatures, and go back to an earlier signed version of a document.

To work with digital signatures in a document, you use a signature handler plug-in with Acrobat. You add, validate, and manage your signatures using commands and tools in the Acrobat interface, but the signature handler determines the nature of the signatures—their appearance on the page, the exact information stored in them, and the attributes and method used for their validation. You can use a variety of signature handlers with Acrobat, providing both mathematical and biometric validation schemes. The flexibility of this structure allows you to use whichever signing method your company or regulations require, with Acrobat providing a consistent and convenient front end.

About digital signatures

A digital signature, like any other signature, identifies a person or entity signing a document. In Acrobat, a digital signature can appear on a page in many different forms— a handwritten name, a logo or other graphic, or some text explaining the purpose of the signing. The particular appearance of the signature is determined by the signature handler.

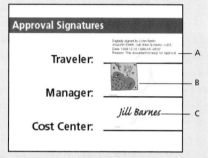

A. Text signature B. Graphic signature
C. Handwritten name signature

–From the Adobe Acrobat User Guide, Chapter 14

Setting file security

Sometimes you may want to lock a PDF document to prevent it from being edited. For example, now that you have gathered all the review comments for the marketing plan, you'll want to protect the compiled file from accidental changes.

Setting file security

1 Choose File > Save As, and choose Standard from the Security menu.

A dialog box appears asking you to specify up to two passwords—one for opening the file and one for changing security options to the file. These passwords are case sensitive.

2 For Open the Document, enter **Circus**, and press Tab.

3 For Change Security Options, enter **ferris**.

4 For Do Not Allow, select Changing the Document, Selecting Text and Graphics, and Adding or Changing Annotations and Form Fields. Click OK.

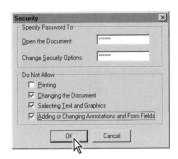

A dialog box appears asking you to confirm your Open password.

5 Type **Circus** and click OK.

Another dialog box appears asking you to confirm your Security password.

6 Type **ferris** and click OK.

7 Name the document **Mktplan2.pdf**, and save it in the Lesson07 folder. Then close the document.

Testing file security

1 Choose File > Open. Select Mktplan2.pdf, located in the Lesson07 folder, and click Open.

A dialog box appears asking you for the Open password.

2 Enter **Circus** and click OK.

Notice that most commands under the Edit and Document menus are dimmed, indicating that you cannot invoke them. Notice that most of the tools in the tool bar are also dimmed.

3 Choose File > Document Info > Security.

A dialog box summarizes the security settings that have been placed on the document. Notice that the document has both Open and Security passwords, and that no actions except for printing the document are allowed.

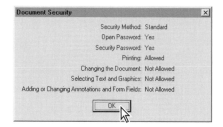

4 Click OK when you have finished viewing the information.

5 Choose File > Save As, and click Settings.

A dialog box appears asking you for the Security password.

6 Enter **ferris** and click OK.

7 Under Do Not Allow, deselect Adding or Changing Annotations and Form Fields, and click OK. Then click Save, and click Yes (Windows) or Replace (Mac OS) to confirm replacing the existing file.

8 Click the small triangle to the right of the file annotation tool ( ), and hold down the mouse button. Drag to select the notes tool ( ). Notice that you can now add a note to the document.

9 Close the Mktplan2.pdf file. You do not need to save your changes.

In this lesson, you have learned how to use and create annotations, and how to assign security settings to a file.

Exploring on your own

Now that you have learned how to add a stamp to a document, try adding custom stamps to the Acrobat stamp library and using them as annotations. All stamp files must be saved as PDF files, and each page of a PDF document can be used as an individual stamp. We've provided a PDF file with two images that you can use for practice, or you can use your own artwork or photo images saved as PDF files.

1 Choose File > Open. Select Stamps.pdf, located inside the Lesson07 folder, and click Open.

You'll prepare the Stamps.pdf file to be added to the Acrobat stamp library.

The Acrobat stamp library consists of several PDF files, which contain one or more stamps. Each PDF file has a category name, which appears in the Category menu in the Stamp Properties dialog box. Acrobat uses the document title of a PDF file as the category name. You'll specify a document title for the Stamps.pdf file using the General Info dialog box.

2 Choose File > Document Info > General.

3 Type **JugglerToys** in the Title text box, and click OK.

To be recognized by Acrobat, each stamp in a stamp file must be named. The name of each stamp should be in the following format:

<CategoryName><StampName>=<StampLabel>

The CategoryName is the name of the stamp category in English, the StampName is the name of the stamp in English, and the StampLabel is the name of the stamp in your native language. Acrobat uses the StampLabel as the name of the stamp listed in the Stamp Properties dialog box. This naming convention ensures that stamps can be easily identified when distributed to users of other languages.

You'll name each stamp in the Stamps.pdf file using Acrobat's Page Templates feature.

4 If needed, go to page 1. Choose Tools > Forms > Page Templates.

5 Type **JugglerToysLibrary=Library** in the Name text box, and click Add. Click Yes to confirm creating a new template using the current page. Then click Close (Windows) or Done (Mac OS) to close the Document Templates dialog box.

6 Click the Next Page button (▶) to go to page 2.

7 Choose Tools > Forms > Page Templates. Type **JugglerToysInternal=Internal** in the Name text box, and click Add. Click Yes. Then click Close (Windows) or Done (Mac OS).

To be part of the Acrobat stamp library, all stamp files must be saved in the Stamps subfolder of the Plug-ins folder for Adobe Acrobat. You'll save the Stamps.pdf file in this location.

8 Choose File > Save As, and save the Stamps.pdf file in the Stamps subfolder of the Plug-ins folder for Adobe Acrobat.

9 Choose File > Close to close the Stamps.pdf file.

Now that you have added custom stamps to the Acrobat stamp library, you can use them as annotations. You'll apply the custom stamps to the marketing plan.

10 Choose File > Open. Select Mktplan1.pdf, located inside the Lesson07 folder, and click Open.

11 Hold down the mouse button on the notes tool ( ) to display the set of hidden tools, and drag to select the stamp tool ( ). Click in the bottom left corner of the page.

The Confidential stamp appears. You'll change the stamp using the Stamp Properties dialog box.

12 Choose Edit > Properties.

13 For Category, choose JugglerToys. Select Library from the list in the left pane of the dialog box. Then click OK.

Click in bottom left corner of page.   *Change stamp using Stamp Properties dialog box.*

The first page of the Stamps.pdf file appears in the marketing plan as a custom stamp.

If needed, you can easily adjust the size and position of the stamp. To resize the stamp, drag one of the corner handles. To move the stamp, position the stamp tool inside the stamp and drag.

Drag corner handle to resize stamp.   *Drag stamp to move it.*

14 Select the hand tool (🖑), and click in the blank space in the document to deselect the stamp.

15 Apply the Internal stamp from the JugglerToys category to the marketing plan. When you have finished, close the Mktplan1.pdf file. You do not need to save your changes.

Review questions

1 How do you change the author name of the current annotation? How do you change the author name for all subsequent annotations?

2 What font is used in a note window when viewed on your computer? On someone else's computer?

3 How do you add a stamp to a document? How do you change the stamp?

4 What type of file can you attach to a document as a file annotation?

5 What are three ways you can mark up text in a document?

6 How do you create a file that contains just the text of the notes added to a PDF document?

7 What types of security passwords can you assign to a document?

Review answers

1 To change the author name of the current annotation, select the annotation, choose Edit > Properties, and enter text in the Author text box. To change the author name for all subsequent annotations, choose File > Preferences > Annotations, and enter text in the Author text box.

2 On your computer, the note window uses the font that you have specified in the Annotations Preferences dialog box. On someone else's computer, the note window uses the font that he or she has specified.

3 To add a stamp, select the stamp tool, and click inside an existing PDF document. To change the stamp, choose Edit > Properties, and select a new stamp from the Stamp Properties dialog box.

4 You can attach any file type as a file annotation. However, to open the file, your reader must have an application that can recognize the attachment.

5 Using Acrobat's text markup tools, you can highlight, strike through, and underline text.

6 Choose Tools > Annotations > Summarize Annotations.

7 You can assign a password that lets users open the document and one that lets users change the security options for the document.

Lesson 8

Creating Forms

Acrobat lets you create form fields that can be filled out by a user in Acrobat or Acrobat Reader. If all the proper software and hardware components are in place, form data can be submitted over the World Wide Web and collected in a database just like HTML forms. In this lesson, you'll fill out form fields, create them, and learn about submitting forms over the Web.

In this lesson, you'll learn how to do the following:

- Fill out a PDF form.

- Export form data.

- Import form data.

- Add form fields, and format those fields.

- Use the forms grid.

- Validate form fields to restrict entries to specific values or characters.

- Perform mathematical calculations on two or more numeric form fields.

This lesson will take about 50 minutes to complete.

If needed, remove the previous lesson folder from your hard drive, and copy the Lesson08 folder onto it.

Working with forms online

With Adobe Acrobat, it's easy to convert your existing paper and electronic forms to PDF, and then use Acrobat to create PDF form fields. Using an existing form lets you maintain your organization's corporate identity and branding, and saves you from having to re-create the form design itself.

Many forms require the same information—name, address, phone number, and so on. Wouldn't it be nice if you could enter that data once and use it again and again with the various forms that you have to fill out? Acrobat's ability to import and export form data makes it possible for you to populate different forms with the same set of data.

In this part of the lesson, you'll fill out a Travel Authorization form with personal information, export the data, and then import the data into an Expense Report form.

Filling out a form

1 Start Acrobat.

2 Choose File > Open. Select Travel.pdf in the Lesson08 folder, located inside the Lessons folder within the AA4_CIB folder on your hard drive, and click Open. Then choose File > Save As, rename the file **Travel1.pdf**, and save it in the Lesson08 folder.

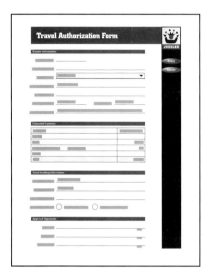

This electronic form was designed using a page-layout application and then converted to PDF. Form fields have been created so that you can fill out the form from within Acrobat. For the purposes of this lesson, some form fields have already been filled out for you.

3 Select the hand tool (☝).

4 Move the pointer to the right of the Today's Date line. When the pointer changes to an I-beam, click to set an insertion point. Enter the current date in numeric month/day/year format; for example, 3/01/1999. (Be sure to enter the day as two digits and the year as four digits to match the field's format and to avoid generating an error message.) Press Tab.

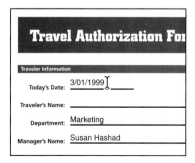
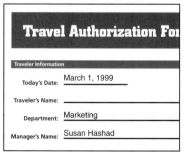

Notice that your date entry automatically updates to a longer date format. Acrobat lets you specify format options, such as currency formats and numbers of decimal places, for data entered in a form field.

5 Enter your name in the Traveler's Name field, and press Tab.

Pressing Tab lets you advance in order through a series of fields. You can set the Tab order of fields when you create a form.

6 Press the triangle to the far right of the Department field to display the *combo box* of department names. Select Engineering from the list.

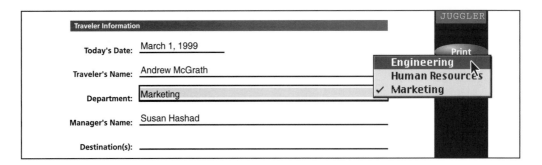

A combo box presents a choice of items in a pop-up menu. You can only select one item from a combo box.

7 Press Tab until you arrive at the Destination(s) field, and enter **Orlando, FL**. Then press Tab until you arrive at the Airfare field of the Estimated Expenses section.

8 Enter **250** for the Airfare field, and press Tab twice.

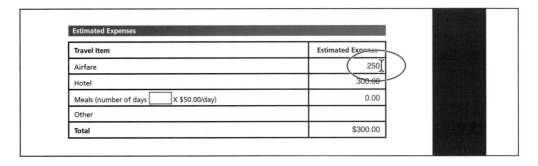

Notice that the airfare price automatically updates to a U.S. dollar currency format with two decimal places. Notice also that the Total field automatically recalculates the sum of total expenses.

This section of the form includes a preformatted mathematical calculation in the Meals field, which multiplies the number of travel days by $50.00 (the budget allotted for meals per day). You'll enter a new number of days to see the calculation. Later in this lesson, you'll learn to set up predefined and custom calculations for numeric fields.

9 In the Meals field, enter **6** for the number of days and press Tab twice.

Estimated Expenses	
Travel Item	**Estimated Expense**
Airfare	$250.00
Hotel	300.00
Meals (number of days 6 X $50.00/day)	300.00
Other	
Total	**$850.00**

Notice that the amount for Meals in the Estimated Expense column changes to $300.00 (6 x $50.00). The calculation is performed automatically when you enter a new value in the number of days field.

10 Press Tab until you arrive at the Confirmation No. field, and try entering **56T123**.

Notice that you cannot enter alphabetic characters. This field has been formatted to accept only numeric entries. Delete the current contents of the field, and reenter a confirmation number of **567123**.

11 For Payment Method, click one of the radio buttons to make a payment choice. You can select only one radio button in a set.

The Travel Authorization form was designed to be filled out electronically and then printed for final signature approvals and submission. For the purposes of this lesson, you'll save the form in its current state without printing it.

12 Choose File > Save As, make sure that Optimize is selected, and save Travel1.pdf in the Lesson08 folder. Click Yes (Windows) or Replace (Mac OS) to confirm replacing the file. The Save As command lets you save a smaller, optimized version of your finished file.

Exporting form data

Now that you have filled out the Travel Authorization form, you'll export the data to a file that contains just the data you entered.

1 Choose File > Export > Form Data. Name the file **Info.fdf** and save it in the Lesson08 folder (.fdf stands for Forms Data Format, the file format for exported form data).

2 Choose File > Close to close the Travel1.pdf file. You don't need to save the file because the data you entered has already been saved in the exported Info.fdf file.

Importing data

Now you'll open another form, and import the Info.fdf file to populate the common fields with the travel data you just entered.

You can import a form data file repeatedly to fill in multiple forms as long as those forms have the same field names as the original form from which you exported your data. A worldwide standard for naming seems unlikely, but it is certainly possible to create a standard within an organization. You can consistently name fields that ask for the same information with the same name. For example, an address field can always be named *Address,* and a home phone field can always be named *Home Phone* (keep in mind that form field names are case sensitive).

1 Choose File > Open. Select ExpFinal.pdf in the Lesson08 folder, located inside the Lessons folder within the AA4_CIB folder on your hard drive, and click Open.

2 Select the form tool ( ) to display the form fields that have been created in the document. Form fields appear as boxes with highlighted field names.

3 Select the hand tool, and choose File > Import > Form Data. Select Info.fdf in the Lesson08 folder, and click Select (Windows) or Open (Mac OS).

The values you entered in the Travel Authorization form for the Traveler's Name, Manager's Name, Department, and Airfare form fields are automatically imported into the corresponding fields in the Expense Report form. (Estimated Airfare from the Travel Authorization form is placed in the first Airfare field in the Transportation section of the Expense Report.)

This Expense Report form contains a number of other premade, formatted fields.

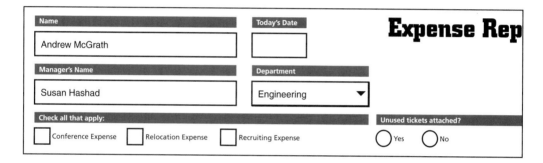

4 Select the hand tool, and experiment with filling out the Expense Report form. Later in the lesson you'll learn how to create the various types of form fields that appear in the Expense Report.

5 Choose File > Close to close the form without saving it.

Adding form fields

In this part of the lesson, you'll work with an earlier, partially created version of the Expense Report form. You'll create text fields, check boxes, a combo box, and radio buttons. You'll also learn how to validate entries in the fields and calculate the sum of numeric entries in two fields.

You create form fields by using the form tool to draw the area and location of each form field.

Adding and formatting text fields

A *text field* lets users enter alphabetic or numeric values. You can specify formatting for data entered into text fields. For example, you can specify how many decimal places to display for numbers or percentages, or the month, day, and year format for dates.

1 Choose File > Open. Select Expense.pdf in the Lesson08 folder, located inside the Lessons folder within the AA4_CIB folder on your hard drive, and click Open. Then choose File > Save As, rename the file **Expense1.pdf**, and save it in the Lesson08 folder.

2 Select the zoom-in tool (🔍), and marquee-zoom to magnify the Transportation section of the form.

3 Select the form tool (🖳) in the tool bar. As you can see from the field names and borders that appear, some form fields have already been added for you.

4 Drag to draw a box inside the first cell under Date in the Transportation section. The field box should sit inside the solid black lines so that any text the user enters remains within the boundaries.

Transportation						
Date	Description	Airfare	Fares (Taxi, Bus, Ferry, Parking, & Tolls)	Personal Auto (enter Miles only) Miles Expense		Rental Auto
		Airfare.line1		Miles.line	Personal	RentalAuto.line1
Total						

The Field Properties dialog box appears. This dialog box lets you specify form field options such as appearance, format, and mathematical calculations.

▣ For a complete description of all the available options, see "Setting form field options" in Chapter 9 of the online Adobe Acrobat User Guide.

5 For Name, enter **Date.line1**, and for Type, choose Text.

6 Click the Appearance tab. Deselect Border Color and Background Color. Make sure that Text Color is set to black, and choose a sans serif font and type size. (We used 10-point Helvetica.)

Because the boundaries of the Date field are defined by the form design, you don't need to outline the field with color.

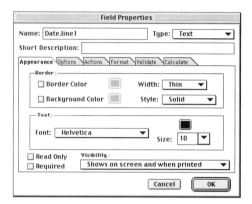

7 Click the Format tab. For Category, select Date. For Date Options, select 1/3/81. Leave the default settings selected for other options, and click OK to add the Date text field to the form.

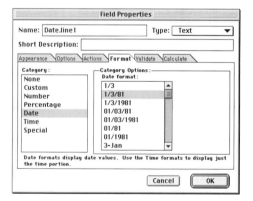

Now you'll create another text field for the Description column.

8 Drag to make a box inside the first cell under Description in the Transportation section.

9 For Name, enter **Description.line1**, and for Type, choose Text. Accept the defaults for other options, and click OK.

Transportation						
Date	Description	Airfare	Fares (Taxi, Bus, Ferry, Parking, & Tolls)	Personal Auto (enter Miles only) *Miles* *Expense*		Rental Auto
Date.li	Description.line1	Airfare.line1		Miles.line	Personal	RentalAuto.line1
Total						

10 Click the Actual Size button (□). Select the hand tool, and experiment with entering values in the fields you just created, pressing Enter or Return after each value. Notice that the Date value automatically updates to the specified date format.

Validating form fields

You use validation to restrict field entries in text or combo box fields to specific values or characters. For example, you can restrict a numeric entry to a certain range. Use validation properties to ensure that users enter appropriate data in form fields.

1 Use the zoom-in tool (🔍) to magnify the Transportation section of the form.

2 Select the form tool (📋), and drag to make a box inside the first cell under Fares in the Transportation section.

3 For Name, enter **Fares.line1**, and for Type, choose Text.

4 Click the Options tab and select Right for Alignment. All text you enter will align with the right border of the field.

5 Click the Format tab. For Category, select Number. For Decimal Places, choose 2.

You'll designate the Fares field to accept only values between 1 and 1000.

6 Click the Validate tab. Select Value Must Be Greater Than or Equal To, and enter **1**. Then enter **1000** for the value Less Than or Equal To. Leave the default settings selected for other options, and click OK.

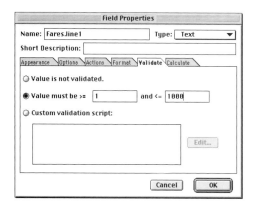

7 Click the Actual Size button (◻). Select the hand tool and click in the Fares field.

8 Enter **1500**, and press Enter or Return to test the validation for the field.

An alert box appears indicating that the value must be between 1 and 1000.

9 Enter **85** in the Fares field.

The value is accepted and appears in the Fares field formatted as a dollar amount.

10 Choose File > Save to save the Expense1.pdf file.

Using the forms grid

To aid form field creation, you'll display the forms grid. The forms grid helps you align, size, and place form fields precisely.

1 Use the zoom-in tool (🔍) to magnify the Transportation section of the form.

2 Choose View > Show Forms Grid.

Although the grid is displayed on-screen, it will not print with the rest of the PDF form.

Notice that many of the cell boundaries in the form follow the lines of the grid. By aligning form field boundaries with the grid, you can ensure consistent size and even spacing between the fields.

3 Choose View > Snap to Forms Grid.

4 Select the form tool (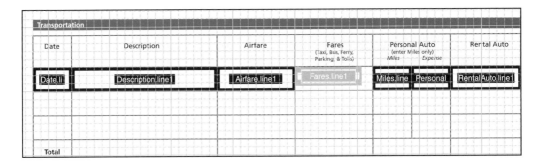), and click the Fares.line1 field to select it.

You can use the form tool to edit the location, size, and properties of a field at any time. You'll resize the Fares.line1 field so that it fills the area of the cell.

5 Position the pointer over a corner of the field to display the double-headed arrow. Then drag to resize the form field. Notice that the field boundary automatically snaps to grid lines.

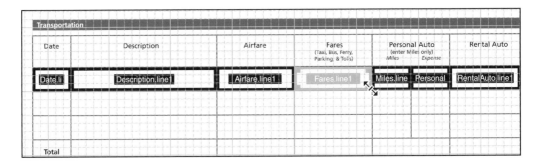

6 Drag the remaining corners of the field to align its boundaries with the cell boundaries.

If desired, you can select and resize the Description.line1 and Date.line1 fields.

Adding check boxes

Check boxes allow a user to make multiple selections from a group of items. Adding check boxes to this form will let users select the purpose of their travel (Conference, Relocation, or Recruiting Expense).

1 Click the Fit in Window button (⬜). Then select the zoom-in tool (🔍), and marquee-zoom around the area under the phrase "Check all that apply."

Notice that the square boxes in this section follow the lines of the grid, for precise sizing and alignment. You'll hide the grid to remove the display of distracting grid lines from the form.

2 Choose View > Show Forms Grid. This command toggles between displaying and hiding the grid lines.

Although you have hidden the display of the grid, the snap-to-grid behavior is still active.

3 Select the form tool ( ), and drag to make a box inside the square just to the left of Conference Expense. Notice that the field automatically snaps to the edges of the square.

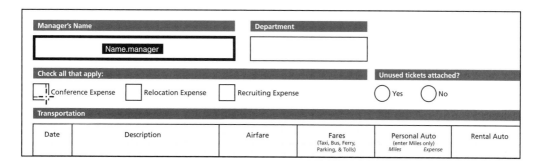

4 For Name, enter **Conference**, and for Type, choose Check Box.

5 Click the Options tab. For Check Style, choose Check (the default style); for Export Value, enter **Yes**.

An export value is the information used by a Common Gateway Interface (CGI) application on a Web server to identify the selected field.

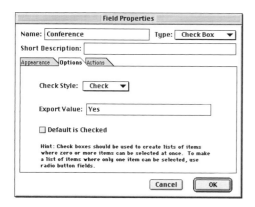

6 Click the Appearance tab. Deselect Border Color and Background Color, and click OK to add the check box to the form.

7 Drag to draw a field inside the square next to Relocation Expense. Name the new field **Relocation**, accept the current formatting and appearance options, and click OK.

Instead of creating the third check box with the form tool, you'll duplicate one of the existing fields.

8 Click to select the Relocation field you just created. (Selected fields appear highlighted in red.) Choose Edit > Copy.

9 Choose Edit > Paste to paste a duplicate of the Relocation field in the center of the document window.

You can move a form field and edit its properties at any time with the form tool.

10 Position the pointer inside the duplicate field, and drag it inside the square next to Recruiting Expense. Notice that it snaps to the grid lines.

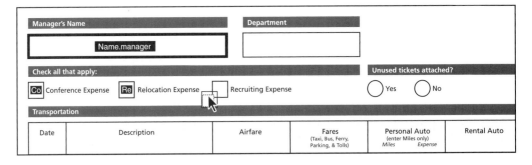

11 Double-click inside the duplicate field to open the Field Properties dialog box.

Because you duplicated this field, it has the same name value as the Relocation field. Each check box field must have a distinct name value to work properly.

12 For Name, enter **Recruiting**. Accept the current formatting and appearance options, and click OK.

13 Click the Actual Size button (🗋). Select the hand tool, and click inside the newly created check box fields. Notice that you can select more than one check box.

Adding a combo box

A *combo box* contains a list of items that appear in a pop-up menu. You'll create a combo box for the Department section of the form.

1 Use the zoom-in tool (🔍) to magnify the top left portion of the form.

2 Select the form tool (📋), and drag to draw a box inside the cell under Department.

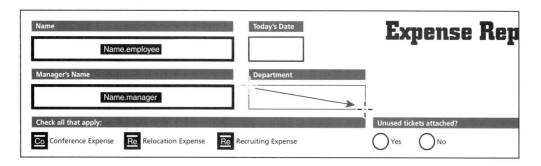

3 For Name, enter **Department**, and for Type, choose Combo Box.

4 Click the Options tab.

Now you'll enter the names of the items you wish to appear in the combo box.

5 For Item, enter **Engineering**, and click Add.

Engineering is added to the combo box list at the bottom of the dialog box, and the Item field is cleared for you to enter additional items.

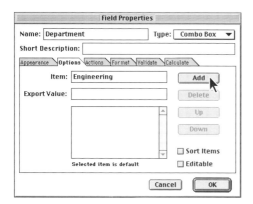

6 For Item, enter **Marketing**, and click Add.

7 For Item, enter **Human Resources,** and click Add.

Note: Be sure to click Add after typing each item name to add it to the combo box list. Do not press the Enter or Return key; if you do, you'll exit the dialog box.

All three items now appear in the combo box list, in the order in which you added them.

8 Select the Sort Items option to rearrange the listed items in alphabetical order.

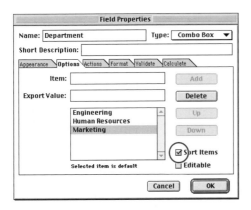

9 Select Marketing to make it the default choice.

10 Click the Appearance tab. Deselect Border Color. Select Background Color and then click the color box next to it to choose a color:

• In Windows, click Define Custom Colors. Enter **255** for Red, **255** for Green, and **204** for Blue. Then click OK.

• In Mac OS, scroll up to select the CMYK Picker. Enter **0%** for Cyan, **0%** for Magenta, **20%** for Yellow, and **0%** for Black. Then click OK.

11 In the Field Properties dialog box, choose a sans serif font and type size. (We used 10-point Helvetica.) Then click OK.

12 Click the Actual Size button (⬜). Select the hand tool, position the pointer over the triangle in the new field, and click to view the pop-up list of items.

Adding radio buttons

Unlike check boxes, which let you make multiple selections from a group of items, radio buttons let you select only one item.

When creating radio buttons, keep in mind that the fields must share the same name but have different export values. For example, for the field "Unused tickets attached?" you can have two values: "Yes" or "No." Now you'll set up that radio button.

1 Use the zoom-in tool (🔍) to magnify the top right portion of the form.

2 Select the form tool (📋), and drag a box that surrounds the circle just to the left of the word "Yes" at the top right of the form.

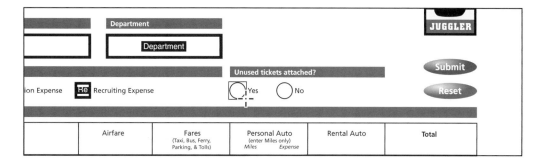

3 For Name, enter **Unused Tickets**, and for Type, choose Radio Button.

4 Click the Options tab. For Radio Style, choose Circle. For Export Value, enter **Yes**.

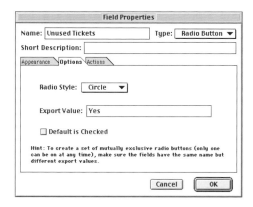

5 Click the Appearance tab. Deselect Border Color and Background Color. For Width, choose Thin, and for Style, choose Solid. Click OK.

Instead of using the form tool to create the other radio button, you'll save time by simply copying the field you just created. When you duplicate a form field, you must remember to edit the appropriate field properties for the new field.

6 Click in a blank area of the form with the form tool to deselect all the fields.

7 Move the pointer inside the Yes field you just created and hold down Control (Windows) or Option (Mac OS). Begin dragging the field to the circle next to No (a hollow arrow appears, indicating that you are making a copy). Then as you drag, hold down Shift to constrain the motion of the duplicate field along the same horizontal or vertical line as the original field.

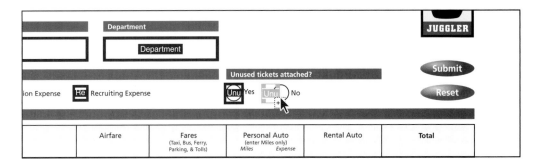

8 Double-click the field next to No to open the Field Properties dialog box. Click the Options tab, enter **No** as the export value, and click OK.

9 Click the Actual Size button (◻). Select the hand tool, and click inside the newly created radio button fields. Notice that you can only select one item at a time.

Because you have set the fields to snap to the grid, the radio buttons should line up evenly with the preexisting black circles on the form.

10 Choose File > Save to save the Expense1.pdf file.

Calculating form fields

You can perform mathematical calculations on two or more existing numeric field entries and display the results. You perform calculations within text or combo box fields. You can apply predefined operations, or you can create custom operations using the JavaScript programming language.

In the first part of this section, you'll create a Total field that adds values from the Airfare, Fares, Personal Auto, and Rental Auto fields in the Transportation section of the form. Then you'll set a custom calculation for the Personal Auto field.

Specifying a predefined calculation

Acrobat lets you assign common mathematical operations to numeric fields—including addition, multiplication, averaging, and finding maximum and minimum values.

1 Use the zoom-in tool to magnify the Transportation section of the form.

2 Select the form tool (⌨), and drag to draw a box inside the first cell under Total at the right of the Transportation section.

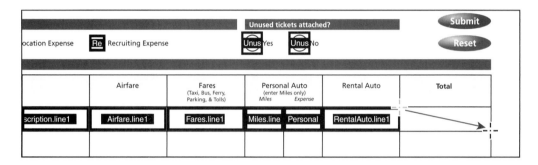

3 Enter **Total.line1** for the name, and for Type, choose Text.

A field must be formatted as a number in order to perform calculations for the field. Now you'll format the Total field as a number.

4 Click the Format tab. For Category, select Number. For Decimal Places, choose 2; for Currency Symbol, choose Dollar.

5 Click the Calculate tab, and select Value Is the <operation> of the Following Fields.

6 Choose sum (+) from the pop-up list (the default setting), and click Pick.

7 In the Select a Field dialog box, select Airfare.line1 in the scroll list and click Add (Windows) or Pick (Mac OS).

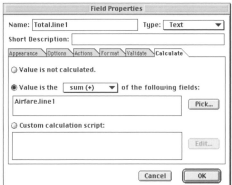

8 Repeat step 7 three times, adding Fares.line1, PersonalAuto.line1, and RentalAuto.line1 to the calculation list.

Values used for calculation must be formatted as numbers in the same way that you formatted the Total field. The Fares.line1, PersonalAuto.line1, and RentalAuto.line1 fields have been preformatted as numbers.

9 Click Done.

The Airfare.line1, Fares.line1, PersonalAuto.line1, and RentalAuto.line1 fields appear in the message box next to the Pick button. If you made a mistake in adding fields, you can select the value in the message box and delete it or click Pick to add more fields.

10 Click OK to verify the calculation settings and close the Field Properties dialog box.

11 Select the hand tool. The Total field should now contain the value $85.00 (from the 85.00 in the Fares field). Because the other numeric fields are still empty, they do not affect the value in the Total field.

12 Now enter **250** in the first cell under Airfare, and press Tab, Enter, or Return to update the Total field.

	Airfare	Fares (Taxi, Bus, Ferry, Parking, & Tolls)	Personal Auto (enter Miles only) Miles Expense		Rental Auto	Total
	250.00	85.00				$335.00

Specifying a custom calculation

Now you'll specify a custom JavaScript calculation for the Personal Auto column to calculate the personal transportation expense (number of miles driven multiplied by the expense per mile).

The Miles and Expense fields have been preformatted as numbers. You'll open the Field Properties dialog box for the Expense field and apply the custom calculation option to the field.

1 Select the form tool (📋), and double-click the PersonalAuto.line1 field under Personal Auto.

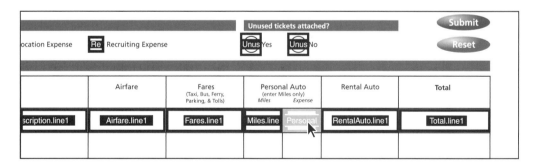

2 Click the Calculate tab. Select Custom Calculation Script and then click Edit.

To create a custom calculation, you write instructions in JavaScript to tell Adobe Acrobat what operations to perform. You'll enter JavaScript code to multiply the number of miles driven by 32 cents (the allowable expense per mile for personal auto usage).

3 Enter the JavaScript code exactly as it appears below, including a line break after the first semicolon:

var a = this.getField("Miles.line1");
event.value = a.value * .32;

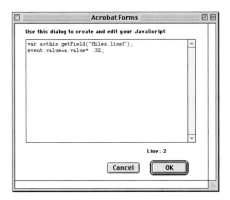

For more information on writing in JavaScript, refer to JavaScript documentation.

4 Click OK. Then click OK again.

Now you'll enter values to test the calculating operations.

5 Click the Actual Size button (□). Select the hand tool and click in the first Miles cell under Personal Auto.

6 Enter **100** and press Enter or Return.

	Airfare	Fares (Taxi, Bus, Ferry, Parking, & Tolls)	Personal Auto (enter Miles only) Miles	Expense	Rental Auto	Total
	250.00	85.00	100	32.00		$335.00

The mileage value appears in the Miles column, and the value 32.00 (100 times .32) appears as the Personal Auto expense.

However, notice that the Total field still displays $335.00, the total excluding the Personal Auto expense. In the next section, you'll fix the calculation order so that the Total field takes the Personal Auto expense into account.

Setting the calculation order

The Total field displays the wrong value because Acrobat is performing the two assigned calculations in the incorrect order. In other words, Acrobat is calculating first the Total, and then the Personal Auto expense. You'll reverse this calculation order so that the Total field displays the correct value.

By default, the calculation order follows the tab order of the fields. For more information on tab order, see "Exploring on your own" on page 208.

1 Choose Tools > Forms > Set Field Calculation Order.

2 Select PersonalAuto.line1, and click Up to move the field to the top of the Calculated Fields list. Then click OK.

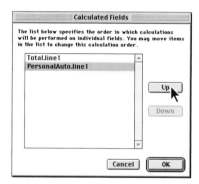

3 In the form, delete 100 from the Miles field under Personal Auto. Then enter **200** for Miles, and press Enter or Return.

Notice that the Total field now shows the correct sum, taking into account the Personal Auto calculation.

4 Choose File > Save to save the Expense1.pdf file.

Creating a Reset Form field

You can specify a Reset Form action to clear the data that has already been entered in a form. You might reset a form to clear a mistake, or to clear the form for another user to fill in.

You'll add the Reset Form action as a button field that clears the form when clicked by the user. For this part of the lesson, you'll turn off the snap-to-grid behavior. To learn more about creating buttons for PDF documents, see Lesson 9, "Adding Buttons."

1 Choose View > Snap to Forms Grid.

2 Select the form tool (⬚), and drag a box around the Reset item at the top right of the form.

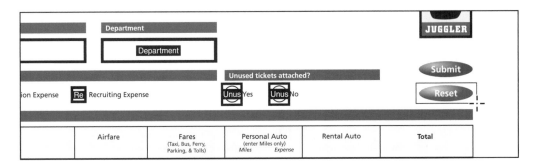

3 For Name, enter **Reset**, and for Type, choose Button.

4 Click the Appearance tab. Deselect Border Color and Background Color, and for Style, choose Solid.

5 Click the Options tab. For Highlight, choose None, and for Layout, choose Text Only.

6 Click the Actions tab. Select Mouse Up to create an action that occurs when the mouse button is released while the pointer is on the Reset button. Then click Add.

The Add an Action dialog box appears, letting you specify the action that will occur after the button is clicked.

7 For Type, choose Reset Form, and click Select Fields.

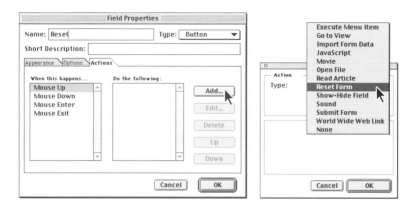

8 In the Field Selection dialog box, select All Fields, and click OK. Click Set Action, and then click OK to add the Reset button to the form.

9 Select the hand tool and click the Reset button to test it.

The fields in the form are cleared.

10 Choose File > Save As, make sure that Optimize is selected, and save Expense1.pdf in the Lesson08 folder. Click Yes (Windows) or Replace (Mac OS) to confirm replacing the file. The Save As command lets you save a smaller, optimized version of your finished file.

Submitting forms over the Web

PDF forms can be used for submitting and collecting information over the Web. For this process to work, you must have a Common Gateway Interface (CGI) application on the Web server to collect and route the data to a database. The field names in the forms must also match those set in the CGI application. Any existing CGI application that collects data from forms (in HTML or FDF format) can be used to collect data from PDF forms.

Keep in mind that CGI scripts must be built outside of Acrobat and require some knowledge of computer programming. CGI applications are usually set up by a Web server administrator. For information on creating and managing a form database, see the FDF (Forms Data Format) Toolkit. If you do not have the FDF Toolkit, contact the Adobe Developer Association, or check the Web site at partners.adobe.com/supportservice/devrelations/memberapp.html.

Filling out the fields

Now you can experiment with filling out the fields that you have just created and resetting the form. (Because you haven't set up a CGI application on a Web server, you won't be able to submit the form data.) When you are finished experimenting with the form, choose File > Close to close the file without saving it.

You have just learned how to create and use PDF forms. Now you can use your new skills to get your existing and future forms online. Work with your Web administrator to collect the data from those forms and keep your databases up to date.

Exploring on your own

You can determine the order in which a user tabs through form fields on a single page. The default tab order is the order in which the form fields were created. You can set the tab order of the Expense Report form so that users tab through fields from left to right, and top to bottom.

1 Select the form tool ( ).

2 Choose Tools > Forms > Fields > Set Tab Order.

The form fields display numbers indicating the current tab order.

3 To reorder the tabs, click the form fields in the order that they should be numbered. Start with the Name field, and proceed by rows from left to right.

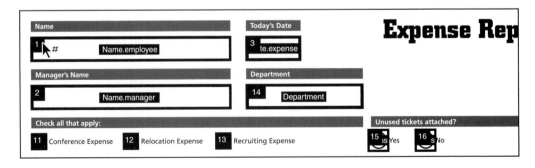

4 Click outside a form field, or switch tools to exit Set Tab Order.

Review questions

1 What is the difference between a check box and a radio button?

2 When will a user be able to submit a form over the Web?

3 Which fields will populate in a form if you use the Import > Form Data command?

4 What is a combo box?

5 How do you copy a form field by dragging?

6 How do you restrict entries in text or combo box fields?

7 How do you perform mathematical calculations on two or more numeric fields?

Review answers

1 You can select multiple check boxes, whereas you can select only one radio button in a series.

2 Users can submit a form over the Web after a CGI (Common Gateway Interface) application is set up on a Web server to handle the form data.

3 When you import data from a form data file, the fields that share names in common with the imported data fields will be populated.

4 A combo box consists of a pop-up list of items from which users can choose only one item.

5 To copy a form field, select the form tool and make sure that all form fields are deselected. Hold down Ctrl (Windows) or Option (Macintosh) and drag the desired field to create and move a copy.

6 To restrict field entries in text or combo box fields and ensure that users enter appropriate data in the form fields, you use validation properties.

7 You perform calculations within text or combo box fields by either applying predefined operations, or creating custom operations using the JavaScript programming language.

Lesson 9

Adding Buttons

Buttons provide an effective way for you to add creative and stylish interactive features to your PDF documents. Like bookmarks and links, buttons let you jump to different destination views and play actions. In addition, you can customize the appearance of buttons by importing icons.

In this lesson, you'll learn how to do the following:

- Activate existing buttons in a document.
- Add your own buttons to a document.
- Duplicate a button across multiple pages.
- Add buttons that show and hide other button fields.
- Add a button that links to the World Wide Web.
- Set the opening display of a document.

This lesson will take about 30 minutes to complete.

If needed, remove the previous lesson folder from your hard drive, and copy the Lesson09 folder onto it.

Using and adding buttons

Like bookmarks and links, buttons can link to a particular destination or play an action. But unlike bookmarks and links, buttons offer the following three additional capabilities:

- Buttons can activate a series of actions, not just a single action.
- Buttons can have alternate appearances, according to the mouse behavior over the buttons.
- You can duplicate buttons across a range of pages, thereby simplifying the task of adding repeat buttons to a document.

In Acrobat, buttons are a type of form field. You use the form tool to add buttons to a PDF document. For detailed information on other types of form fields, see Lesson 8, "Modifying PDF Documents."

Using buttons

In this lesson, you'll work with the camping section of the Mount Rainier Field Guide. This document already contains some buttons that help ease navigation to informational sections such as the index and the Welcome page. You'll try out these existing buttons and then add your own buttons.

1 Start Acrobat.

2 Choose File > Open. Select Visit.pdf in the Lesson09 folder, located inside the Lessons folder within the AA4_CIB folder on your hard drive, and click Open. Then choose File > Save As, rename the file **Visit1.pdf**, and save it in the Lesson09 folder.

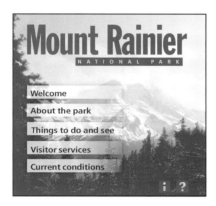

3 Take a moment to page through the document. Click the Fit in Window button ( ) to fit the document pages in the window. Select the hand tool ( ) in the tool bar, and notice the two buttons that appear in the bottom right corner of each page.

4 Go to page 3 of the document.

5 Move your pointer over the "i" button at the bottom of the page. The hand pointer turns into a pointing finger, indicating that you are positioned over a button.

6 Click the "i" button to jump to the index for this document.

Click "i" button.   *Result*

7 Click the Go to Previous View button ( ) to return to page 3.

8 Now click the "?" button at the bottom of the page to go to the Welcome page.

These easily recognizable buttons let you jump to their respective informational sections from any page in the document.

Adding buttons

Now you'll add a button of your own, and then duplicate it across the relevant pages. You'll add a "home" button that brings the user back to page 1 of the document—the "home" page.

1 Go to page 4 of the document.

2 Select the form tool (⬚) in the tool bar. The field borders for the two existing buttons appear, enclosing the names of the buttons.

3 Drag to make a box about the same size as and to the left of the other buttons at the bottom of the page.

The Field Properties dialog box appears. This dialog box lets you name, format, and assign actions to the new button.

4 For Name, type **Home**, and for Type, choose Button.

5 Click the Options tab.

6 For Highlight, choose Push, and for Layout, choose Icon only.

Drag to create new form field.

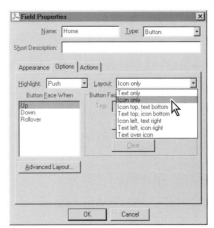
Specify properties in Field Properties dialog box.

The Highlight option determines the highlight appearance of the button when it is activated, and the Layout option determines the graphic layout of the button. Buttons can display as a line of text, an icon, or a combination of both. You can use text and icons that already exist in the document, or you can import text and icons to represent the buttons. You can only import icons that have been saved in PDF. See the following illustration for examples of the different layout options.

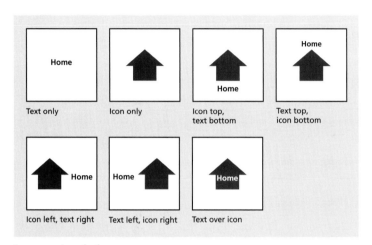

Layout options for buttons

You can specify up to three icons for the same button—one icon for each of the following button states:

• Up indicates the button display when the mouse is not interacting with the button.

• Down indicates the button display when the mouse is pressed over the button.

• Rollover indicates the change in the button display when the cursor moves across the button.

7 For Button Face When, select Up. Under Button Face Attributes, click Select Icon.

8 Click Browse.

9 Select Home.pdf in the Buttons folder, located inside the Lesson09 folder, and click Open.

The Home.pdf file contains some premade "home" icons for your use. A preview of the first page of the file appears in the Select Appearance dialog box.

10 Click OK to accept the displayed image as the Up icon.

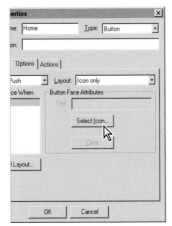

Click Select Icon.   Click Browse.   Select Home.pdf and click OK.

Now you'll use another page from Home.pdf as the button icon when the mouse is pressed over the button.

11 For Button Face When, select Down. Under Button Face Attributes, click Select Icon.

The Home.pdf preview appears in the Select Appearance dialog box.

12 Click in the scroll bar until you see "2 out of 2" in the preview window, and click OK to accept the displayed icon.

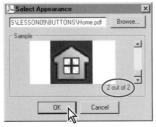

Click in scroll bar.   When you see "2 out of 2," click OK.

Storing similar button icons as separate pages in a PDF file makes it easy for you to scroll through the previews until you find the icon that you want.

When you create a button icon, keep in mind that the icon will automatically shrink to fit the field that you create for the button area in the document. You should create button icons at approximately the size that you wish to display them in your document.

 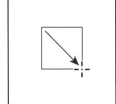 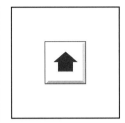

Original size of button icon   *Button field size*   *Resulting button*

Note: *When creating a button icon in your drawing or photo-editing application, be sure to place it on a page that is at least 1-by-1 inch—the minimum size page allowed as a PDF document. If you want the icon to appear smaller than 1-by-1 inch, you can draw a smaller field with the form tool, assign the icon to the field, and let the icon shrink to fit the field.*

For more information on creating your own button icons, see "Exploring on your own" on page 232.

13 Click the Appearance tab.

14 Deselect Border Color and Background Color. For Style, choose Solid.

Now you'll assign the appropriate "home" action to your button.

15 Click the Actions tab.

You specify different actions to occur for behaviors of the mouse over the button. The following list describes the various mouse behaviors to which you can assign button actions:

• Mouse Up specifies releasing the mouse button.

• Mouse Down specifies depressing the mouse button.

• Mouse Enter specifies moving the mouse into the button field.

• Mouse Exit specifies moving the mouse out of the button field.

We recommend assigning most actions to the Mouse Up behavior. This way, if users decide that they do not want a particular action to occur, they can simply drag their pointer away from the button field to avoid causing the action.

16 Select Mouse Up, and click Add.

17 For Type, choose Execute Menu Item. Click Edit Menu Item.

18 Choose Document > First Page, and click OK.

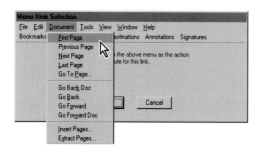

19 Click Set Action. Then click OK.

The button is added to the document page.

20 Select the hand tool (🖑), move the pointer over the new home button, and hold down the mouse.

Notice that the appearance of the button changes when you depress the mouse.

21 Release the mouse to jump to the first page of the document.

22 Click the Go to Previous View button (◀) to return to page 4.

If needed, you can easily adjust the size and position of the home button so that it matches the other two buttons on the page. To resize the home button, select the form tool, click the button to select it, and drag one of the corner handles. To move the home button, position the form tool inside the button and drag.

23 Choose File > Save to save the Visit1.pdf file.

Duplicating the button

Now that you have created a button that returns the user to the home page, you'll duplicate the button to other pages in the document. Duplicating a button saves you from the tedious work of recreating the button for each relevant page.

1 Select the form tool ( ), and click the home button once to select it. Handles appear at the four corners of the button field.

2 Choose Tools > Forms > Fields > Duplicate.

3 In the Duplicate Field dialog box, click From. Type **2** for the start of the page range, press Tab, and type **9** for the end of the page range. Then click OK. You do not need a home button on the first page.

Click home button to select it.

Enter page range in Duplicate Field dialog box.

4 Select the hand tool ( ), and click the Next Page button a few times to see the duplicated home button.

5 Click the home button at the bottom of the current page. You go to the home page.

6 Choose File > Save As, make sure that Optimize is selected, and save Visit1.pdf in the Lesson09 folder. Click Yes (Windows) or Replace (Mac OS) to confirm replacing the file. The Save As command lets you save a smaller, optimized version of your finished file.

Be sure to save the Visit1.pdf file in the Lesson09 folder. As you will see in the next part of this lesson, the Visit1.pdf file contains a link to another PDF document in the Lesson09 folder. PDF documents that are linked to each other must remain in their relative folder locations.

Note: When you duplicate buttons across pages that have been rotated, the buttons may appear in unexpected locations. If this happens, delete the buttons from the problematic pages, and readd the buttons manually.

Adding a print button

1 Go to page 4 of the document. If needed, click the Fit in Window button (▣) to fit the entire page in the window.

2 Click the Information Sheet link to open the Camping.pdf document.

Click Information Sheet link.   *Result*

Notice that the campgrounds page plays a sound clip as an open page action. Enhancing files with sounds and movies is discussed in Lesson 14, "Adding Page Actions, Movies, and Sounds to PDF Files."

This page contains important information about the campgrounds in the park. You'll add a button that opens the Print dialog box so that users can print the page for handy reference.

3 If needed, scroll down to display the bottom of the page.

4 Select the form tool (), and drag a box in the bottom right corner of the page, as shown in the following illustration.

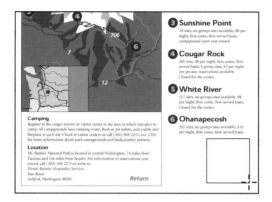

5 For Name, type **Print,** and for Type, choose Button.

6 Click the Options tab.

7 For Highlight, choose None, and for Layout, choose Icon top, text bottom.

8 Under Button Face Attributes, for Text, type **Print this page**. Click Select Icon.

9 Click Browse.

10 Select Printer.pdf in the Buttons folder, located inside the Lesson09 folder, and click Open.

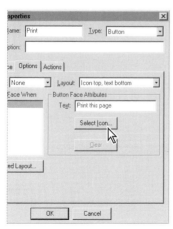

Click Select Icon.

Click Browse.

Select Printer.pdf and click OK.

11 Click OK to accept the previewed icon.

Buttons do not have to have alternate appearances. In this case, you'll give this button only one appearance.

12 Click the Appearance tab.

13 If needed, deselect Border Color and Background Color, and for Style, choose Solid.

14 Under Text, for Font, choose a font (we used Helvetica Bold). For Size, choose 12. The text color should be black. If needed, click the color box to access the system palette and set the color to black.

15 To prevent the button from appearing on a printout, follow the instructions for your computer platform:

• In Windows, under Common Properties, for Form Field, choose Visible but doesn't print.

• In Mac OS, for Visibility, choose Shows on screen, hidden when printed.

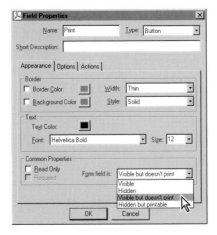

16 Click the Actions tab.

17 Select Mouse Up, and click Add.

18 For Type, choose Execute Menu Item. Then click Edit Menu Item.

19 Choose File > Print, and click OK.

20 Click Set Action. Then click OK. The button is added to the page.

21 Select the hand tool, and click your new button.

Note: If the text is cut off, you'll need to resize the button field. To resize the field, select the form tool, click the field, and drag one of the handles. Select the hand tool to view the results.

22 The Print dialog box appears. If you would like to print this document, click OK (Windows) or Print (Mac OS). If not, click Cancel.

Buttons can execute any menu item in the Acrobat or Reader menus. But keep in mind that Reader users do not have access to all of the menu items available in Acrobat. If you are not sure if a button will execute a menu item when activated in Reader, try it out.

Editing a button

You can easily change the appearance or action of an existing button.

1 Select the form tool (🖳), and double-click the Print button to open the Field Properties dialog box.

2 Click the Options tab.

3 For Layout, choose Text top, icon bottom. Click OK.

4 Select the hand tool. As you can see, the button layout has changed.

Before

After

5 Continue to experiment with the button layout by selecting the form tool and double-clicking the button field, or go on to the next section.

Using the Show/Hide Field action

Buttons can be used to show or hide a form field. Because form fields can include a combination of text and graphics, you can alternate showing and hiding a form field to create an interesting visual effect. In this section, you'll see how the Show/Hide Field action works, and then set up a field to show and hide another field.

We have already set up a field to show and hide another field in the campgrounds page. The hidden field is shown when your pointer enters the border of the other field. The field is hidden again when your pointer exits the border.

1 Click the Fit in Window button (◱). Then click the Fit Width button (▣).

2 If needed, select the hand tool (🖐). Move your pointer over the "1" button in the map. As you do, an illustration of the Ipsut Creek Campground is displayed in the upper right corner of the page.

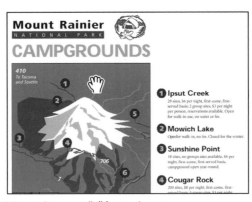

Move pointer over "1" button in map.   *Result*

3 Move your pointer away from the "1" button. The Ipsut Creek Campground illustration is hidden again.

Assigning the Show/Hide Field action

To create the same effect for another campground, you'll add two new form fields.

1 Select the form tool (🗒). The existing form fields appear in the page.

First you'll create the field that will be shown and hidden.

2 Drag to draw a box in the upper right corner of the page that just encloses the existing Ipsut Creek Map button field.

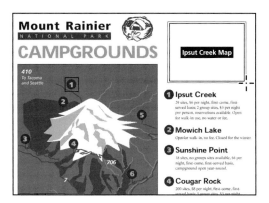

3 For Name, type **Mowich Lake Map**, and for Type, choose Button.

4 Click the Options tab.

5 For Highlight, choose Push, and for Layout, choose Icon only.

6 For Button Face When, select Up. Under Button Face Attributes, click Select Icon.

7 Click Browse.

8 Select Mowich.pdf, located inside the Lesson09 folder, and click Open.

9 Click OK to accept the previewed image as the button.

10 Click the Appearance tab.

11 If needed, deselect Border Color and Background Color, and for Style, choose Solid. Click OK.

Now you'll create the button on the campgrounds map that will activate the Show/Hide Field action.

12 Drag a box around the "2" icon in the map.

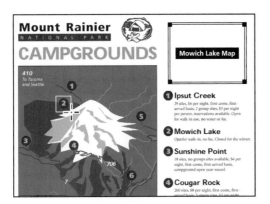

13 For Name, type **2**, and for Type, choose Button.

You won't assign an icon or appearance to this button. Instead, you'll assign actions to occur when the mouse enters and exits the border of the field.

14 Click the Actions tab.

15 Select Mouse Enter, and click Add.

16 For Type, choose Show/Hide Field. Click Edit.

17 Click Show, select Mowich Lake Map, and click OK.

18 Click Set Action.

19 Select Mouse Exit, and click Add.

20 For Type, choose Show/Hide Field. Click Edit.

21 Click Hide, select Mowich Lake Map, and click OK.

22 Click Set Action. Then click OK.

23 Select the hand tool, and pass the pointer back and forth over the "2" button in the map. (You have to pass the hand over the "2" button to hide the map for the first time.)

Notice that the Mowich Lake map appears and disappears as the mouse enters and exits the field's border.

Adding a text-only button that links to the World Wide Web

As you have seen, buttons do not have to have icons—they can have no appearance or consist only of a text display. In this part of the lesson, you'll add a text-only button that links to the World Wide Web.

1 Scroll down to view the bottom part of the campgrounds page.

2 Select the form tool ( ).

3 Drag to draw a rectangular box along the bottom edge of the page, as shown in the following illustration.

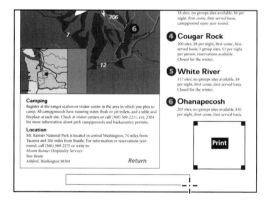

4 For Name, type **URL**, and for Type, choose Button.

5 Click the Options tab.

6 For Highlight, choose None, and for Layout, choose Text only.

7 Under Button Face Attributes, for Text, type **Mount Rainier Web Site**.

You'll give this button a beveled, gray appearance.

8 Click the Appearance Tab.

9 Under Border, select Border Color and Background Color. Click the appropriate color box to access the system palette and set the Border Color to light gray and the Background Color to light gray.

10 For Width, choose Thin, and for Style, choose Beveled.

11 Under Text, for Font, choose a font (we used Helvetica Bold). For Size, choose 12. The text color should not be light gray. If needed, click the appropriate color box to access the system palette and choose a color other than light gray.

12 Follow the instructions for your computer platform:

• In Windows, under Common Properties, for Form Field, choose Visible but doesn't print.

• In Mac OS, for Visibility, choose Shows on screen, hidden when printed.

13 Click the Actions tab.

14 Select Mouse Up, and click Add.

15 For Type, choose World Wide Web Link. Then click Edit URL.

16 Type a URL for the destination of the link in the URL text box (we used http://www.adobe.com), and click OK.

17 Click Set Action. Then click OK.

18 Select the hand tool (✍), and click your new button. If you have a connection to the Internet, you can connect to the Web site.

19 In Acrobat, choose File > Save As, make sure that Optimize is selected, and save Camping.pdf in the Lesson09 folder. Click Yes (Windows) or Replace (Mac OS) to confirm replacing the file.

20 Choose File > Close to close the campgrounds page.

Determining the opening display of a document

In some cases, you may want to control how a particular document displays when it is opened. For example, you may want the document to open in Full Screen mode or to a specific page other than the first page. You can set these preferences easily using the Open Info dialog box.

1 If Visit1.pdf is not already open, choose File > Open, select Visit1.pdf in the Lesson09 folder, and click Open.

2 Choose File > Document Info > Open.

The Open Info dialog box appears. This dialog box contains a number of display options for the current document.

⬚ For information on all the options available in the Open Info dialog box, see "Defining opening views" in Chapter 13 of the online Adobe Acrobat User Guide.

3 Under Window Options, select Open in Full Screen Mode, and click OK.

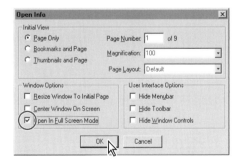

4 Choose File > Save As, rename the file **Visit2.pdf**, and save it in the Lesson09 folder.

5 Choose File > Close to close the file.

6 Choose File > Open, and reopen Visit2.pdf in the Lesson09 folder.

Notice how the document opened in Full Screen mode, hiding the menu, command, tool, and status bars.

7 Press Enter or Return to progress through the document.

You can use Full Screen mode for online presentations or just to enhance the display of a document on-screen.

8 Press Esc to exit Full Screen mode.

9 Choose File > Close to close the file.

In this lesson, you learned how to add navigational aids, execute menu items, and show and hide fields using buttons. Buttons add a new dimension to the level of interactivity that you can use in your PDF documents. As you experiment further with buttons, you'll find new ways to use them to enhance your documents.

Exploring on your own

Now that you have learned how to add buttons to a document, try creating your own button icons. All button icon files must be saved as PDF files, and each page of a PDF document can be used as an individual button icon.

First, use your favorite drawing or photo-editing application to create an image, or locate an existing image file. Be sure to save the image file in one of the following formats: BMP, GIF, JPEG, PCS, PhotoCD®, PICT (Mac OS only), PNG, or TIFF. Then follow the steps below to import the image, and crop it in Acrobat if necessary.

1 In Acrobat, choose File > Import > Image.

2 Select your image file. Click Open (Windows), or Add and Done (Mac OS).

The image is converted to PDF and placed in a new document. If you want to use only a portion of the page as the button icon, you need to crop the page. Acrobat's crop tool allows you to adjust page margins by setting specific parameters or by visually setting page boundaries. You cannot undo a crop operation.

3 Select the crop tool ( ) in the tool bar, and drag a rectangle around the button icon on the page.

4 Double-click inside the rectangle to display the Crop Pages dialog box.

5 Use the left, right, top, and bottom increment arrows to adjust the page margins.

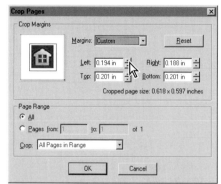

Drag rectangle around button icon.

Adjust page margins in Crop Pages dialog box.

6 Click OK to accept the new page margins.

7 Choose File > Save to save the file.

8 If you want, you can add more button icons to your button icon file by importing additional images to the current document, cropping them if necessary, and saving your file.

9 Choose File > Close to close the file.

Now that you have created your own button icons, you can add buttons with these icons to an existing PDF document by following the general instructions in "Adding buttons" on page 216.

Review questions

1 In what file format must a graphic be saved before you can use it as a button icon?

2 If your original button icon is 5 inches by 5 inches in your graphics application and the field you draw in a PDF file is 3 inches by 3 inches, at what size will the button icon appear in the PDF file?

3 What is a mouse behavior?

4 How can you make a button quit Acrobat or Reader?

5 Which style gives the appearance of a button without using an icon?

Review answers

1 To use a graphic as a button icon, the graphic must be in PDF.

2 The button icon will be 3 inches by 3 inches in the PDF file. The original icon is resized to fit the button field you draw.

3 Mouse behavior refers to the position of the mouse or mouse button in relation to the button field; this position determines when the specified button action occurs. You can specify an action to occur when the mouse button is released or depressed, or when the mouse enters or exits the button field.

4 To make a button that quits Acrobat or Reader, create a button and choose Execute Menu Item as the action type. In the Menu Selection dialog box, choose File > Exit (Windows) or File > Quit (Mac OS).

5 To create a button appearance without adding an icon, choose Beveled for Style under the Appearance tab.

Lesson 10

Creating PDF Documents from Paper and the Web

Acrobat lets you create editable and searchable PDF documents by converting or "capturing" scanned documents and Web pages. You can use the resulting PDF documents for a variety of archival, presentation, and distribution needs.

In this lesson, you'll learn how to do the following:

- Capture a PDF Image file.

- Show and correct Capture suspects.

- Convert a Web page to PDF using Web Capture (Windows only).

This lesson will take about 35 minutes to complete.

If needed, remove the previous lesson folder from your hard drive, and copy the Lesson10 folder onto it.

Capturing a fax image file

You can use the Import feature to convert image files, such as TIFF images or scanned paper documents, to PDF Image Only pages. In PDF Image Only format, all elements on a page can only be edited as bitmap images; text characters cannot be searched or edited. If your imported document contains text, you may want to convert the document to PDF Normal format so that the text can be edited and searched in Acrobat. You use the Capture feature to convert documents to PDF Normal format.

We've provided a fax document, scanned and saved as a TIFF image file, for you to import and capture.

Scanning text you plan to capture

- *For normal text, set up the scanner to create black-and-white (or 1-bit) images.*

- *Black-and-white images and text must be scanned at 200 to 600 dpi. Color images and text must be scanned at 200 to 400 dpi.*

Note: Pages scanned in 24-bit color, 300 dpi, at 8.5-by-11 inches are very large files (24 MB); your system must have at least twice that amount of virtual memory available to be able to scan. If you're scanning in color, check that you have at least 50 MB of space available on your hard drive before beginning the scanning process.

- *For color or grayscale pages with large type, consider scanning at 200 dpi for faster processing.*

- *For most pages, scanning at 300 dpi produces the best captures. However, if a page has many unrecognized words or very small text (9 points or below), try scanning at a higher resolution (up to 600 dpi). Scan in black and white whenever possible.*

- *Do not use dithering or halftone scanner settings. These settings can improve the appearance of photographic images, but they make it difficult to recognize text.*

• *For text printed on colored paper, try increasing the brightness and contrast by about 10%. If your scanner has color-filtering capability, consider using a filter or lamp that drops out the background color.*

• *If your scanner has a manual brightness control, adjust it so that characters are clean and well formed. If characters are touching because they are too thick, use a higher (brighter) setting. If characters are separated because the characters are too thin, use a lower (darker) setting.*

Note: The Capture Pages command is designed primarily for black-and-white text, but it can be adjusted to work with color text if there is a high contrast and a minimum of background color or graphics. Capture Pages handles text that is rotated by as much as 7°. For complex color OCR work, see the Adobe Web site (www.adobe.com) for information on the full Acrobat Capture product.

Characters that are too thin, well-formed characters, and characters that are too thick

–From the online Adobe Acrobat User Guide, Chapter 4

Importing the fax

1 Start Acrobat.

2 Choose File > Import > Image.

3 Open the fax document:

• In Windows, select Fax.tif in the Lesson10 folder, located inside the Lessons folder within the AA4_CIB folder on your hard drive, and click Open.

• In Mac OS, select Fax.tif in the Lesson10 folder, located inside the Lessons folder within the AA4_CIB folder on your hard drive, and click Add. Then click Done.

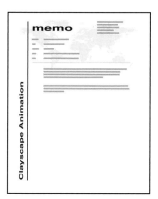

The fax image file is imported as a new PDF Image Only document.

4 Select the touchup text tool (𝕋), and click in the fax text.

Notice that you cannot edit the text in the document. The TIFF file has been imported as a PDF Image Only file; that is, all elements in the document, including the text, behave as bitmap pictures.

5 Choose File > Save As, rename the file **Fax1.pdf**, and save it in the Lesson10 folder.

You'll convert the file to PDF Normal format using the Capture Pages command. A PDF Normal document contains editable text that can be altered, scaled, and reformatted.

Capturing the fax image

1 Choose Tools > Paper Capture > Capture Pages.

You can restrict the capture to certain pages of the document and specify other capture settings.

2 Select Current Page to capture the page currently displayed on-screen.

3 Click Preferences. In the Preferences dialog box, choose English (US) for the language and Normal for the style.

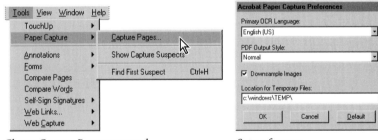

Choose Capture Pages command.   *Set preferences.*

4 Click OK to exit the Preferences dialog box, and click OK again to capture the fax document.

5 Select the touchup text tool (T), and click in the document. Notice that you can now edit all horizontal text. The vertically oriented text along the side of the page is still treated as a bitmap image.

About PDF file types

You can use Acrobat with a scanner to create a PDF file from a paper document. The resulting file is a PDF Image Only file—that is, a bitmap picture of the pages that can be viewed in Acrobat but not searched.

If you want to be able to search, correct, and copy the text in an Image Only file, you must "capture" the pages in the file to convert the file to PDF Normal. When you capture pages, Acrobat applies optical character recognition (OCR) and font and page recognition to the text images and converts them to scalable text. You can also convert a file to PDF Original Image with Hidden Text when you capture pages. This type of file has a picture of the pages in the foreground, with the scalable captured text behind it.

PDF Normal files are generally the smallest files, making them ideal for online distribution. PDF Original Image with Hidden Text files are recommended when you need to have searchable text but must keep the original scanned image of a page for legal or archival purposes.

On an Asian-language system, or on a nonnative system with the Asian languages installed, you can scan (but not capture) documents with Asian text.

–From the online Adobe Acrobat User Guide, Chapter 4

Cropping the file

Now you'll crop the captured file to a standard page size.

Note: You must capture a file before cropping or rotating it. If you capture a file after you crop or rotate it, you'll lose the changes you have made to the file.

1 Click the Fit in Window button (🔳).

Look at the page status bar. Notice that the page size is 9-by-11 inches. You'll crop the page to standard letter size, 8.5-by-11 inches.

2 Choose Document > Crop Pages.

3 In the Crop Pages dialog box, enter **0.25** for both Left and Right, and click OK. If needed, click OK again to the confirmation message to crop the page.

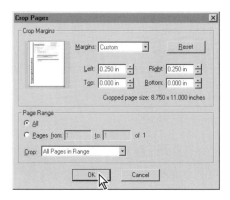

4 Choose File > Save to save the Fax1.pdf file.

Correcting suspects

The Capture Pages command converts a bitmap text image into its equivalent text characters. If Acrobat suspects that it has not recognized a word correctly, it displays the bitmap image for the word in the document and hides its best guess for the word behind the bitmap. You can view these *suspect* words in the captured document.

Showing suspects

Choose Tools > Paper Capture > Show Capture Suspects.

The suspect words appear highlighted in the document. Next, you'll examine each suspect and correct or accept Acrobat's best guess for the word.

Correcting suspects

1 Choose Tools > Paper Capture > Find First Suspect.

The original bitmap word appears enlarged in the Capture Suspect window, and Acrobat's best guess for the word appears highlighted in the document. You can correct a suspect word by typing in the desired characters, or you can accept Acrobat's best guess for the word.

2 If needed, click Accept & Next until you arrive at the suspected word "office." If needed, zoom in on the document page to view Acrobat's best guess for the suspect.

Since Acrobat's guess is obviously wrong, you'll type in the correct word.

3 Type **offices** on the keyboard. Notice that the word is updated in the document as you type. Then click Accept (Windows) or Accept & Next (Mac OS) to convert the image text to the word you just typed.

4 Choose File > Save As, make sure that Optimized is selected, and save Fax1.pdf in the Lesson10 folder. Click Yes (Windows) or Replace (Mac OS) to confirm replacing the file. The Save As command lets you save a smaller, optimized version of your finished file.

5 Choose File > Close to close the file.

If you are working in Mac OS, skip to the review questions at the end of the lesson. If you are working in Windows, proceed to the next section.

Converting a Web page to PDF (Windows)

In Windows, you can use Acrobat to download pages from the World Wide Web and convert them to PDF. You can define a page layout, set display options for fonts and other visual elements, and create bookmarks for Web pages that you convert to PDF.

Because captured Web pages are in PDF, you can easily save, distribute, and print them for shared or future use. Acrobat gives you the power to convert remote, minimally formatted files into local, fully formatted PDF documents that you can access at any time.

Note: To convert Web pages to PDF, Acrobat utilizes technology provided by Microsoft Internet Explorer. As a result, you must have Internet Explorer configured on your system, though it need not be set as your default browser. For example, you can capture Web pages with Netscape Navigator as your default browser, as long as Internet Explorer is installed on your system.

About PDF documents converted from Web pages

In most respects, a PDF document created from HTML Web pages is like any other PDF document. You can navigate through the document and add annotations and other enhancements to it. Any Weblinks on the pages are still active in PDF—just click a link to download the link's pages, and add them to the end of the document.

Depending on the options you select when downloading Web pages, a PDF document created from Web pages can display special structured bookmarks that retain Web information, such as the URLs for all links on the pages. You can use these structured bookmarks to navigate, to reorganize or delete pages, and to download more pages, and you can add more structured bookmarks to represent paragraphs, images, table cells, and other items on the pages.

Note that one "Web page" may correspond to more than one PDF page. This is because Acrobat divides long HTML pages into standard-size pages (depending on the PDF page layout settings) that can print predictably.

–From the online Adobe Acrobat User Guide, Chapter 5

Setting options for converting Web pages

You set options for capturing Web pages before you download the pages. Here, you'll set options for the structure and appearance of your captured pages.

1 Choose File > Open Web Page.

Note: *If the Open Web Page command does not appear under the File menu, choose File > Preferences > Web Capture, and deselect Consolidate Menu Items in Top-level Menu. When this option is selected, all commands pertaining to Web capture appear under a separate Web menu.*

2 Click Conversion Settings.

3 In the Conversion Settings dialog box, click the General tab.

4 Under General Settings for Generated PDF, select the following options:

• Create Bookmarks to New Content to create a structured bookmark for each downloaded Web page, using the page's HTML title tag as the bookmark name. Structured bookmarks help you organize and navigate your captured pages.

• Add PDF Structure to store a structure in the PDF file that corresponds to the HTML structure of the original Web pages.

• Put Headers and Footers on New Page to place a header with the Web page's title and a footer with the page's URL, page number in the downloaded set, and the date and time of download.

• Save Refresh Commands to save a list of all URLs in the PDF file for the purpose of refreshing pages.

5 Under Content-Type Specific Settings, select HTML and click Settings.

6 Click the Layout tab and look at the options available.

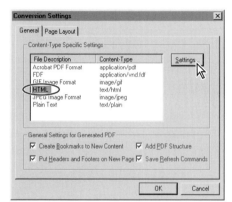

Conversion Settings dialog box

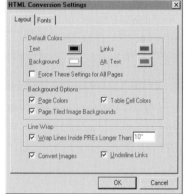

Layout options for HTML conversion

You can select colors for text, page backgrounds, links, and Alt text (the text that replaces an image on a Web page when the image is unavailable). You can also select background display options. For this lesson, you'll leave these options unchanged and proceed to selecting font options.

7 Click the Fonts tab.

8 Under Font for Body Text, click Choose Font.

9 In the Choose Font dialog box, choose a sans serif font from the Font list. (We chose Helvetica.) Choose 12 from the Size list, and then click OK.

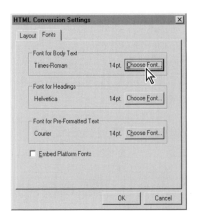

10 Under Font for Headings, click Choose Font.

11 In the Choose Font dialog box, choose a thick sans serif font from the Font list. (We chose Arial Black.) Choose 14 from the Size list.

12 Click OK, and click OK again to accept the HTML conversion settings.

13 In the Conversion Settings dialog box, click the Page Layout tab.

You can choose from standard page sizes in the Page Size pop-up list, or define a custom page size. You can also define margins and choose page orientation.

14 Under Margins, enter **0.5** for Left, Right, Top, and Bottom.

15 Click OK to accept the settings and return to the Open Web Page dialog box.

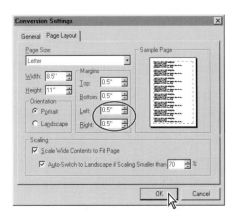
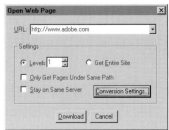

Tips for capturing Web pages

When you capture Web pages, it is important to remember that a Web site can have more than one level of pages. The opening page is the top level of the site, and any links on that page go to other pages at a second level. Links on the second-level pages go to pages at a third level, and so on. In addition, links may go to external sites (for instance, a link at a Web site on tourism may connect to a Web site for a travel agency). Most Web sites can be represented as a tree diagram that becomes broader as you move down the levels.

Be aware of the following when converting Web pages with Acrobat:

• Acrobat can download HTML pages, JPEG and GIF graphics (including the first frame of animated GIFs), text files, image maps, and password-secured areas from a Web site.

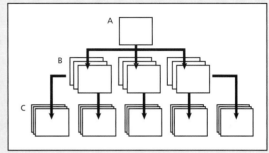

A. First level B. Second level C. Third level

• HTML pages can include tables, links, most types of frames (except certain complex frames, such as cascading stylesheets), background colors, text colors, and forms. HTML links are turned into Weblinks, and HTML forms are turned into PDF forms.

• JavaScript cannot be downloaded.

• To convert Japanese Web pages to PDF, you must have the Asian system files installed. This feature is not supported for the other Asian languages.

Important: *If you're converting Web sites to PDF, you need to be aware of the number and complexity of pages you may encounter when downloading more than one level at a time. In addition, downloading pages over a modem connection will usually take much longer than downloading them over a high-speed connection.*

–From the online Adobe Acrobat User Guide, Chapter 5

Converting a Web page with Acrobat

Now you'll enter a URL in the Open Web Page dialog box and capture some Web pages.

Note: *If you are working from within a company network, you may encounter a firewall that limits your access to external Web pages from Acrobat. For instructions on configuring your system to bypass a company firewall, consult your network administrator.*

1 If the Open Web Page dialog box is not open, choose File > Open Web Page.

2 For URL, enter the address of the Web site you'd like to capture. (We used the NASA Mars Global Surveyor site at http://www.jpl.nasa.gov/mgs/overvu/overview.html.)

You control the number of captured pages by specifying the levels of site hierarchy you wish to capture, starting from your entered URL. For example, the top level consists of the page corresponding to the specified URL; the second level consists of pages linked from the top-level page, and so on.

3 Select Levels, and enter **2** to retrieve two levels of pages in the Web site.

4 Select Only Get Pages Under Same Path to capture only pages that are subordinate to the URL you entered.

5 Select Stay on Same Server to download only pages on the same server as the URL you entered.

6 Click Download. The Download Status dialog box displays the status of the download in progress. When downloading and conversion are complete, the captured Web site appears in the Acrobat document window, with bookmarks in the Bookmark palette. Structured bookmark icons differ from the plain icons for regular bookmarks.

Specifying URL to be downloaded   *Downloading in progress*

The captured Web site is navigable and editable just like any other PDF document. Acrobat formats the pages to reflect the page-layout conversion settings, as well as the look of the original Web site. Some of the longer Web pages may be spread across multiple PDF pages to preserve the integrity of the page content.

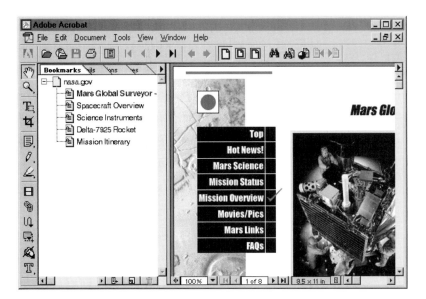

Now you'll use the Bookmarks palette to navigate to another captured page.

7 Select the hand tool (🕘), and click a bookmark in the Bookmarks palette.

The page corresponding to the bookmark appears in the Acrobat window.

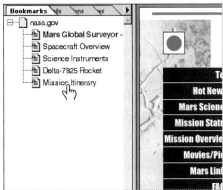

Clicking a structured bookmark . . .   *. . . links to the corresponding page.*

You can also click a Web link in the document that links to an unconverted page to download and convert that page to PDF. In order to convert linked pages to PDF, you must set Web Capture preferences to open Weblinks in Acrobat (the default setting) rather than in your default browser.

8 Choose File > Preferences > Web Capture.

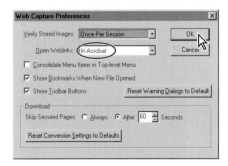

9 For Open Weblinks, choose In Acrobat. Then click OK.

10 Navigate through the captured Web site until you find a Weblink to an unconverted page, and click the link. (The pointer changes to a pointing finger with a plus sign when positioned over a Weblink.)

Note: If the Specify Weblink Behavior dialog box appears, make sure that Open Weblink to Acrobat is selected, and click OK.

The Download Status dialog box again displays the status of the download. When download and conversion are complete, the linked page appears in the Acrobat window, with a bookmark for the page added to the Bookmarks list.

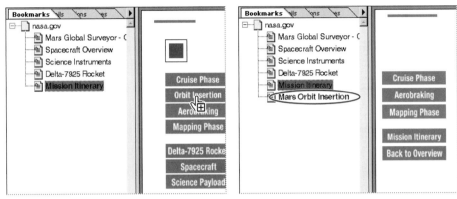

Clicking a Weblink . . .   *. . . converts the target page to PDF.*

11 Choose File > Save As, rename the file **Web1.pdf**, and save it in the Lesson10 folder. Then close the file.

Review questions

1 What are the properties of a PDF Image Only file? A PDF Normal file?

2 How do you make a scanned page searchable and editable in Acrobat?

3 What is a "suspect" word?

4 How do you control the number of Web pages captured by Acrobat?

5 How do you convert destinations of Web links automatically to PDF?

Review answers

1 In a PDF Image file, all the pictures and text are treated as images. You cannot edit the text using the touchup text tool or search the text using the Find or Search command. A PDF Normal file contains searchable and editable text.

2 To convert a scanned PDF Image file to a searchable, editable PDF Normal file, apply the Capture Pages command. This command uses optical character recognition to convert bitmap text to searchable, editable text.

3 A suspect is a word that has probably been recognized incorrectly by the Capture Pages command. Acrobat provides its best guess for the characters in the suspect word and lets you correct its mistakes.

4 You can control the number of captured Web pages by specifying the following options:

• The Levels option lets you specify how many levels in the site hierarchy you want to capture.

• The Only Get Pages Under Same Path option lets you download only pages that are subordinate to the specified URL.

• The Stay on Same Server option lets you download only pages that are stored on the same server as the specified URL.

5 To convert the destination of a Web link to PDF, first choose File > Preferences > Web Capture, and choose In Acrobat for Open Weblinks. Then click the Web link in the PDF file to convert the link's destination to PDF.

Lesson 11

Building a Searchable PDF Library and Catalog

Converting all of your electronic and paper publications to PDF lets you distribute and search large collections of documents quickly and easily. You can use Acrobat Catalog to create a full-text index of your PDF publications, and then use the Search command in Acrobat or Acrobat Reader to search the entire library almost instantly.

In this lesson, you'll learn how to do the following:

• Build an index using Acrobat Catalog.

• Use the Search command to locate information contained in the files indexed by Catalog.

• Set Search options.

• Refine a search.

• Use Document Info fields to conduct a search.

• Search for information using Boolean expressions.

• Choose Catalog options.

• Search for a phrase.

This lesson will take about an hour to complete.

If needed, remove the previous lesson folder from your hard drive, and copy the Lesson11 folder onto it.

Building an index

You use Acrobat Catalog to build full-text indexes of PDF document collections. A full-text index is a searchable database of all the text in a document or set of documents. Your documents should be complete in content and electronic features such as links, bookmarks, and form fields before you use Catalog to index them. In this lesson, you'll work with chapter files from the book, *Hawaii: The Big Island Revealed*, by Andrew Doughty and Harriett Friedman.

You'll create an index of these files and then search that index to find exciting information about what to do on your next trip to Hawaii.

1 From the desktop, open the Hawaii folder in the Lesson11 folder, located inside the Lessons folder within the AA4_CIB folder on your hard drive. Notice the files contained within this folder. All of the PDF files in this folder will be indexed by Catalog.

Before you index a document collection, you need to organize the documents on the disk drive or network server volume, make sure the filenames comply with cross-platform conventions, break large documents up into smaller files (to enhance search performance), and complete Document Info fields in each document, if appropriate. (See "Using Document Info fields to search" on page 265.)

2 Start Acrobat Catalog.

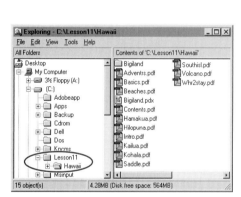

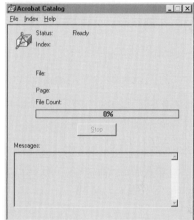

Files contained in Hawaii folder   *Acrobat Catalog*

3 In Mac OS, choose Edit > Preferences, make sure that Make Include/Exclude Folders DOS Compatible is deselected, and click OK.

4 Choose Index > New (Windows) or File > New (Mac OS). For Index Title, enter **Hawaii: The Big Island**.

The Index Description box provides users with more information about the documents included in the index.

5 Click inside the Index Description box, and enter information about the index you are building. (We entered "The Ultimate Guidebook. The most comprehensive, yet easy to use guidebook ever written for the Big Island.")

6 Under Include Directories, click Add.

Now you'll select the folder or folders that contain the documents to be indexed.

7 Click to select the Hawaii folder in the Lesson11 folder, and then click OK (Windows) or click Select "Hawaii" (Mac OS).

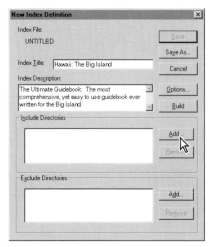

Entering index description   *Folder where you'll save results*

By default, Catalog indexes subdirectories, but you can exclude subdirectories using the Exclude Directories option. You can also add more than one directory to the index. For this lesson you'll index one directory.

8 Click Build.

9 Open the Hawaii folder so that you can save the index within that folder. Name the index **Guide.pdx**, and click Save. The file extension PDX identifies a file as an Acrobat index.

To make searches more efficient, you can save the index within the folder of information it's indexing. In Windows, the folder must be on the disk or network server volume where the documents to be indexed are stored. In Mac OS, the folder may be put on a different disk or network server volume from that of the indexed documents, if you don't plan to move the index and documents. (In that case, you would choose Edit > Preferences > Index > Allow Indexing on a Separate Drive.) Setting index options, such as Case Sensitive, Sounds Like, and Word Stemming, can also enhance how well an index can be searched. For more information, see "Creating a new index and choosing options" on page 268.

10 Exit or quit Catalog after "Index Build Successful" appears in the Catalog message window.

Structuring PDF collections for indexing

When you define and build an index, Catalog creates an index folder in which it puts an index definition file and a support folder. The index definition file has the same name as the index folder but has a .pdx extension. The folder has the same name as the PDX file and contains related folders that are automatically generated by Catalog.

Catalog places the PDX file (onlinepr.pdx in this example) and the support folder (onlinepr in this example) in the folder that contains the indexed document collection. The following guidelines apply:

• *The entire index—both the PDX file and the support folder—must be located inside a single folder.*

• *The indexed documents must reside on a single disk drive or network server volume, and the index must be on the same drive or volume as the indexed documents (Windows).*

Consider creating a separate PDF file for each chapter or section of a document. When you separate a document into parts and then search it, search performance is optimized.

–From the online Adobe Acrobat User Guide, Chapter 11

Searching an index

Now you'll use the Search command in Acrobat to perform searches of the PDF documents you just indexed with Catalog. You'll also use the Search command to limit and expand the definition of the term for which you are searching.

By searching a full-text index, you can quickly search a collection of PDF documents; in contrast, the Find command works only with a single PDF document and reads every word on every page, a much slower process.

For information on the Find command, see "Finding words in PDF documents" in Chapter 1 of the online Adobe Acrobat User Guide.

1 Start Acrobat.

2 Begin the search by using the Search button () in the command bar:

• In Windows, choose Window > Show Command Bar if the command bar is not visible. Then click the Search button. In Windows, the command bar is visible whenever Acrobat is open and Window > Show Command Bar is selected.

• In Mac OS, choose File > Open. Select Basics.pdf in the Hawaii folder, located inside the Lesson11 folder, and click Open. Then click the Search button. In Mac OS, a document must be open in Acrobat for the command bar to appear. (You open the Basics.pdf document only to view the command bar, not as part of the search.)

The Adobe Acrobat Search palette appears. First you'll select an index to search.

3 Click Indexes to display the Index Selection dialog box.

4 Click Add.

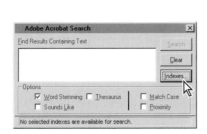

Adobe Acrobat Search palette

Index Selection dialog box lists available indexes

5 Select the Hawaii folder, located inside the Lesson11 folder, and click Open.

6 Select Guide.pdx, located inside the Hawaii folder, and click Open. The Hawaii: The Big Island index now appears under the list of available indexes.

7 Deselect any other indexes in the list by clicking the boxes next to them to clear the checkmark. Then click OK.

Acrobat searches only the selected index or indexes in the Available Indexes list. Here, you'll search only for entries in the Hawaii index.

To find information contained in the Hawaii index, you enter a word or phrase representing the desired topic.

8 In the Find Results Containing Text box, enter **hiking**.

9 For Options, select Word Stemming, and deselect all other search options.

The Word Stemming option tells Search to look also for words that share the same word stem as "hiking," such as "hike" or "hiked."

[?] For detailed information on each search option, see "Setting the search options" in Chapter 12 of the online Adobe Acrobat User Guide.

10 Click Search.

Looking at the Search Results list

The Search Results palette lists the documents that contain the word or words you searched for. The palette also displays how many documents were searched and how many were found to contain the words. In this example, 13 documents were searched, with 11 containing variations of the word "hiking."

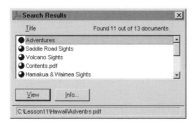

The documents are listed by relative ranking—documents with solid circles have more occurrences of the search words relative to the other documents in the list.

Acrobat Search uses five icons to indicate a document's relevance ranking:

Relevance ranking from most (solid circle) to least (empty circle)

If needed, use the scroll bar or resize the Search Results palette to view the entire list. You can open any of the documents in the list and view the highlighted search words.

1 Select the Adventures entry at the top of the list, and click View to display the corresponding document. If needed, click the Fit in Window button ( ) to view the entire document page.

Notice the highlighted occurrences of the word "hike." Because the Adventures document contains many occurrences of the searched word, it is ranked near the top of the Search Results list. If desired, use the zoom-in tool ($\mathcal{Q}$) to magnify a section in which "hike" is highlighted.

> **MAUNA ULU CRATER**
> This short hike is no
> frightened or the faint
> Ulu erupted between 1
> When it was all over, it
> maw 400 feet deep and
> (That's a guess—it get
> time.) This crater is acc
> minute hike from Chain
> in Hawai'i Volcanoes Na
> map on following page

2 Click the Search Results button (⊞) to redisplay the Search Results list. If needed, drag the Search Results list by its title bar to reposition the list so that it doesn't obscure the document.

3 Scroll to the bottom of the list, and double-click Kohala Sights to open that document. If needed, click the Fit in Window button to view the highlighted occurrence of "hiking."

The Kohala Sights document is ranked at the bottom of the Search Results list because it has fewer occurrences of the searched word than the other files in the list.

4 Choose File > Close to close the Kohala Sights document.

Narrowing the search

To make searching more effective, you should define your search criteria as much as possible. So far, you have found 11 documents that contain some information about hiking on the island of Hawaii. Now you'll refine your search to list only those documents that contain information about hiking near volcanoes.

1 Click the Search button.

2 In the Find Results Containing Text box, after "hiking," enter the words **and volcanoes**.

3 For Options, deselect Word Stemming to search only for the specific words you entered.

You are about to do a refined search. A refined search tells Search to look only at the documents in your current results list and to apply the new search criteria (instead of searching the index completely from scratch).

4 Hold down Ctrl (Windows) or Option (Mac OS) to change the Search button in the dialog box to Refine, and click Refine.

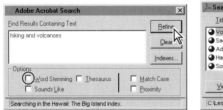
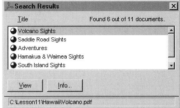

Word Stemming option deselected   *Results of refined search*

Notice that 6 documents out of the 11 in the last Search Results list meet the new search criteria. Using very specific search criteria helps you quickly identify which documents, if any, contain the information for which you are looking.

Also note that you've eliminated five documents with this search, but that the ranking of the remaining six documents is very close.

5 Close the Search Results palette.

Affecting the ranking order

You need to know which, if any, of the six listed documents is the best candidate for information about hiking near volcanoes. You can affect the relative ranking order by using any of the options displayed in the Adobe Acrobat Search dialog box.

1 Click the Search button (🔍) in the command bar.

2 For Options, select Proximity. This option finds documents in which the search words occur within three pages of each other. If the words are more than three pages apart, the search criteria aren't met and the document won't be listed in the Search Results window.

3 Hold down Ctrl (Windows) or Option (Mac OS) to make the Search button change to Refine, and click Refine.

Notice that the Search Results list has narrowed the field to three documents with very different relative rankings.

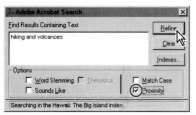

Refining search to narrow results   *Result*

4 Select Volcano Sights in the list and click View, or double-click Volcano Sights. To view the whole document page, click the Fit in Window button.

Notice that nearby occurrences of "hiking" and "volcano" are highlighted. You can zoom in on the highlighted text to read the information.

5 Choose File > Close to close the document.

Using Document Info fields to search

In addition to conducting a search based on specific words, you can search a collection of documents using any one of the Document Info fields. In this section, you'll search for documents that have a specific entry in their Subject fields.

First, you'll make sure that the Adobe Acrobat Search dialog box displays Document Info fields.

1 Choose File > Preferences > Search to display the Acrobat Search Preferences dialog box.

2 For Query, select Show Fields, and click OK.

3 Click the Search button ( ) in the command bar.

The Adobe Acrobat Search dialog box now displays Document Info fields in which you can enter additional search information. For example, when creating an index for a document, you can enter relevant information in the Title, Subject, and Keywords fields to make a search more efficient. Users can then search for this specific information.

4 If needed, click Clear to clear the text and Document Info fields.

5 For Subject, enter **beaches**, and click Search. Three documents meet the search criteria.

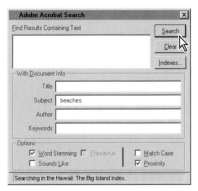

Entering search criteria   *Search results*

6 Double-click Beaches to open that document. To view the whole page, click the Fit in Window button ().

7 Click the Next Highlight (▸🖹) button to open the next document in the Search Results list. Once you click the Next Highlight button, the Previous Highlight (🖹◂) button becomes available. You use the Next Highlight and Previous Highlight buttons to browse through a Search Results list.

Note: *Alternatively, use the Next and Previous Documents commands in the Edit > Search menu to browse the search results.*

8 Choose File > Close to close the document.

Searching with Boolean expressions

You can use AND, OR, and NOT operators to build a logical expression (called a *Boolean expression*) that searches for words in a specific relation to each other. For example, earlier in this lesson you used the AND operator to build an expression that searched for occurrences of both "hiking" and "volcanoes" in the same document.

Using the OR operator

Use OR to find documents containing any of two or more search terms. Maybe you aren't sure what you want to do one day on your vacation—you could go diving or to Kailua.

1 Click the Search button (🔍) in the command bar.

2 Click Clear to clear the text and Document Info fields. Deselect all search options.

3 In the Find Results Containing Text box, enter **diving or Kailua.**

4 Click Search.

OR Boolean expression   Results

The Search Results palette lists nine documents that contain information about either diving or Kailua. You can open any of the documents to find information about one subject or the other, but not necessarily both.

5 Close the Search Results palette.

Using the AND operator

If you plan it right, you might be able to go diving and see Kailua in one day trip. Use AND to find documents containing two or more search terms.

1 Click the Search button (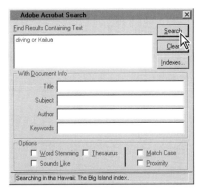) in the command bar.

2 Click Clear. Under Find Results Containing Text, enter **diving and Kailua.**

3 Click Search. Three documents contain information about both diving and Kailua.

4 Double-click Beaches to open that document. Zoom in on the bottom right quarter of the displayed pages to learn about a small cove near Kailua that is excellent for scuba diving.

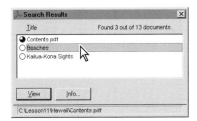

You can also search with the NOT Boolean operator, combine Boolean operators, and search with wildcard characters.

▣ For more information on searching with Boolean operators, see "Tips on defining search queries" in Chapter 12 of the online Adobe Acrobat User Guide.

5 Choose File > Close and close all open files (Windows) or close all open files except the Basics.pdf file (Mac OS).

Searching on the Web

An index created by Catalog is not searchable over the Web or a company intranet, but your documents can be indexed by a Web search engine that supports indexing PDF documents. You must first set up the search-engine software that can search PDF files on your Web server. Users can then run a search from your Web page.

Many companies develop search engines that can automatically and continuously update a search index of both PDF and HTML documents on a Web server. For a current list of these companies, see "Searching PDF Files on the Web" on the Acrobat Web page at http://www.adobe.com/acrobat/moreinfo, and click a specific link.

Choosing Catalog options

You can change the Catalog default options to minimize the size of an index as much as possible, for example, if you plan to post an index (and its associated files) on a network file server where space is at a premium.

In Windows, the defaults are fixed. You can change them for a particular definition, but not permanently. In Mac OS, you can change the defaults for most of the options in the Index Defaults group of preferences.

Creating a new index and choosing options

In this section, you'll create another index of the documents contained in the Hawaii folders and choose Catalog options to reduce the size of that index.

1 Start Acrobat Catalog.

2 Choose Index > New (Windows) or File > New (Mac OS).

3 For Index Title, enter **The Island**.

4 Click Options.

The Options dialog box lets you change Acrobat Catalog defaults for a particular index definition. You can exclude specified terms (called *stopwords*) and numbers, and turn off the Match Case, Sounds Like, and Word Stemming features. If the collection contains PDF files created by version 1.0 of Acrobat PDF Writer or Acrobat Distiller, you can select the Add IDs to Acrobat 1.0 PDF Files option to add unique IDs to the file to assist Search in locating a document.

Use the Words To Not Include In Index section to enter stopwords—words that you exclude from an index to minimize its file size. Stopwords usually are words that would not be entered as search terms, including articles such as "the" and "a", conjunctions such as "but" and "or", and prepositions such as "for" and "by."

Excluding stopwords from an index makes the index typically 10% to 15% smaller. However, searches won't find phrases (that is, words enclosed in quotation marks) that contain the stopwords. To help users, you should list the stopwords in the index description.

5 For Word, enter the following words, clicking Add after each entry: **the, The, and, And, a, A, but, But, or, Or, for, For, by, By.**

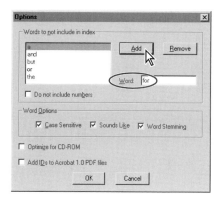

Note: If stopwords include words that are also used in Boolean expressions, such as "and" and "or," the Search feature won't be able to perform logical searches with those Boolean operators.

You can add up to 500 stopwords to an index. Stopwords can be up to 24 characters long. If you want to stop a word completely, you must enter all capitalization possibilities such as "the" and "The."

6 Select Do Not Include Numbers. This option excludes numbers such as phone numbers, part numbers, and address numbers from an index.

Excluding numbers from an index about Hawaii is appropriate because users of the index will not be looking for specific numbers. Excluding numbers from an index of an auto parts manual, where it is likely people will be searching for numbers, is not appropriate.

7 Select all of the Word Options. These options let you use some of the options in the Search dialog box.

[?] For more information on Word options, see "Setting the search options" in Chapter 12 of the online Adobe Acrobat User Guide.

8 Deselect Optimize for CD-ROM.

Intended for indexes placed on a CD, this option arranges index files for the fastest possible access. Additionally, this option makes it easier to modify Document Info fields or security settings after you have indexed a document by bypassing a default alert message.

9 Deselect Add IDs to Acrobat 1.0 PDF Files, because this collection doesn't contain any 1.0 PDF files. Click OK.

10 In the Index Definition dialog box next to the Include Directories box, click Add. Select the Hawaii folder, located in the Lesson11 folder, and then click OK (Windows) or click Select "Hawaii" (Mac OS).

11 In the Index Description text box, add information on what stopwords were included. (For example, we entered: "The following stopwords have been excluded from this index: the, The, and, And, a, A, but, But, or, Or, for, For, by, By.")

12 Click Build. Open the Hawaii folder so that you can save the index within that folder. Name the index **Island.pdx**, and click Save.

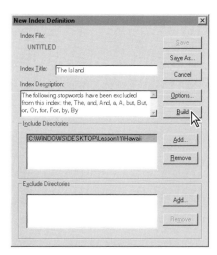

13 Exit or quit Catalog.

Comparing index sizes

Indexes consist of an index definition file (PDX) and a folder that contains the supporting data files that are needed to return search results. This folder must travel with the PDX file at all times. An index definition file also contains relative paths between the PDX file and the folders containing the indexed documents. These relative paths must also always be maintained to complete successful searches.

When you set options in Catalog to reduce the size of your index, you are actually reducing the size of the supporting data files and not the index definition file itself. Now you'll compare the sizes of the folders that hold the supporting data files to see how the folder size is reduced.

1 From the desktop, open the Hawaii folder, located in the Lesson11 folder. Among the files, you should see two folders, named Guide and Island.

2 Display the folder size:

• In Windows, right-click the Guide folder and choose Properties.

• In Mac OS, click once to select the Guide folder, and choose File > Get Info.

3 Write down the folder's size. In Mac OS, close the Get Info window.

4 Repeat steps 2 and 3 for the Island folder.

As you can see, the Island folder is smaller than the Guide folder. If these indexes were larger, you would see an even greater difference in the size of the folders.

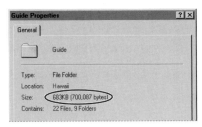 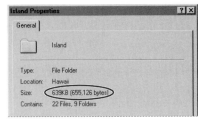

Guide folder size   *Island folder size*

Tips for updating indexes

You must update an index if documents are added to or removed from the collection, or if the hierarchy of the indexed folders has changed.

You should also consider updating an index when documents in the indexed document collection have changed, or data values for the new field are added because a new Document Info field has been defined.

You can reduce the index update time by following these guidelines:

• Don't support the Sounds Like, Case Sensitive, or Word Stemming search options.

• Use stopwords and exclude numbers.

• Install Acrobat Catalog on the system where the indexed documents are stored. If the program and documents are on different systems and it is feasible to move the documents temporarily, move them to the Catalog system for updating, then move them back.

–From the online Adobe Acrobat User Guide, Chapter 11

Searching for a phrase

By using the Search button in Acrobat or Reader, you can search for a phrase that contains two or more words, such as *Marriage license*. But when you search for a phrase containing words that might be confused with Boolean operators such as *and*, *or*, and *not*, or parentheses, you must enclose the phrase in quotation marks.

1 In Acrobat, click the Search button ( ) in the command bar.

2 Click Indexes.

3 If the *Hawaii: The Big Island* index created in this lesson is not in the available indexes list, click Add. Select Guide.pdx, located in the Hawaii folder inside the Lesson11 folder, and click Open.

Now you'll add the index created in this lesson with stopwords.

4 Click Add. Select Island.pdx, located in the Hawaii folder inside the Lesson11 folder, and click Open. *Hawaii: The Big Island* and *The Island* are listed as available indexes.

5 Deselect *The Island* so that the index remains in the list, but won't be searched. Click OK.

6 In the Find Results Containing Text box, enter **Mauna Loa and Mauna Kea**; then click Search. (These are the two biggest volcanoes on Hawaii.)

The Search Results palette lists eight documents that contain information about the two volcanoes. The search engine returned all documents that contained both Mauna Loa and Mauna Kea to the Search Results list, even if both names weren't in the same sentence. But what if you remember seeing something about the two volcanoes in the same sentence and want to find the phrase *Mauna Loa and Mauna Kea*? If that is the case, you need to add quotation marks.

7 Click the Search button in the command bar.

8 In the Find Results Containing Text box enter **"Mauna Loa and Mauna Kea"** (with quotation marks) and click Search.

Now the Search Results list returns two documents that contain the phrase "Mauna Loa and Mauna Kea."

9 Double-click Saddle Road Sights to view the information. Close the file when you have finished viewing it.

Seeing the effects of stopwords

As mentioned earlier, excluding certain words from an index results in a smaller index. But searching for phrases that contain stopwords will fail and index users won't be able to find phrases that contain the stopwords.

1 Click the Search button (![icon]) in the command bar.

2 In the Adobe Acrobat Search dialog box, click Indexes.

3 Deselect *Hawaii: The Big Island* so that the index remains in the list, but will not be searched.

4 Select *The Island*. Click OK.

5 In the Find Results Containing Text box enter **Mauna Loa and Mauna Kea** (no quotation marks) and click Search. The Search Results palette lists eight documents that contain information about these two volcanoes.

6 Click the Search button in the command bar.

7 Now enter **"Mauna Loa and Mauna Kea"** and click Search.

Remember that you excluded *and* from the index as a stopword. As a result, the current search found no documents that matched your query. The use of stopwords prevents you from locating phrases (as defined by quotation marks) containing words included as stopwords, even though these phrases exist in the document collection.

8 Click OK to close the alert box.

9 Exit or quit Acrobat.

This completes the lesson. You've learned how to build an index using Acrobat Catalog and how to perform various searches. For additional practice in building indexes from a series of PDF files, see Lesson 13, "Distributing PDF Documents."

Exploring on your own

If you're including PDF files on a CD, Adobe recommends that you also include an index to help your users access your information with ease and efficiency. You can practice building an index for a CD from PDF files.

For additional practice, you can update an index (called scheduling an index build). Scheduling index builds or updates lets you keep your indexes up to date and use system resources when they are usually not needed for other tasks. Catalog must be running to execute the build or update.

1 Start Catalog.

2 Choose Index > Schedule.

3 For each index you want to build, click Add, and select the name of the index-definition (PDX) file. (If you have about 6 MB of free RAM, you can add up to 128 indexes.)

For example, select Island.pdx in the Hawaii folder, located inside the Lesson11 folder.

4 Click Open.

5 Select a build time: Every, Once, or Continuously.

• If you select Once or Continuously, the index begins building or updating immediately.

• If you select Continuously, Catalog updates the indexes in the order they are listed in the Indices to Build list.

• If you select Every, enter a numeric time interval, and then choose Minutes, Hours, or Days from the menu. If you want to delay processing the selected indexes until a specified time, select Starting At, and use the Up and Down Arrow keys to select the time. Select Every for updates at regular intervals. Then enter a time interval in the format hh:mm:ss (for hours:minutes:seconds). If you want to delay processing the selected indexes until a specified time, select Starting At and use the arrow keys or type in a number to select the time.

Catalog updates are incremental, to minimize updating time and permit searching to go on uninterrupted during updates.

6 Click Start.

Note: To save the schedule information and enter Scheduled Build mode later, click Save in the Scheduled Builds dialog box.

7 Click Stop to halt the update process.

Review questions

1 How can you distinguish an index file from a PDF file?

2 What does the Search Results palette display?

3 How does the Word Stemming option expand your search results?

4 What key do you press to do a refined search?

5 Why should you enter Document Info field information in all your PDF documents?

6 Give two examples of Boolean expressions and what they do.

7 What are stopwords?

8 How can an index user find out which, if any, stopwords were excluded from an index?

9 When would you not include numbers in an index?

10 Can you schedule an index to build every 30 minutes?

11 When should you purge an index?

12 What is the difference between searching for a phrase with quotation marks and without quotation marks?

Review answers

1 In Acrobat, the file extension PDX identifies a file as an Acrobat index.

2 The Search Results palette lists the documents that contain the word or words you searched for, and displays how many documents were searched and how many were found to contain the words.

3 The Word Stemming option tells Search to look also for words that share the same word stem. For example, the word "hiking" also includes the word stems "hike" or "hiked."

4 A refined search is one in which Search looks only at the documents in your current results list and applies the new search criteria (instead of searching the index completely from scratch). To do a refined search, hold down Ctrl (Windows) or Option (Mac OS) to change the Search button in the dialog box to Refine.

5 To give users more ways to search for information in a PDF file, you should fill in the Title, Subject, and Keywords text boxes in the Document Info dialog box with the relevant information. Users can search for this specific information and use the title, subject, and keywords as they would index terms to refine their searches.

6 AND, NOT, and OR are Boolean expressions used in searches, as follows:

• AND combines two or more search terms.

• OR searches for any of two or more search terms.

• NOT excludes terms from searches.

7 Stopwords are words that you exclude from an index to minimize the size of the index file or reduce it by 10% to 15%. Stopwords are usually words that would not be entered as search terms; for example, articles such as "the" and "a," conjunctions such as "but" and "or," and prepositions such as "for" and "by."

8 Listing the stopwords in the index description helps users find out what stopwords were excluded from the index.

9 You should exclude numbers from an index that doesn't pertain specifically to numbered information, such as in a guide book or descriptive text. But you should include numbers in an index if users would be searching for numbers, for example, for technical specifications, addresses, part numbers, or phone numbers.

10 You can schedule an index to build at regular intervals, including every 30 minutes, or once only or continuously.

11 To compensate for incremental Catalog updates that increase the size of the index, you should purge and rebuild an index periodically to reclaim disk space and speed up searches.

12 Searching for a phrase enclosed in quotation marks finds the verbatim phase. Searching for a phrase without quotation marks finds the terms within close proximity in the document.

Lesson 12

Customizing PDF Output Quality

You control the output quality of your files by specifying appropriate compression and resampling options used by Acrobat Distiller to convert the files to PDF. In addition to default options designed to produce satisfactory results for common output needs, Distiller lets you customize individual conversion options for your specific needs.

In this lesson, you'll learn how to do the following:

• Choose Acrobat Distiller compression and resampling options.

• Compare the output of PDF files converted with different options.

• Set up watched folders for batch-processing of PDF files.

• Convert PostScript files to PDF using the drag-and-drop method.

This lesson will take approximately 50 minutes to complete.

If needed, remove the previous lesson folder from your hard drive, and copy the Lesson12 folder onto it.

Controlling PDF output quality

Acrobat Distiller produces PDF files that accurately preserve the look and content of the original document. Distiller also uses various methods to compress text, line art, and bitmap images so that they use less file space in the resulting PDF file. In this lesson, you'll learn how to choose and customize compression options to create the PDF quality and file size appropriate to your output needs.

In Lesson 3, "Creating PDF from Authoring Programs," you learned how to convert a source document directly to PDF using Distiller. Behind the scenes of this conversion process, Distiller creates an intermediate file in PostScript format before producing the final PDF file. For greater control over the creation of PDF files, you may want to create your own PostScript file from the source document and then process the PostScript file manually using Distiller. Creating PostScript files manually gives you greater control over page descriptions and compression options, and allows you to automate the creation of PDF files using watched folders. Although you'll not do so in this lesson, you can easily create PostScript files from many source applications.

For information on setting up your system to create PostScript files, see "Creating PostScript files with Distiller" in Chapter 2 of the online Adobe Acrobat User Guide.

About compression and resampling

Distiller lets you choose from a variety of file compression methods designed to reduce the file space used by color, grayscale, and monochrome images in your document. Which method you choose depends on the kind of images you are compressing.

In addition to choosing a compression method, you can *resample* bitmap images in your file to reduce the file size. A bitmap image consists of digital units called *pixels,* whose total number determines the file size. When you resample a bitmap image using Distiller, the information represented by several pixels in the image is combined to make a single larger pixel. This process is also called *downsampling* because it reduces the number of pixels in the image.

Using default compression settings

In this part of the lesson, you'll apply default compression settings to a sample file using Distiller's predefined ScreenOptimized, PrintOptimized, and PressOptimized job options. These options use preset compression methods to control the quality of the resulting PDF document for different distribution and printing needs.

Processing the color file with default settings

You'll convert a sample PostScript file to PDF three times, using a different predefined set of job options each time. You convert PostScript files to PDF by opening them in Acrobat Distiller.

1 Start Distiller.

2 Choose ScreenOptimized from the Job Options menu.

The ScreenOptimized setting creates output appropriate for on-screen display, such as on the World Wide Web.

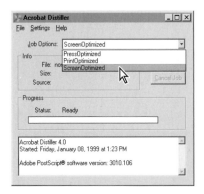

3 Choose File > Open. Select Color.ps in the Lesson12 folder, located inside the Lessons folder within the AA4_CIB folder on your hard drive, and click Open.

4 Name the resulting PDF file **Color1.pdf**, and save it in the Lesson12 folder. Notice that Distiller shows the status of the conversion process to PDF.

5 Repeat steps 2 through 4, but this time choose PrintOptimized from the Job Options menu, name the resulting PDF file **Color2.pdf**, and save it in the Lesson12 folder.

The PrintOptimized setting creates output appropriate for printing on a typical desktop laser printer.

6 Repeat steps 2 through 4, but this time choose PressOptimized from the Job Options menu, name the resulting PDF file **Color3.pdf**, and save it in the Lesson12 folder.

The PressOptimized setting creates output appropriate for printing to high-end presses.

Comparing the color files

Now you'll open the three PDF files in Acrobat and compare their quality and file size.

1 Start Acrobat.

2 Open the PDF files you just created: Color1.pdf, Color2.pdf, and Color3.pdf, located in the Lesson12 folder.

3 Choose Window > Tile > Vertically to display the files side by side. If needed, use the scroll bars to display the same area in each of the files.

At 100% magnification, all three images should look very similar.

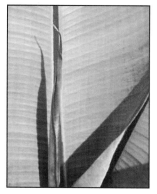
Color1.pdf

Color2.pdf

Color3.pdf

4 Use the magnification pop-up menu to display each image at 200% magnification. Scroll as needed so that you can see the same area in each of the files.

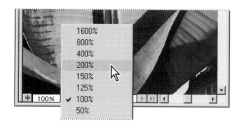

In comparison with the other images, Color1.pdf (the screen-optimized file) has a more jagged display quality. Since Color1.pdf is intended for low-resolution, on-screen use, it does not require as detailed a display quality. Screen-optimized files will also display more quickly than higher resolution images.

5 Now display Color2.pdf and Color3.pdf at 800% magnification, and scroll as needed to display the same area in the two files.

Notice that Color2.pdf (the print-optimized file) now has a coarser display quality than Color3.pdf (the press-optimized file). Since Color3.pdf is intended for high-resolution printing, it contains the most detailed image quality.

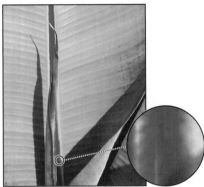

Color2.pdf   *Color3.pdf*

6 Choose Window > Close All to close all three files without saving them.

Now you'll compare the file sizes of the three PDF files.

7 In Windows, use Windows Explorer to open the Lesson12 folder, and note the sizes of the three files. In Mac OS, open the Lesson12 folder, shift-click both Color2.pdf and Color3.pdf, and choose Get Info from the File menu. Notice that Color1.pdf has the lowest image quality and the smallest file size, while Color3.pdf has the highest image quality and the largest file size.

PDF creation involves a trade-off between image quality and file compression. More compression means smaller file sizes but also coarser image quality, while finer image quality is achieved at the expense of larger file sizes. For information on the default job options, see "Creating a PDF file with Acrobat Distiller" on page 76.

Using custom compression settings

The default Distiller job options are designed to produce good results in most cases. However, you can set job options manually if you are dissatisfied with the results produced by the default settings or if you want to fine-tune the compression methods used by Distiller. In this part of the lesson, you'll practice applying custom compression and resampling settings to the color PostScript file.

Changing the job options

By combining the appropriate compression and downsampling job options, you can greatly reduce the file size of the PDF document without losing noticeable detail in the image. You'll apply your custom settings to the original high-resolution PostScript file Color.ps.

1 In Distiller, choose ScreenOptimized from the Job Options menu.

2 Choose Settings > Job Options, and click the Compression tab.

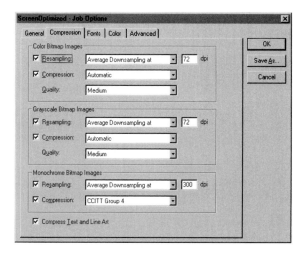

The default compression values associated with the ScreenOptimized setting are displayed. You already saved the file color1.pdf at 72 dots per inch (dpi) resolution. You'll now adjust several options to produce your own custom setting for optimizing on-screen PDF display.

3 In the Color Bitmap Images area, enter **144** for the resampling value.

This will downsample the original PostScript color image file down to a resolution of 144 dpi. Options you enter in the Color Bitmap Images section of the dialog box will affect only color images. Any changes you make to the grayscale or monochrome options will have no effect on color images. Distiller recognizes the type of PostScript image file, and applies the appropriate color, grayscale, or monochrome compression settings.

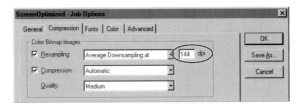

Now you'll save the custom setting that you have specified so that you can use it again in the future.

4 Click Save As. Name the custom setting **ScreenOptimized(1).joboptions,** and click Save.

Your custom setting will now be available from the Job Options menu, along with the default settings.

5 Click OK to exit the job options.

About methods of compression

Distiller applies ZIP compression to text and line art; ZIP or JPEG compression to color and grayscale bitmap images; and ZIP, CCITT Group 3 or 4, or Run Length compression to monochrome images.

• ZIP is a compression method that works well on images with large areas of single colors or repeating patterns, such as screen shots and simple images created with paint programs, and for black-and-white images that contain repeating patterns. Acrobat provides 4-bit and 8-bit ZIP compression options. If you use 4-bit ZIP compression with 4-bit images, or 8-bit ZIP with 4-bit or 8-bit images, the ZIP method is lossless, which means it does not remove data to reduce file size and so does not affect an image's quality. However, using 4-bit ZIP compression with 8-bit data can affect the quality, since data is lost.

• The JPEG (Joint Photographic Experts Group) compression method is suitable for grayscale or color images, such as continuous-tone photographs that contain more detail than can be reproduced on-screen or in print. JPEG is lossy, which means that it removes image data and may reduce image quality, but it attempts to reduce file size with the minimum loss of information. Because JPEG eliminates data, it can achieve much smaller file sizes than ZIP compression.

Acrobat provides five JPEG options, ranging from Maximum quality (the least compression and the smallest loss of data) to Minimum quality (the most compression and the greatest loss of data). The loss of detail that results from the Maximum and High quality settings are so slight that most people cannot tell an image has been compressed; at Minimum and Low, however, the image may become blocky and acquire a mosaic look. The Medium quality setting usually strikes the best balance in creating a compact file while still maintaining enough information to produce high-quality images.

• The CCITT (International Coordinating Committee for Telephony and Telegraphy) compression method is appropriate for black-and-white images made by paint programs and any images scanned with an image depth of 1 bit. CCITT is a lossless method.

Acrobat provides the CCITT Group 3 and Group 4 compression options. CCITT Group 4 is a general-purpose method that produces good compression for most types of monochrome images. CCITT Group 3, used by most fax machines, compresses monochrome bitmaps one row at a time.

• Run Length is a lossless compression option that produces the best results for images that contain large areas of solid white or black.

–From the online Adobe Acrobat User Guide, Chapter 3

Processing the color file with custom settings

Now you're ready to try out your new job option setting.

1 In Distiller, choose File > Open. Select Color.ps in the Lesson12 folder, located inside the Lessons folder within the AA4_CIB folder on your hard drive, and click Open.

2 Name the resulting PDF file **Color4.pdf**, and save it in the Lesson12 folder.

3 In Acrobat, open Color4.pdf and then open Color1.pdf, the other screen-optimized PDF file.

4 Choose Window > Tile > Vertically to display the files side by side, and view both files at 200% magnification. If needed, use the scroll bars to display the same area in each of the files.

Notice that Color4.pdf is smoother than Color1.pdf. Because Color4.pdf has a higher resolution (144 dpi rather than 72 dpi), it contains more pixel detail and finer image quality.

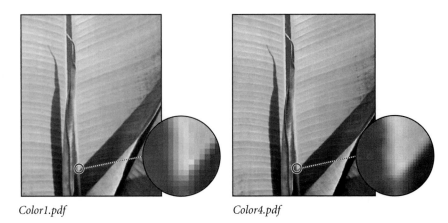

Color1.pdf   *Color4.pdf*

5 Choose Window > Close All to close the files without saving them.

6 In Windows Explorer (Windows), compare the file sizes of the two images. In Mac OS, use Get Info again, and notice that Color4.pdf is somewhat larger than Color1.pdf.

Processing grayscale and monochrome images

If you want, you can experiment with applying default compression and resampling settings to a grayscale and a monochrome PostScript image file. This part of the lesson is optional; if desired, you can skip to the next section to examine a gallery of different PDF output qualities.

1 Follow the instructions in "Processing the color file with default settings" on page 283, this time using the files Gray.ps and Mono.ps instead of Color.ps. These files are located in the Lesson12 folder.

2 Compare their quality and file sizes, the same as you did for the Color1.pdf, Color2.pdf, and Color3.pdf files in "Comparing the color files" on page 284.

Comparing color, grayscale, and monochrome images

Now you'll examine a gallery that shows the same area from each of the three images that you have worked on. The images have been converted with the ScreenOptimized job option in Distiller using a variety of compression and downsampling settings appropriate for display on different devices.

1 In Acrobat, choose File > Open. Select Compare.pdf in the Lesson12 folder, located inside the Lessons folder within the AA4_CIB folder on your hard drive, and click Open.

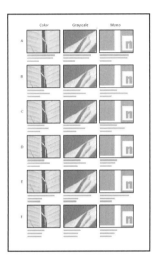

2 Zoom in as needed to compare detail between the different image versions.

You'll notice that images with larger file sizes do not necessarily yield better display quality. Downsampling a monochrome file may not significantly reduce its size. When converting your images to PDF, choose compression and resampling options that will give you adequate quality at the smallest file size possible.

Using watched folders

To automate the process of creating PDF files, you can set up a *watched folder* on your system or network server. When Distiller watches a folder, it periodically checks the folder for PostScript files. When a PostScript file is saved or copied into a watched folder, Distiller automatically converts the file to PDF and moves it to an Out folder.

In this part of the lesson, you'll set up a watched folder on your machine and use it to convert a PostScript file to PDF.

Setting up a watched folder

You'll configure Distiller to check a folder periodically for PostScript files, and to process these files for on-screen PDF output.

1 Create a folder on your desktop, and name it **Watch**.

2 In Distiller, choose ScreenOptimized from the Job Options menu.

3 Choose Settings > Watched Folders.

The Watched Folders dialog box lets you specify how frequently Distiller checks a watched folder and how to handle files after they are processed.

4 Click Add.

5 Select the Watch folder on your desktop, and click OK (Windows) or click Select "Watch" (Mac OS).

The Watch folder appears in the Watched Folder list.

6 Select Watch from the list. For Check Watched Folders Every, enter **10** to process PostScript files every 10 seconds. Under Post-Processing, choose Moved to "Out" Folder.

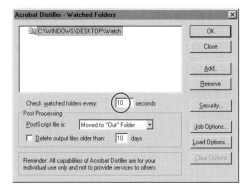

7 Click Job Options. You can set different options for each watched folder.

8 Click the Compression tab to display the compression and resampling options. Under Color Bitmap Images and Grayscale Bitmap Images, choose High for the compression quality. Then click OK.

9 Click OK again to close the Watched Folders dialog box.

Converting a file using a watched folder

Your new Watch folder has an In folder and an Out folder in it, as well as a job options file. You'll place a sample PostScript file in the In folder. When Distiller is finished processing the file, you'll retrieve the resulting PDF file from the Out folder.

1 In Windows Explorer (Windows) or the Finder (Mac OS), open the Watch folder.

2 Open the Lesson12 folder. Drag Drop.ps from the Lesson12 folder to the In folder within the Watch folder.

If Distiller is still visible, you should be able to see information about the processing in the Distiller window.

3 Open the Out folder within the Watch folder. You should now have a Drop.pdf file and a Drop.ps file in this folder.

4 Double-click Drop.pdf to view it in Acrobat.

5 When you are finished viewing the file, close it and drag it to the Lesson12 folder.

6 Exit or quit Acrobat.

Removing watched folders

If you no longer need Distiller to watch a particular folder, you should remove it from the list of watched folders. If you do not remove it from the list, Distiller will waste resources checking that folder and ultimately slow down the processing of other tasks.

If you haven't done so already, you should drag Drop.pdf to the Lesson12 folder.

1 In Distiller, choose Settings > Watched Folders.

2 Select Watch from the list.

3 Click Remove, and then click OK.

4 Exit or quit Distiller.

In this lesson, you learned several methods to convert PostScript files to PDF, and how to manage output quality. The method you use depends on your system resources and working habits. You may not always use the same settings. You should experiment to find the best solution for your needs.

Exploring on your own

Dragging one or more PostScript files onto the Acrobat Distiller window will launch Distiller and begin the conversion to PDF. You can also drag the file onto the Distiller icon.

By default, Distiller does not display the Save As dialog box when you use the drag-and-drop method. Instead, it places PDF files into the same folder as the source PostScript files and adds the extension .pdf or .PDF to the original filename. It also uses the current job options defined in Distiller.

1 In Windows Explorer (Windows) or the Finder (Mac OS), open the folder containing the PostScript file you want to process.

2 Drag the PostScript file from the source folder to the Distiller window or icon.

3 When Distiller is finished processing, double-click the resulting PDF file located in the source folder to view it in Acrobat.

Note: To display the Save As dialog box by using the drag-and-drop method, select the PostScript file, hold down Ctrl (Windows) or Option (Mac OS), and drag to the Distiller window.

Review questions

1 How do you specify different compression and resampling methods in Distiller?

2 What is resampling? What is downsampling?

3 How often does Distiller check a watched folder for a PostScript file?

4 When you drag and drop a PostScript file onto the Distiller window, where is the resulting PDF file saved?

Review answers

1 You can specify default compression and resampling methods by choosing a predefined setting (ScreenOptimized, PrintOptimized, PressOptimized) from the Job Options menu. You can also specify custom settings by choosing Settings > Job Options.

2 Resampling refers to reducing the number of pixels in an image to minimize the file size. Multiple pixels in the original image are combined to make a single, larger pixel that represents approximately the same image area. Downsampling is the same as resampling.

3 Distiller checks watched folders as frequently as you specify. Choose Settings > Watched Folders, and enter a value for Check Watched Folders Every.

4 When you drag and drop a PostScript file onto the Distiller window, the resulting PDF file is saved by default in the source folder containing the PostScript file.

Lesson 13

Distributing PDF Documents

Platform independence and small file sizes make PDF an attractive format in which to distribute your documents on the Web, an intranet, or a CD. In this lesson, you'll put the finishing touches on a collection of documents to finalize them for electronic distribution.

In this lesson, you'll learn how to do the following:

- Examine the issues associated with distributing PDF documents.

- Collect documents for distribution.

- Compare image quality and file size between two PDF documents.

- Examine sample *Welcome* documents.

- Add links to a *Welcome* document.

- Add document information to a PDF document.

- Index a document collection with Acrobat Catalog.

- Test PDF documents in a staging area.

- Examine a Web server administrator's checklist.

This lesson will take about 45 minutes to complete.

If needed, remove the previous lesson folder from your hard drive, and copy the Lesson13 folder onto it.

Distributing PDF documents

PDF's ability to faithfully maintain the formatting of a document while offering smaller file sizes, searchable text, printability, and integration with the most popular Web browsers, makes it a popular choice for distributing documents on the Web, company intranets, CDs, and via e-mail. Of course, you could simply create your PDF documents and send them out to the world without any more effort than printing. But with a little extra effort, you can make the information in your documents more accessible to your users and thereby make the documents more successful.

Collecting the documents to publish

The first step is to create or collect your PDF documents. In this project, you'll use documents from the Seybold 98 Internet Publishing archives to prepare, arrange, stage, and test for distribution. In this case, you can assume that the contents of the documents you are going to use are complete.

You should be at the point where you would normally print the final copy of those documents. But you must first check a few things—image quality, file size, and filenames—to ensure that the documents you distribute have the desired quality, are as efficient as possible, and work across computer platforms.

Checking image quality and file size

Making bitmap images small enough for network distribution or for mass storage on CD volumes generally requires compression—saving images in a way that uses less disk space.

For continuous-tone images such as photographs, JPEG Medium compression (the Acrobat Distiller and PDF Writer default) saves a lot of space with little loss of quality. You can choose different compression settings to fine-tune the balance between image quality and file size.

In this part of the lesson, you'll open and view an image that has had no compression applied to it, and then choose a compression setting in Distiller and process the PostScript version of that image. You'll then compare the image quality and file size of the original file with the compressed file.

1 Start Acrobat.

2 Choose File > Open. Select Image.pdf in the Lesson13 folder, located inside the Lessons folder within the AA4_CIB folder on your hard drive, and click Open. Then choose File > Save As, rename the file **Image1.pdf**, and save it in the Lesson13 folder.

3 Position the pointer on the triangle next to the Magnification pop-up menu in the status bar, and choose 400% to zoom in on the image.

Examine the image. No compression was applied to this file when it was converted to PDF.

Uncompressed Image1.pdf at 100% magnification

400% magnification

Choosing a compression setting

Now you'll choose a compression setting in Distiller and convert the PostScript version of this file to PDF again.

1 Start Acrobat Distiller.

2 In the Distiller window, choose Settings > Job Options, and click the General tab. For Compatibility, choose Acrobat 3.0 (the default setting).

？ For information on compatibility settings, see "Setting the General job options" in Chapter 3 of the online Adobe Acrobat User Guide.

3 Click the Compression tab.

4 In the Color Bitmap Images section, select the following options:

• In Windows, deselect Resampling; in Mac OS, deselect Average Downsampling At.

• Select Compression and choose Automatic.

• For Quality, choose Medium.

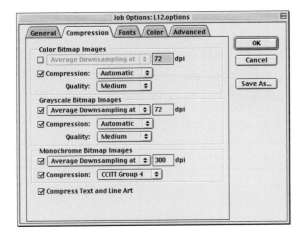

5 Click Save As. Name the Job Options settings **Image.options**, save the job options in the Settings folder, and click Save.

Before continuing, in Windows, you can choose to save Job Options settings; in Mac OS, you must save the settings.

6 Click OK.

The Automatic Compression option determines the best compression method for color and grayscale bitmap images (JPEG or ZIP) and applies the correct setting. For example, JPEG compression is used for images with smooth color changes, such as scanned photographs. ZIP compression is used for images with sharp color changes, such as screen shots of dialog boxes.

The image in this file has smooth color changes; therefore, JPEG Medium will be applied to this image.

🔲 For more information on compression settings, see "Applying compression and resampling to PDF files" in Chapter 3 of the online Adobe Acrobat User Guide.

Now you'll use Distiller to convert a version of the Image document that was saved as a PostScript file. Converting a file to PostScript and then using Distiller to convert it to PDF requires more manual steps than other conversion methods. But it gives you better control over the conversion settings by letting you choose specific resampling and compression methods for bitmap images in the documents; lets you maintain all the formatting, graphics, and photographic images from the original document; preserves EPS graphics; and lets you convert PostScript files to PDF in a batch process.

Now you'll compare the file that has had compression applied against the uncompressed file.

7 In Distiller, choose File > Open. Select Image.ps in the Lesson13 folder, located inside the Lessons folder within the AA4_CIB folder on your hard drive, and click Open. Rename the file **PSImage.pdf**, and save it in the Lesson13 folder.

Distiller converts the file, displaying information about the conversion.

8 Exit or quit Distiller.

Comparing the files in Adobe Acrobat

Now you'll compare the image quality and file size of the original file with the compressed file.

1 In Acrobat, choose File > Open. Select PSImage.pdf, which you just converted to PDF and saved in the Lesson13 folder, and click Open.

2 Choose Window > Tile > Vertically to compare Image1.pdf and PSImage.pdf. (Only Image1.pdf and PSImage.pdf should be open. If other files are open, close them, and choose Window > Tile > Vertically again.)

3 Choose 400% magnification from the status bar at the bottom of the PSImage.pdf document. Adjust your viewing area to view the same portion of the image in each file.

Uncompressed Image1.pdf   *Compressed PSImage.pdf*

As you can see, it's very difficult to detect any quality degradation in the PSImage.pdf file that had the default compression applied to it. But you can also see a significant difference in the file size—Image1.pdf is 1 MB and PSImage.pdf is 64K.

4 When you have finished viewing the files, choose Window > Close All.

Checking filenames

Adobe recommends that your filenames consist of one to eight characters (no spaces) followed by an extension (a period and from one to three characters) of your choice. Use .pdf as the file extension for your PDF documents. Most Web browsers, Web servers, and versions of Microsoft Windows have been configured to associate .pdf files with Adobe Acrobat, Acrobat Reader, or the Web Capture command. If properly configured, these applications will launch the appropriate program when PDF files are encountered.

You can view PDF documents in Web browsers compatible with Netscape Navigator 3.0 (or later) or Internet Explorer 3.0 (or later). The Web browser you use, the Web server, and several other factors determine how your system handles the PDF documents.

For more information on viewing PDF documents in Web browsers, see "Viewing PDF documents on the Web" in Chapter 1 of the online Adobe Acrobat User Guide.

Naming PDF files for cross-platform compatibility

When you name PDF documents and build indexes for cross-platform document collections, the safest approach is to observe MS-DOS® filenaming conventions. Although Acrobat has a sophisticated mapping filter for identifying formats of indexed documents, ambiguities caused when names created for one platform are mapped to usable names on another platform can slow down the searches. There may even be cases where this prevents documents from being located.

Consider the following guidelines when naming PDF files and documents:

• If you are using the Mac OS version of Catalog to build a cross-platform indexed document collection, and if you don't want to change long PDF filenames to MS-DOS filenames, select Make Include/Exclude Folders DOS Compatible in the Index group of preferences before you build your index. If you check this preference, you must use MS-DOS filenaming conventions for the folder names (8 digits with 3 digit extension); however, you do not have to use these conventions for the names of the files inside the folders.

• If you are using Mac OS with an OS/2® LAN Server, and if you want to be sure that the indexed files are searchable on all PC platforms, either configure LAN Server Macintosh (LSM) to enforce MS-DOS filenaming conventions, or index only FAT volumes. (HPFS volumes may contain unretrievable long filenames.)

• If you are indexing PDF documents with long filenames that will be truncated for Windows use, be consistent in your use of either the Windows or Mac OS version of Catalog to build or update the index.

• If you are creating documents that will be searched only by Macintosh users, do not use deeply nested folders or pathnames longer than 256 characters.

• If you are planning to deliver the document collection and index on an ISO 9660-formatted CD, you should use ISO 9660 filenames. With the Macintosh version of Catalog, check Log Compatibility Warnings in the Logging preferences to be warned of noncompliant filenames. For more information, see "Naming PDF documents" in Chapter 11 of the online Adobe Acrobat User Guide.

Important: *Avoid using extended characters, such as accented characters and some non-English characters, in the names of files and folders used for the index or the indexed files. The font used by Catalog does not support character codes 133 through 159.*

–From the online Adobe Acrobat User Guide, Chapter 11

Preparing a Welcome document

In many cases, you may want to distribute material in a collection of PDF documents rather than in a single document. Users may have difficulty, when first opening a CD or visiting a Web site, determining where to start or what's in the document collection. It often helps other users if you include a "welcome" PDF page in your collection, to point them in the right direction.

On the Web or an intranet, you might want to use an HTML Web page as your welcome document. The page typically gives an overview of the documents and provides links to specific places in them.

◯ *On CD volumes, you should also include a ReadMe text file that contains Acrobat Reader installation instructions and any necessary last-minute information about the CD.*

Adding links to a Welcome document

A *Welcome* document has been provided for you to use with this lesson. The Welcome document includes a table of contents for the Seybold 98 Internet Publishing newsletters. Now you'll open the document and add cross-document links to some of the documents in the Lesson13 folder.

1 In Acrobat, choose File > Open. Select Welcome.pdf in the Lesson13 folder, located inside the Lessons folder within the AA4_CIB folder, and click Open. Then choose File > Save As, rename the file **Welcome1.pdf**, and save it in the Lesson13 folder.

2 If desired, resize the Welcome1.pdf document.

Now you'll use the link tool to add some cross-document links.

3 Select the link tool (✋), and drag a link rectangle to enclose "January."

4 For Appearance Type, choose Invisible Rectangle.

5 For Action Type, choose Go to View.

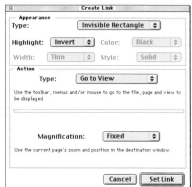

6 With the Create Link dialog box still open, choose File > Open, select ip0198.pdf in the Seybold Reports folder, located inside the Lesson13 folder, and click Open. The file opens in front of the Welcome1.pdf document.

7 In the Create Link dialog box, choose a magnification level with which you are comfortable, as follows:

• Fixed displays the destination at the magnification level and page position in effect when you create the bookmark or link. Use the zoom-in or zoom-out tool, the view buttons in the tool or status bar, or the scroll bar to adjust the view before accepting this setting.

• Fit View displays the visible portion of the current page as the destination. The magnification level and window size vary with monitor resolution.

• Fit in Window displays the current page in the destination window.

• Fit Width displays the width of the current page in the destination window.

• Fit Height displays the height of the current page in the destination window.

• Fit Visible displays the width of the visible contents of the current page in the destination window.

• Inherit Zoom displays the destination window at the magnification level the readers are using when they click the bookmark or link.

8 Click Set Link. The Welcome1.pdf document appears frontmost on-screen.

9 Using the hand tool, click the link to test it.

10 Using the link tool, add a second link by dragging a link rectangle to enclose "April." Then in the Create Link dialog box, do the following:

• For Appearance Type, choose Invisible Rectangle.

• For Action Type, choose Go to View.

• Choose File > Open, select ip0498.pdf in the Seybold Reports folder, located inside the Lesson13 folder, and click Open.

• Accept the magnification level you chose in step 7.

• Click Set Link.

11 Using the hand tool, click the link to test it.

12 Choose File > Save to save the Welcome1.pdf file.

13 Close all of the files except the Welcome1.pdf file. The files must be closed before they can be batch processed, which you'll do later in the lesson.

Adding Document Info data to PDF files

Document information screens provide users with basic information about a file and another way to index a file in a collection of documents. The Title, Subject, Author, and Keyword fields in the General Document Info dialog box can be entered and edited in Acrobat.

First, take a look at the information loaded in the Document Info fields for the Welcome1.pdf document.

1 Choose File > Document Info > General.

By default, the filename Welcome.ai appears in the Title field and the Subject, Author, and Keyword fields are empty. The other entries represent file information generated by the PDF creator.

Because many Web search engines use the Document Info fields to search for information and display results in a Search Results list, you should fill in Document Info fields for each document you distribute. The filename often is not an adequate description of the document. In addition, you should fill in the Document Info text boxes for all of your files if you plan to index your document collection with Acrobat Catalog. For more information on creating indexes with Acrobat Catalog, see Lesson 11, "Building a Searchable PDF Library and Catalog."

In this lesson, you'll enter Document Info information in only the Welcome1.pdf file. In a normal workflow, you should enter Document Info information for all files in a document collection.

2 In the General Info dialog box, fill in the following text boxes:

• Title. (We entered "Online Press Research Data.")

• Subject. (We entered "Internet Publishing.")

• Author. (For example, enter your name.)

• Keywords. (We entered "Seybold, Internet publishing, Online Press." Be sure to enter a comma and space between each keyword.)

3 Click OK.

4 Save the file and close it.

Once you have finished entering Document Info in all the files in your document collection, you are ready to stage, optimize, and index your documents.

Organizing the staging area

When you have collected all the PDF documents and the Acrobat Reader installer, set up a staging area (that is, a central location or folder) for the collection on a network file server. Then test the document links, bookmarks, actions, forms, and indexes on the server to make sure everything works the way you planned.

In a normal workflow, you should set up a staging area on a network file server if possible, and keep a copy of the original files in another location. Backup copies can save you from having to re-create files if, by chance, they are mistakenly deleted or corrupted. For this lesson, you'll use the Lesson13 folder as the staging area.

Organizing the documents in folders lends an intuitive organization and leads readers to the information they need. Before you publish your document collection, consider asking others to use the folder structure in your staging area to make sure your organization is easy to understand.

Optimizing PDF documents

Optimization consolidates and reorders your PDF documents, and in most cases, reduces their file size significantly. Acrobat removes duplicate background objects (text, line art, and images), replacing them with pointers to the first occurrences of those objects. Optimizing also reorders objects in the PDF file format for *page-at-a-time downloading* over the Internet. With page-at-a-time downloading (also called byte-serving), the Web server sends only the requested page of information to the user, not the entire PDF document. This is especially important with large documents, which can take a long time to download from the server.

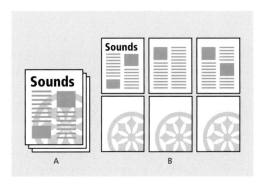
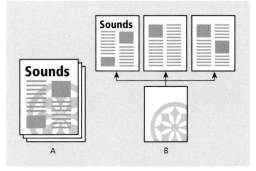

Not optimized
A. *Original page* **B.** *Repeated background*

Optimized
A. *Original page* **B.** *Repeated background*

You can optimize a file every time you choose the Save As command by selecting the Optimize option (selected by default), or you can optimize a collection of documents all at once by choosing File > Batch Process. In this section, you'll batch-optimize the files in the Lesson13 folder all at once.

1 In Acrobat, choose File > Batch Process.

2 Select the Lesson13 folder:

• In Windows, double-click to select the Lesson13 folder, and click OK.

• In Mac OS, click to select the Lesson13 folder, and click Select "Lesson13."

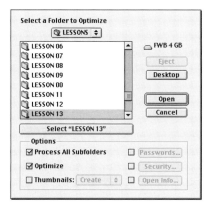

The Batch Processor Progress dialog box appears, with a message box and an optimization status bar displaying the progress of the optimization process.

3 When all files in the folder have been processed, click Close.

The files are almost ready for distribution.

Optimizing PDF documents for the Web

You can choose these additional options when batch processing:

• *Process All Subfolders also optimizes PDF documents in any subfolders in the selected folder.*

• *Thumbnails creates or deletes thumbnails in the documents. If you create or delete thumbnails for optimized documents, the documents are reoptimized.*

PDF documents that are already optimized, are read-only, require an open password, or are stored in a location for which you do not have write access are not optimized (unless you are creating or deleting thumbnails in optimized files). The Optimize.log file, located in the folder that contains the optimized documents, lists any documents that were not optimized in the process.

To stop the batch optimization process:

Click Stop in the Batch Processor Progress dialog box. The process stops after the document currently being optimized has been completed (which may take some time). Any documents processed before you click Stop are already optimized.

To find out if a PDF document has been optimized:

Choose File > Document Info > General, and look at the Optimized option.

–From the online Acrobat User Guide, Chapter 13

Indexing your document collection

If your document collection will be distributed on a CD, you should index the collection using Acrobat Catalog so that users can search the documents quickly. However, an index created by Catalog is not searchable over the World Wide Web or a company intranet. To make your PDF documents searchable over the Web or your intranet, they must be indexed by a Web search engine that supports indexing PDF documents. For a list of Web search engines that support PDF indexing, see www.adobe.com/proindex/acrobat/websearch.html.

Now you'll index the documents in the Lesson13 folder.

1 Start Acrobat Catalog.

2 In Mac OS, choose Edit > Preferences, make sure that Make Include/Exclude Folders DOS Compatible is deselected, and click OK.

3 In Catalog, choose Index > New (Windows) or File > New (Mac OS), and enter a title for the index. (We used "Online Press.")

4 Enter information about the index in the Index Description box. (We entered "Internet publishing newsletters, Seybold 1998.")

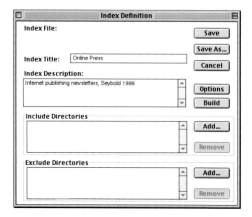

5 Click the Add button in the Include Directories box, and select the Lesson13 folder:

• In Windows, double-click to select the Lesson13 folder, and click OK.

• In Mac OS, click to select the Lesson13 folder, and click Select "Lesson13."

6 Click Build, and name the index **onlinepr.pdx**.

7 Open the Lesson13 folder, save the index inside that folder, and click Save.

8 When the message Index Build Successful appears in the Catalog message window, exit or quit Catalog.

Automatically loading an index

Before you can search an index, that index must be loaded in the available index list. You can load an index manually, or you can associate an index with a file so that the associated index is added automatically to the available index list whenever the file is opened.

In this section, you'll associate the Seybold 1998 Newsletters index with the Welcome1.pdf document, so that whenever the Welcome document is opened, the Seybold 1998 Newsletters index will automatically be available for searching.

1 Return to Acrobat.

2 Choose File > Open, select Welcome1.pdf in the Lesson13 folder, and click Open.

3 Click the Search button (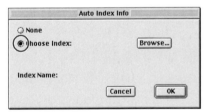) in the command bar, and click Indexes. Notice that the Online Press index is not listed as an available index.

4 Click OK.

5 Click the close box in the Acrobat Search dialog box.

6 Choose File > Document Info > Index.

7 Locate the index:

• In Windows, click Browse.

• In Mac OS, click Choose Index and then click Browse.

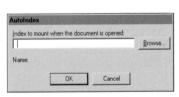

Click Browse and locate index (Windows).

Click Choose Index and Browse (Mac OS).

8 Select onlinepr.pdx, located in the Lesson13 folder. Click Open and then click OK.

Associating index with Welcome1.pdf file in Windows (left) and in Mac OS (right)

9 Choose File > Save As, make sure that Optimize is selected, and save Welcome1.pdf in the Lesson13 folder. Click Yes (Windows) or Replace (Mac OS) to confirm replacing the file. The Save As command lets you save a smaller, optimized version of the finished file.

10 Close the file.

Testing an associated index

Now you'll reopen Welcome1.pdf to see the index automatically associated with the file. It's a good idea to check that the associated index works as expected before distributing your documents.

1 Choose File > Open, and reopen the Welcome1.pdf file.

2 Click the Search button ( ) in the command bar.

3 In the Acrobat Search dialog box, click Indexes.

The Online Press index now appears as an available index in the Index Selection dialog box.

4 Click OK.

5 Enter **multimedia** in the Find Results Containing Text box, and click Search.

The Search Results palette lists 9 of 28 documents containing the term.

6 Select any of the documents in the list, and click View to view the file.

7 When you have finished viewing the file, close it.

Once you have completed all cross-document links and indexed your collection, it is important to maintain relative file relationships. (A relative file relationship keeps the same organization of a file in a folder, within the same hierarchy of folders and subfolders.) Moving a file outside of the folder in which a link was created or that Catalog indexed will alter the relative file relationship. This causes linking and searching to produce error messages instead of link destinations and highlighted search terms.

Adding Acrobat Reader installers

Acrobat Reader is available free of charge for distribution with your documents so that users can view your PDF documents. It's important either to include a copy of the Reader installers on your CD or to point Web users to the Reader installers on the Adobe Web site at www.adobe.com.

If you're including the Reader installers on a CD-ROM, include a ReadMe text file at the top level of the CD that describes how to install Reader and provides any last-minute information. If you're posting the Reader installers on a Web site, include the Reader installation instructions with the link to the downloadable software.

If you're distributing documents on the Web, you'll probably want to point users to the Adobe Web site for the downloadable Reader software.

You may make and distribute unlimited copies of Reader, including copies for commercial distribution, as long as each copy you make and distribute includes all of the following:

• The Acrobat Reader installer, exactly as provided by Adobe.

• The Acrobat Reader Electronic End User License Agreement.

• Copyright and other proprietary notices included in Acrobat Reader.

• The following attribution statement on any media and packaging that includes Reader:

Acrobat® Reader Copyright © 1987–1999 Adobe Systems Incorporated. All rights reserved. Adobe, the Adobe logo, Acrobat, and the Acrobat logo are trademarks of Adobe Systems Incorporated.

The Acrobat Reader Electronic End User License Agreement and proprietary notices are contained in the Reader installer program. You are expressly prohibited from modifying or creating your own installer for the Reader software. Details on the terms of use for the Reader products are found in the Acrobat Reader Electronic End User License Agreement presented during installation of each product.

A special "Includes Adobe Acrobat" logo is available from Adobe for use when distributing Reader. See the Adobe Web site for details.

Testing your document collection

When you have staged your documents and the Reader installers by organizing them in one location, it's important to test your document links, bookmarks, actions, forms, and indexes to ensure that everything works the way you planned.

In this lesson, you tested your document links and the associated index as you prepared the document collection. You can test documents in other collections that you're preparing by opening the documents and randomly testing any links, bookmarks, actions, and forms in the document, and by using the Search command to test any associated indexes.

Double-checking the checklist

You should double-check content, layout, artwork, and so forth of any document that you intend to distribute. As you have seen with this lesson, electronic documents add a few other items to your checklist. We have created a checklist to help you double-check the basics. Of course, feel free to add to the list to help you complete your own projects.

Checklist:

• Content is complete.

• Electronic enhancements, links and bookmarks, and so forth are complete.

• Document Info has been added to all files.

• Filenames have one to eight characters plus a .pdf extension, following the DOS naming conventions.

• Files are organized appropriately.

• Optimization is complete.

- Files are indexed (if intended for CD distribution).

- Files have been tested in staging area.

- The file structure is maintained when delivering your document collection to your Web server administrator or CD creator.

This completes the lesson. You have learned how to organize and prepare documents for conversion to PDF and electronic distribution. For additional practice in building indexes from a series of PDF files, see Lesson 11, "Building a Searchable PDF Library and Catalog."

Review questions

1 Describe three ways you can make a document collection more accessible to users.

2 Why is providing a Welcome document important?

3 Why is it recommended that you name your files with one to eight characters plus a .pdf extension?

4 What does optimization do to your PDF files?

5 Are you allowed to include the Acrobat Reader installers on CDs that you publish?

Review answers

1 You can make the information in a document collection more accessible to users in these ways:

• By compressing files to ensure that they're small enough for network distribution or for mass storage on CD volumes.

• By using filenames that work across computer platforms.

• By including a Welcome document with links to the document contents.

• By ensuring that the collection includes document information such as title, subject, and keywords.

• By organizing the files intuitively.

• By indexing the document collection.

• By optimizing the files for online use.

• By including the Acrobat Reader application for viewing the documents.

• By testing any electronic enhancements such as bookmarks, links, and forms, to make sure that they work as expected.

2 Users may have difficulty determining where to start when first opening a CD or visiting a Web site, or determining what's in the document collection. A Welcome PDF document can give users an overview of a document collection and can include links to specific places in the collection.

3 Naming files with one to eight characters (no spaces) plus a .pdf extension causes properly configured applications to launch the appropriate program when they encounter PDF files. Most Web browsers, Web servers, and versions of Microsoft Windows have been configured to associate .pdf files with Adobe Acrobat, Acrobat Reader, or the Web browser plug-in.

4 When Acrobat optimizes PDF documents, it consolidates background objects (text, line art, and images) to reduce the file size significantly, and reorders objects in the PDF file format for page-at-a-time downloading over the Internet. With page-at-a-time downloading (also called byte-serving), the Web server sends only the requested page of information to the user, not the entire PDF document.

5 Yes, Adobe allows you to distribute the Acrobat Reader installer and application with PDF documents that you publish.

Lesson 14

Adding Page Actions, Movies, and Sounds to PDF Files

By adding movie and sound clips, you can transform your PDF document into a multimedia experience. Movie and sound files can be integrated into PDF documents as playable clips and as link or bookmark actions.

In this lesson, you'll learn how to do the following:

• Assign a page action.

• Add a movie to a document, and set the movie's appearance and playback properties.

• Edit the playback properties of a movie clip.

• Add a link that plays a movie clip.

• Add a link that plays a sound clip.

This lesson will take about 20 minutes to complete.

If needed, remove the previous lesson folder from your hard drive, and copy the Lesson14 folder onto it.

Using movie and sound files

You can use media clips with your PDF documents in a variety of ways. The movie tool in Adobe Acrobat lets you add movies and sounds as playable clips in your document. You can also assign movies and sounds as actions that automatically play when you click a link, bookmark, or button, or when you open or close a page.

When you add a media clip to a PDF document using the movie tool, or when you add a movie clip as an action, the clip does not become part of the document; the document simply contains a pointer that references the media file. If you plan to distribute your PDF document, you must also include these sound or movie files along with the document. However, when you add a sound clip as an action, the sound clip does become part of the PDF file; in this case, you do not have to include the original sound file.

Although you can add movie and sound clips to a PDF document, you cannot create or edit the content of these files using any of the Acrobat programs. You must create your clip using a sound- or video-editing program first, and then save the file in a format that Acrobat can recognize.

For a list of suitable sound and movie formats, see "Integrating media clips into PDFs" in Chapter 10 of the online Adobe Acrobat User Guide.

Opening the work file

In this lesson, you'll work with an online Field Guide for Mount Rainier. The field guide is designed to provide park visitors with an interactive, multimedia tour of Mount Rainier's services, sights, geology, and history. Visitors can use links to follow their own path of interest through the document and view more detailed information about a desired topic.

1 Start Acrobat.

2 Choose File > Open. Select Geology.pdf in the Lesson14 folder, located inside the Lessons folder within the AA4_CIB folder on your hard drive, and click Open. Then choose File > Save As, rename the file **Geology1.pdf**, and save it in the Lesson14 folder.

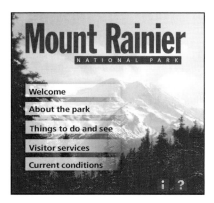

Using page actions

You can add sounds and movies as *page actions* to a PDF document. Page actions occur when a page is opened or closed. First, you'll open a page that has an action assigned to it; then you'll assign your own page action.

Activating a page action

Click About the Park and listen.

A sound plays when the "About the Park" page opens. This is an example of a page action. (You'll hear a sound if you have the proper software and hardware components installed.)

Assigning a page action

Now, you'll add a sound to the history contents page by setting a page action. You should be viewing page 2 of the field guide.

1 Click History.

2 Choose Document > Set Page Action.

3 Select Page Open in the Page Actions dialog box, and click Add.

4 In the Add an Action dialog box, choose Sound for the type of action and then click Select Sound.

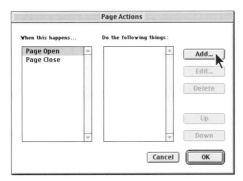 

Add action to occur when page opens.   *Specify type of action.*

5 Select the Sound2.wav (Windows) or Sound2.aif (Mac OS) file in the Lesson14 folder, and click Open.

6 Click Set Action, and then click OK.

You have just assigned a sound to play whenever this page is opened. Now you'll try it out.

7 Click the Next Page (▶) button.

8 Click the Previous Page (◀) button and listen for the sound.

9 Click the First Page (◀) button.

10 Select the page number in the status bar, type **3**, and press Enter or Return to go to page 3.

The sound plays again when you open the history page. From now on, you'll hear the sound whenever you open the page, regardless of the method you use to open it.

11 Choose File > Save to save the Geology1.pdf file.

Actions can also be assigned to occur when a page closes. And you can assign more than one action to occur and control the order in which they occur. To learn how to assign multiple actions to a button, see Lesson 15, "Enhancing a Multimedia Project."

Using movies in PDF files

You activate a movie in a PDF document much as you activate a link. A certain area on the page is designated as the active area for the movie; clicking in this hot spot plays the movie.

You'll practice activating an existing movie in the field guide and also adding a new movie to the document.

Playing a movie

You should be viewing page 3 of the field guide.

1 Click Geologic History to find out more about the park's natural formations.

The first geologic history screen appears.

2 If necessary, adjust the view magnification to display the entire page on-screen.

The topic window contains page navigation features for moving to the next screen. The Geologic History series spans six screens.

Notice that the page number on the page reads "1 of 6," while the page number in the status bar reads "4 of 11." When you create a custom page-numbering sequence in a document, you can expect this sequence to differ from the default page numbering shown in the status bar, which always regards the first page of a document as page 1. For information on changing the default page numbering shown in the status bar, see "Editing pages" on page 110.

3 Click the forward arrow at the bottom right corner of the page to go to screen 2 of the sequence (page 5 in the status bar). Then click the About Volcanoes graphic to follow its link.

4 Move the pointer over the Volcano Movie graphic. Notice that the pointer changes to a movie frame pointer.

5 Click the Volcano Movie graphic to show the movie clip.

Hand pointer indicates link to page.   *Movie frame pointer indicates link to movie.*

The movie plays inside a *floating window* that appears in front of the document temporarily. You can also have a movie play directly in the document page without a floating window.

6 Click RETURN in the page when you're finished viewing the movie to return to the Geologic History section.

Adding a movie

You'll add a movie about glaciers to the About Glaciers information screen and have it play directly inside its activation area in the document.

1 Click the forward arrow three times to go to screen 5 of the Geologic History sequence (page 8 in the status bar).

2 Click the About Glaciers graphic to view its information screen.

3 If necessary, click the Actual Size button (□) to return to a 100% view.

Because movies have a set number of pixels and therefore a set size, it's important to keep the magnification at 100% to prevent the added movie clip from being scaled inadvertently.

4 Select the movie tool (⊟) in the tool bar.

5 Click in the center of the black box to set the location for the movie. Be sure to click, not drag, with the movie tool.

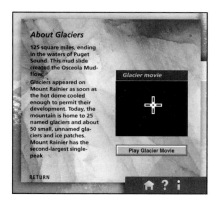

When you click to place a movie, the pixel size of the movie frame determines the activation area for the clip in the document. You can also drag with the movie tool to specify the activation area, but this is not advised, because the movie frame must then be stretched or compressed to fit into the specified area. This resizing often results in distortion and poor image quality.

When you're adding a movie using a floating window, however, you can drag freely with the movie tool to set the activation area. The size of a floating window is determined by its Movie Properties setting, not by the activation area you set by dragging.

6 Select Glacier.mov, located in the Lesson14 folder, and click Open.

The Movie Properties dialog box lets you set the appearance and playback behavior of the movie. You can also specify whether to place a poster (a still image of the first movie frame) in the document.

7 For Title, enter **Glacier.** For Movie Poster, choose Put Poster in Document.

8 Under Player Options, select Show Controller. For Mode, choose Repeat Play. Deselect Floating Window (Windows) or Use Floating Window (Mac OS).

Selecting Show Controller displays the controller bar, which lets the viewer stop, pause, and rewind the movie.

9 Under Border Appearance, choose Invisible for the Width. Then click OK.

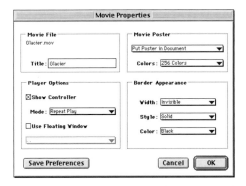

The movie poster appears in the document.

10 Move the pointer over the poster until the arrow (▶) appears, and drag the movie poster to position it inside the Glacier Movie box.

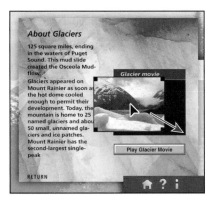

Drag to position new movie poster.

You can also resize the poster by dragging the corners of the poster. However, remember that resizing the movie area may result in a distorted image.

11 Select the hand tool (✋), and test the movie you just added. Use the buttons and the slider in the controller bar to pause, rewind, and advance through the movie.

You can stop a movie at any time by pressing Esc or clicking outside the movie image.

12 Choose File > Save to save the Geology1.pdf file.

Adding a link that plays a movie

In addition to linking different page views, links can be used to perform actions such as playing movie or sound clips. You must first add a movie to a document before you can create a link that activates it, and the link you create must be on the same page as the movie. In this part of the lesson, you'll create a new link that plays the glacier movie that you have already added.

1 Select the link tool (🔗), and drag a marquee around the Play Glacier Movie button.

2 In the Create Link dialog box, under Appearance, choose Invisible Rectangle for the type. Under Action, choose Movie for the type.

3 Click Select Movie. For Select Movie, choose Glacier. For Select Operation, choose Play. Then click OK.

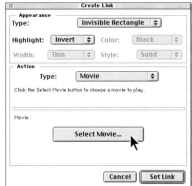

Drag marquee around button.   *Create link to Glacier movie.*

4 Click Set Link.

5 Use the hand tool to test your new link.

Editing movie properties

You can change the playback properties of a movie at any time.

1 Select the movie tool, and double-click within the glacier image to display the Movie Properties dialog box.

2 Under Player Options, deselect Show Controller. For Mode, choose Play Once Then Stop. Then click OK.

3 Select the hand tool, and click Play Glacier Movie to see the modified playback properties.

Tips for adding movie and sound clips

When adding movie and sound clips to PDF documents, consider the following suggestions:

• Use a graphic image for the activation area of the link to a movie. You can do this by inserting an image that you capture from the movie. (Capture the image using a movie authoring application.) Once the image is incorporated into the PDF document, draw a rectangle around it to specify the play area for the movie. Then deselect the Display Poster option from the Movie Properties dialog box, and select Use Floating Window.

• Use a miniature version of the movie poster to create an icon for the movie. The movie can play in a separate window. You can create the icon by adjusting the movie boundaries to less than full size, and then selecting Display Poster. The Use Floating Window option sets the movie to play in a separate window.

• Use a play action other than Play Once Then Stop when a controller bar is used with a clip. Selecting the controller bar stops the clip. Double-clicking inside the movie frame starts it playing again.

• Use movie and sound files that are located on your hard disk or on a CD-ROM with your PDF files. This ensures optimum performance. If you link your PDF documents to movie or sound files residing across a network or on the World Wide Web, performance decreases.

–From the online Adobe Acrobat User Guide, Chapter 10

Using sounds in a document

You can add sound to a PDF document as a page action, as an action associated with a link or a bookmark, or as a sound clip placed with the movie tool.

Activating an existing sound

You'll play a sound clip that was added to the About Mountains information screen using the movie tool.

1 Select the page number in the status bar, type **6**, and press Enter or Return to view the screen containing the About Mountains image.

2 Using the hand tool, move the pointer over the About Mountains image. Notice that the pointer turns into the movie frame pointer.

The movie frame pointer indicates that either a movie or sound clip can be activated.

3 Click the About Mountains image to play the sound that has been added to this location.

Adding a sound as a link action

Next, you'll create a link that plays a sound as an action.

1 Click the forward arrow on the page to view the screen that contains the About Mudflows image (page 4 of the Geologic history section).

You'll add a sound that will be activated by clicking the About Mudflows image.

2 Select the link tool in the tool bar.

3 Drag a marquee that surrounds the About Mudflows image.

4 In the Create Link dialog box, under Appearance, choose Invisible Rectangle for the type. For Highlight, choose None.

5 Under Action, choose Sound for the type, and then click Select Sound.

6 Select the Mud.wav (Windows) or Mud.aif (Mac OS) file in the Lesson14 folder, and click Open.

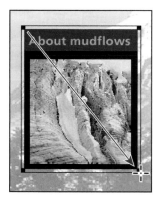

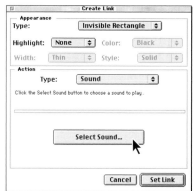

Drag marquee around graphic.   *Create link to Mud sound.*

7 Click Set Link.

8 Select the hand tool, and move the pointer over the About Mudflows graphic. Click the link to play the sound you just added.

9 Choose File > Save As, make sure that Optimize is selected, and save Geology1.pdf in the Lesson14 folder. Click Yes (Windows) or Replace (Mac OS) to confirm replacing the file. The Save As command lets you save a smaller, optimized version of your finished file.

10 Choose File > Close to close the document.

Review questions

1 What kinds of actions can you assign as page actions?

2 When using the movie tool to add a movie to a document, why should you click instead of drag?

3 What is a movie poster?

4 Name three ways in which you can add sound to a PDF document.

5 Can you edit the content of movie and sound clips from within Acrobat?

Review answers

1 You can assign Execute Menu Item, Go to View, Import Form Data, JavaScript, Movie, Open File, Read Article, Reset Form, Show/Hide Field, Sound, Submit Form, World Wide Web Link, and None actions to a page action.

2 If you drag with the movie tool, the movie is resized to fit inside the dragged area on the page, resulting in distorted image quality. Clicking with the movie tool lets you place a movie in its original size on the page.

3 A movie poster consists of a still image of the first movie frame. You can choose whether or not to display a movie poster in the activation area for a movie on the page.

4 You can add sound to a PDF document in these three ways: as a page action, as an action associated with a link or a bookmark, and as a sound clip placed with the movie tool.

5 No, you cannot edit the content of movie and sound clips from within Acrobat.

Lesson 15

Enhancing a Multimedia Project

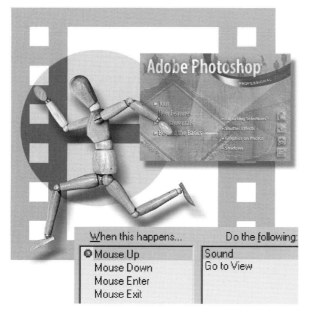

In this lesson, you'll use the skills learned in previous lessons to modify a document that acts as an interface to a software tutorial. You'll enhance the file with buttons, movies, actions, and sounds. Take time to experiment, and have fun.

In this lesson, you'll apply the skills you learned in the previous lessons to create a self-guiding tutorial that was designed to be used online. You'll do the following:

• Add buttons with multiple actions.

• Add a page action.

• Add a movie.

• Choose the opening view of a document.

This lesson will take about 35 minutes to complete.

If needed, remove the previous lesson folder from your hard drive, and copy the Lesson15 folder onto it.

Opening the work file

The document that you'll work with in this lesson is part of an actual Adobe Photoshop tutorial shell. It was created to provide users of the Photoshop tutorial with an interface to the instructional movies and step-by-step lessons.

You'll add some of the elements, such as buttons, that exist in the released version of the shell, and also add some other elements just for this lesson.

1 Start Acrobat.

2 Choose File > Open. Select Tutorial.pdf in the Lesson15 folder, located inside the Lessons folder within the AA4_CIB folder on your hard drive, and click Open. Then choose File > Save As, rename the file **Tutor1.pdf**, and save it in the Lesson15 folder.

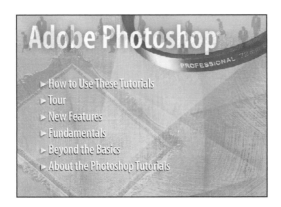

Note: Because there are links to movies in this file, you need to save this file in the Lesson15 folder to maintain the relative relationship between the PDF file and the movie files. If the relative file relationship is not maintained, you'll receive an error message and the movies will not play when activated by an action or clicked.

3 Take a moment to page through the document using the Next Page button (▶) in the command bar.

Notice the Home button that appears on every page except the first and last pages. This button has a Go to View action assigned to it that always returns the user to the home page.

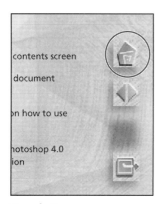

Home button

4 Click the Home button to return to the first page.

Adding a Go to View button

The Go to View action allows you to create a button that links to a page other than the first, last, next, or previous page. First, you create a button on the destination page, and then you duplicate it across the appropriate pages in the document. Then, in some cases, delete it from the destination page.

Note: The Go to View action assigned to a button can only be used to jump to a destination within the same file. If you want a button to open another file, use the Open File action.

In this section, you'll add a button that goes to the How to Use These Tutorials page of the document and then duplicate it across other pages.

1 Go to page 2. This page describes how to use the Photoshop tutorials.

2 Select the form tool (록) in the tool bar.

3 Choose View > Show Forms Grid, and then choose View > Snap to Forms Grid.

4 Move the pointer above the Quit field in the bottom right corner of the page, and drag to draw a rectangle about the same size as the other fields.

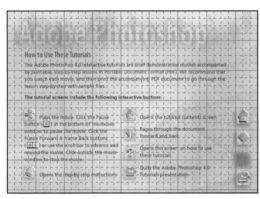
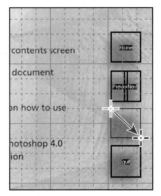

Normal view before selecting form tool   *Drag form tool to create field.*

5 In the Field Properties dialog box, type **How to** in the Name text box, and for Type, choose Button.

6 Click the Options tab. For Highlight, choose None, and for Layout, choose Icon only.

7 Click Select Icon, and then click Browse in the Select Appearance dialog box. Locate and select Qustmks.pdf in the Lesson15 folder, and click Open.

8 Use the scroll bar to view the available question mark icons, select one, and click OK.

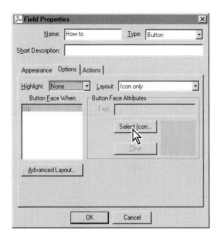

Create button field.   Select a button icon, and click OK.

9 Click the Appearance tab in the Field Properties dialog box. Deselect Border Color and Background Color. For Style, choose Solid.

10 Click the Actions tab. Select Mouse Up, and click Add.

11 In the Add an Action dialog box, choose Go to View for the Type. For Magnification, choose Fit View. Click Set Action.

12 Click OK to close the Field Properties dialog box.

Choose solid border with no added color
for button.   Go to View action is added to button.

13 Select the hand tool (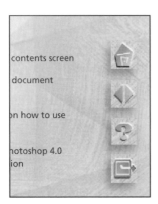) in the tool bar, and view the new button.

14 Choose View > Show Forms Grid to hide the grid. Then choose View > Snap to Forms Grid to deselect it.

Note: If you need to resize the button to match the size of the other buttons, select the form tool and click the button to select it. Then drag a handle to resize the button and drag the center to reposition it. Reselect the hand tool after resizing the button.

You have just added a button with an action to show the current view of page 2 when clicked. Next, you'll assign another action to play a sound when the button is clicked, and duplicate the button across the appropriate pages in the document.

Adding multiple actions to the button

You can assign more than one action to a button, and also sort the order in which those actions occur after assigning them.

1 Select the form tool and double-click the How to button you created.

2 Click the Actions tab in the Field Properties dialog box.

3 Select Mouse Up. Notice that the Go to View action is already listed in the Do the Following column.

4 Click Add. For Type, choose Sound, and then click Select Sound.

5 Locate and select one of the clicking sound files—click1.wav, click2.wav, or click3.wav (Windows) or click1.aiff, click2.aiff, or click3.aiff (Mac OS)—in the Lesson15 folder, and click Open. Then click Set Action.

Now two actions are listed in the Do the Following column—Go to View and Sound. When the button is clicked, the actions will activate in the order listed. But for this tutorial you want the user to hear the sound first, then go to the destination view. So, you'll reorder the actions.

6 Select the Sound entry in the Do the Following column, and click Up. Sound moves up in the list and will now activate before the Go to View action.

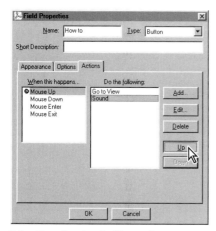

Select Sound action for How to button.

Move Sound up to top of list to change playing order.

7 Click OK.

Duplicating the button

Now that you have formatted the How To button, you'll duplicate it so that the users of this document can easily access the How to Use These Tutorials page from other pages in the document.

1 The How To button should still be selected. If it isn't, select the form tool, and click the button to select it. You know the button is selected when handles appear in the four corners of the button field.

2 Choose Tools > Forms > Fields > Duplicate.

3 In the Duplicate Field dialog box, select From and enter from pages **2** to **9**, and click OK. A duplicate How to button is added to the pages you specified in the same location on each page. Now you'll test the button.

Add button to pages 2 through 9.

4 Select the hand tool.

5 Click the Next Page button (▶) to go to page 3.

6 Click the How to button.

Notice that you hear the clicking sound before you go to the How to Use These Tutorials page. Duplicating buttons makes it easy to add navigational buttons across multiple pages.

7 Choose File > Save to save the Tutor1.pdf file.

Using actions for special effects

Acrobat allows you to add special effects to PDF documents. You can specify that a particular action will occur when a bookmark, link, or form field is selected, or when a page or form is viewed. For example, you can use links and bookmarks to jump to different locations in a document, but you can also use them to play movies, sound clips, execute commands from a menu, or other actions. Page actions are another way of activating special effects in a PDF document. For example, you can specify a movie or sound clip to play when a page is opened or closed.

Here is a list of the actions available in the Add an Action dialog box:

Execute Menu Item *Executes a specified menu command as the action. Click Edit Menu Item, select a menu item, and then click OK.*

Go to View *Jumps to a destination within the current document or in another PDF document. Go to the destination where you want the reader to end up, and set the position and magnification for the view. You can either navigate to the location in the current document or choose File > Open, select a PDF file, and then go to the destination.*

Import Form *Brings in form data from another file, and places it in the active form.*

JavaScript *Runs a specified JavaScript. The Edit button allows you to create or edit a JavaScript action that is activated when the bookmark, link, and so on is selected.*

Movie *Plays a specified QuickTime or AVI movie. Click Select Movie, and select the movie you want to play when the action is activated. The movie must already be added to the PDF document for you to be able to select it.*

Open File *Launches and opens a non-PDF file. Click Select File, locate the file, and click Select. If you are distributing a PDF file with a link to a non-PDF file, the reader needs the native application of the non-PDF file to open it successfully.*

Read Article *Follows an article thread in the active document or in another PDF document. To choose an article from the active document, click Select Article, select an article from the list, and click OK. To choose an article in another PDF document, make the destination file the active document, click Select Article, select an article from the list, and click OK.*

Reset Form *Clears previously entered data in a form. You can control the fields that are reset with the Select Fields dialog box.*

Show/Hide Field *Toggles between showing and hiding a field in a PDF document. Click Edit to select a field and whether to show or hide it.*

Sound *Plays a specified sound file. The sound will be embedded into the PDF document in a cross-platform format that will play in Windows and Mac OS. In Mac OS, you can add QuickTime, System 7 sound files, AIFF, Sound Mover (FSSD), and WAV files. In Windows, you can add AIF and WAV files.*

Submit Form *Sends the form data to a specified URL.*

World Wide Web Link *Jumps to a destination on the World Wide Web. You can use http, ftp, and mailto protocols to define your link.*

None *Specifies no action. This is often used for a bookmark representing a section heading that does not have a specific destination.*

–From the online Adobe Acrobat User Guide, Chapter 10

Combining buttons and page actions

To add some interesting effects to this tutorial shell, you'll add more buttons and page actions, and then combine them to get the final effect. First, you'll watch how combining buttons and page actions can work together.

1 Click the Next Page (▶) button to go to page 3.

2 Move the pointer over the arrow icon to the left of Shutter Effects. Notice that an image appears, and a sound plays.

3 Move the pointer away from the arrow, and the image disappears. The arrow icon has the Show/Hide Field and Sound actions assigned to it.

Position pointer over arrow to play actions.

Move pointer away to hide image.

4 Now click the Shutter Effects link to go to that topic. When the page opens, a short movie plays, then stops.

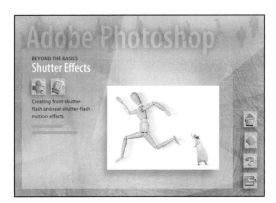

Movie plays when page is opened.

In the next section, you'll edit this file so that the Shadows topic has the same combination of multimedia effects as the Shutter Effects topic.

Creating an image to hide and show

Showing and hiding buttons can be a tricky procedure, but once mastered, it can add interest to any multimedia project. For example, if you don't want to clutter your page with images, but want to entice your users with previews, you can choose to hide the images until you anticipate a user would actually want to see them.

First, you'll create a button to contain an image of a sun for the Shadows topic.

1 Click the Go to Previous View button (◄) to go back to page 3.

2 Select the form tool (▦) in the tool bar. Notice the Mouse field that appears on this page. This field contains the image of the white mouse and running figure that appears when the Shutter Effects arrow icon is activated.

3 Drag to draw a rectangle in an open area on the page that is approximately the same size as the Mouse field. After you have formatted this new field, you'll move it on top of the Mouse field so that the image you are adding appears in the same place as the Shutter Effects image when activated.

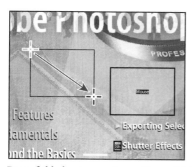

Draw field about same size as Mouse field.

4 In the Field Properties dialog box, type **Sun** in the Name text box. For Type, choose Button.

5 Click the Options tab. For Highlight, choose Push, and for Layout, choose Icon only. Select Up and then click Select Icon.

6 In the Select Appearance dialog box, click Browse, locate and select Shadow.pdf from the list of files in the Lesson15 folder, and click Open. Then click OK to close the Select Appearance dialog box.

7 Click the Appearance tab in the Field Properties dialog box. Make sure that Border Color and Background Color are not selected. For Style, choose Solid. Click OK.

8 Drag the Sun field on top of the Mouse field.

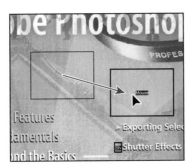

Position Sun field in front of Mouse field.

Adding sound and a Show/Hide Field action

Now you'll add another button field that will show and hide the Sun field, as well as play a sound when you move the pointer over an arrow icon.

1 Using the form tool, drag to draw a rectangle around the arrow icon next to the word "Shadows."

Draw field that covers arrow icon next to "Shadows."

2 In the Field Properties dialog box, type **Shadows** in the Name text box. For Type, choose Button.

This field will be represented by the image of the arrow on the page, so you don't need to set Button or Appearance options.

3 Click the Actions tab, select Mouse Enter, and click Add.

4 In the Add an Action dialog box, choose Show/Hide Field for Type, and click Edit.

5 Click Show, select Sun in the list, and click OK. Then click Set Action.

Now you'll add a sound to play.

6 With Mouse Enter still selected in the Field Properties dialog box, click Add.

7 For Type, choose Sound, and click Select Sound. Select Shadow.wav (Windows) or Shadow.aiff (Mac OS) and click Open. Then click Set Action.

Now you need to assign an action to hide the Sun image when the pointer is not over the arrow icon.

8 In the Field Properties dialog box, select Mouse Exit and click Add.

9 For Type, choose Show/Hide Field, and click Edit.

10 Click Hide, select Sun in the list, and click OK. Then click Set Action.

11 Click OK to close the Field Properties dialog box.

12 Select the hand tool (image) and move the pointer over the arrow icon next to "Shadows," and then move it away from the arrow to see the effect.

Move pointer over Show/Hide field—graphic is displayed and sound is played.

Move pointer away from Show/Hide field—graphic is hidden.

Adding a movie

To complete the combination of multimedia effects, you'll add a movie to the Shadows topic page that will play automatically when the page is displayed.

1 Click the Shadows link to go to that topic.

First, you'll insert the movie in front of the sun image.

2 Select the movie tool (▤) in the tool bar, and click once in the center of the sun image.

Use movie tool to add movie in front of sun image.

3 Locate and select Shadow2.mov from the list of files in the Lesson15 folder, and click Open.

4 In the Movie Properties dialog box, type **Shadow2** in the Title text box. For Movie Poster, choose Don't Show Poster.

5 Under Player Options, deselect Show Controller. For Mode, choose Play Once then Stop. Deselect Floating Window (Windows) or Use Floating Window (Mac OS). Under Border Appearance, for Width, choose Invisible. Click OK.

6 Drag the movie field to adjust its position over the sun image.

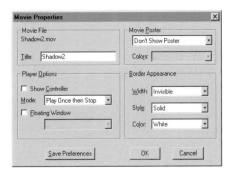

Now you'll set a page action to play the movie when the page is displayed.

7 Select the hand tool, and choose Document > Set Page Action.

8 In the Page Actions dialog box, select Page Open, and click Add.

9 In the Add an Action dialog box, choose Movie for Type, and click Select Movie. For Select Movie, choose Shadow2. For Select Operation, choose Play. Click OK and then click Set Action.

10 Click OK to close the Page Actions dialog box.

Now let's try it out.

11 Click the Go to Previous View button (◆).

12 Move the pointer over the arrow icon to the left of the word "Shadows" to see the effect you added earlier again.

13 Click the Shadows link. The short movie plays immediately after the page opens.

14 Choose File > Save to save the Tutor1.pdf file.

Choosing the opening view

The opening view of a document should be determined by the design, audience, and purpose of the document. The actual Photoshop tutorial shell was designed to teach users how to use Photoshop, not Acrobat. To focus the users on the content of the shell rather than on the program running it, the designers decided to limit the window elements with which a Photoshop user could interact. In this section, you'll learn how to choose opening view options, and see the effects of your choices.

Hiding the tool bar and window controls

You'll change the opening view of the tutorial shell so that the window resizes to fit the page, is centered in the screen, and does not show the command bar, tool bar, or window controls.

1 Choose File > Document Info > Open.

2 Select the following options:

• Resize Window to Initial Page

• Center Window on Screen

• Hide Toolbar

• Hide Window Controls

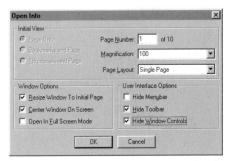

*Select Hide Toolbar to hide both command and
tool bar when document is opened.*

3 Click OK.

4 Choose File > Save As. Name the file **Tutor2.pdf**, and save it in the Lesson15 folder.

Because the changes only take effect when you open the file, you must close it and reopen it to see the changes.

5 Choose File > Close. Then choose File > Open and reopen the Tutor2.pdf file.

6 Notice the changes in the opening view of the file.

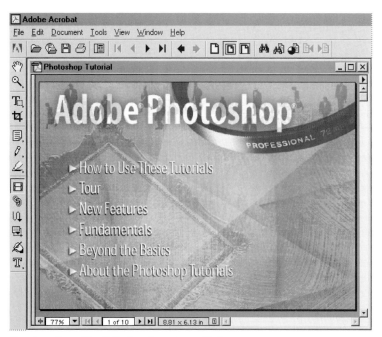

Opening view with all display elements enabled

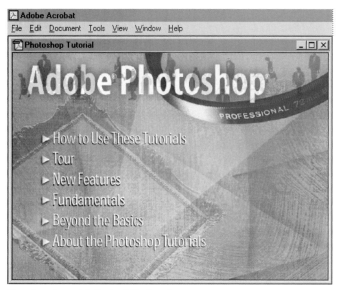

Opening view with limited display elements

Adding a quit button

To further distance a document from the program running it, you can disable the menu bar. But if you disable the menu bar, you need to add buttons that allow users to quit the file they are reading.

First, you'll add a quit button.

1 Press the Right Arrow key on your keyboard to go to the next page in the document, and then click the Quit button in the bottom right corner of the document to go to the Quit page.

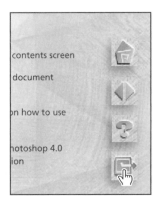

2 Choose Window > Show Tool Bar.

3 Select the form tool (⬚) in the tool bar and draw a rectangle around the word "Yes" on the page.

4 In the Field Properties dialog box, type **Yes** in the Name text box, and choose Button for the Type. Click the Actions tab, select Mouse Up, and click Add.

5 In the Add an Action dialog box, choose Execute Menu Item for the Type, and click Edit Menu Item.

6 In the Menu Selection dialog box, choose File > Exit (Windows) or File > Quit (Mac OS), and click OK.

7 Click Set Action and then click OK.

Adding a go to previous view button

Next, you'll add a go to previous view button to the Quit page.

1 Using the form tool, draw a rectangle around the word "No" on the page.

2 In the Field Properties dialog box, type **No** in the Name text box, and for Type, choose Button. Click the Actions tab, select Mouse Up, and click Add.

3 In the Add an Action dialog box, choose Execute Menu Item, and click Edit Menu Item.

4 In the Menu Selection dialog box, choose Document > Go Back and click OK.

5 Click Set Action and then click OK.

Hiding the menu bar

Now you'll choose the settings to hide the menu bar and reopen the document. With the tool bar, window controls, and menu bar all hidden, you'll use the buttons in the document to navigate.

1 Choose File > Document Info > Open.

2 Select Hide Menu Bar, and click OK.

3 Choose File > Save As, make sure that Optimize is selected, and save Tutor2.pdf in the Lesson15 folder. Click Yes (Windows) or Replace (Mac OS) to confirm replacing the file. The Save As command lets you save a smaller, optimized version of your finished file.

4 Before closing the document, select the hand tool.

The hand tool remains selected when you reopen the document even when the tool bar is not showing.

5 Choose File > Close.

6 Choose File > Open and reopen Tutor2.pdf. Notice that the menu bar is now hidden.

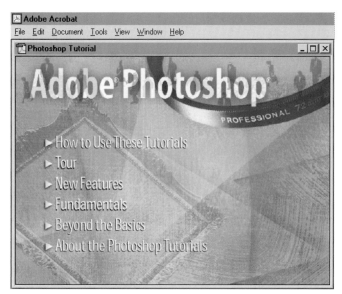

Opening view with menu bar visible

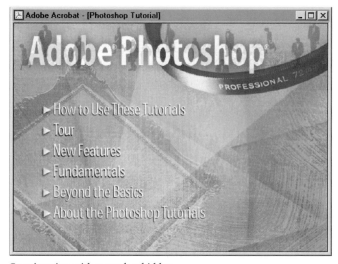

Opening view with menu bar hidden

7 Click the Beyond the Basics link, and click the Quit button in the bottom right corner of the page.

8 Click No. You return to the Beyond the Basics page.

9 If you wish to quit Acrobat, click the Quit button again and then click Yes.

Exploring on your own

Many types of presentations may improve when the document takes over the entire screen, and hides the menu bar, command bar, tool bar, and other window controls. This is useful for presentations that aren't interactive or that have all the controls and buttons built into the PDF pages.

To learn how to set up a full-screen presentation, you'll use the tutorial shell from this lesson. You'll set it up to work as a full-screen slide show on your computer with pages that turn automatically, as in a stand-alone kiosk display.

1 If necessary, start Acrobat and choose File > Open to open the Tutor2.pdf file you saved earlier in the Lesson15 folder.

2 Press F7 to display the menu bar, and choose File > Document Info > Open.

3 Under Window Options, select Open in Full Screen Mode and click OK.

The next time the file is opened, the image and a solid background will automatically fill the entire screen. (If you want the image to be larger, you may need to increase the magnification in the Open Info dialog box.)

4 Choose File > Preferences > Full Screen.

5 Under Navigation, select Advance Every 5 Seconds. Make sure that Escape Key Exits is selected.

Full-screen mode also lets you choose special effects for transitions between pages.

6 For Default Transition, choose Dissolve and then click OK.

7 Choose File > Save As, make sure that Optimize is selected, and save the file as **Tutor3.pdf** in the Lesson15 folder.

8 Choose File > Close.

9 Choose File > Open and reopen the Tutor3.pdf document.

10 To stop the slide show, press Esc. To stop the slide show and quit Acrobat, click the Quit button on one of the pages, and then click Yes.

Take some time to experiment with the actions that you can assign to buttons, links, bookmarks, and pages. You may find that actions add a new level of communication possibilities and fun to your PDF documents that you never thought possible.

Review questions

1 How do you create buttons for multiple pages that all go to the same page view when clicked?

2 When selected, what does the Hidden option on the Appearance tab of the Field Properties dialog box do?

3 What actions can you assign to a button?

4 To what other types of elements can you assign actions?

5 What happens to the display of a movie when you use the Floating Window option in the Movie Properties dialog box?

6 Is there a way to display the menu bar, command bar, or tool bar if they are hidden from view? (Hint: Keyboard shortcuts are listed for each in the Window menu.)

Review answers

1 First go to the page view that you want to be displayed when the buttons are clicked, and create a button field with a Go to View action set for the current page. Then duplicate the button field (choose Tools > Forms > Fields > Duplicate) and specify the pages onto which you want to copy the button. If you wish, delete the original button.

2 The Hidden option on the Appearance tab of the Field properties dialog box makes the field invisible until another action shows it.

3 You can assign the following actions to a button: Execute Menu Item, Go To View, Import Form Data, Movie, Open File, Read Article, Reset Form, Show/Hide Field, Sound, Submit Form, World Wide Web link, and None.

4 Besides buttons, you can assign actions to links, bookmarks, page actions, and other types of form fields.

5 The movie plays inside a floating window that appears in front of the document temporarily rather than on the document page.

6 Yes. To show the menu bar, press F7. To show the command bar, press F8. To show the tool bar, press F9.

Index

Production Notes

This Adobe Acrobat 4.0 Classroom in a Book was created electronically using Adobe Acrobat and Adobe FrameMaker. Art was produced using Adobe Illustrator, Adobe ImageReady®, Adobe PageMaker, and Adobe Photoshop. The Minion® and Frutiger* families of typefaces were used throughout the book.

All resemblance to real entities is unintended and purely coincidental.

Aesop's Fables retold by Adobe Systems Inc. from the public domain.

Use of the Jet Propulsion Laboratory Website was approved by Caltech/JPL.

Hawaii: The Big Island Revealed© Andrew Doughty and Harriett Friedman; used by permission.

Seybold Internet Publishing archives used by permission.

Images

Illustrations and photographic images are intended for use with the Adobe Acrobat 4.0 Classroom in a Book only.

Photography Credits

Dean Dapkus: Tour (Chez Maison).

Julieanne Kost: Tour (background; Dinh's Garden; Fragrant Harbor; Giuletta's; Ranch House Grill).

Lisa Milosevich: Lesson 12 (woman with computer; plant).

Ray Weisgerber and Steve Frayson: Lesson 9 (Mt. Rainier).

Adobe Typefaces Used

Adobe Myriad® Condensed Semibold and Adobe Garamond® were used throughout the book and CD.

Adobe Certified Expert Program

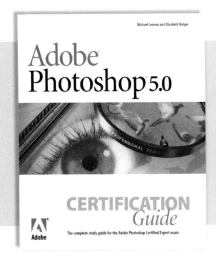

The Adobe Photoshop 5.0 Certification Guide contains comprehensive study material as well as Practice Proficiency Exams to help better prepare users for the Adobe Photoshop Proficiency Examination!

What is an ACE?

An Adobe Certified Expert is an individual who has passed an Adobe Product Proficiency Exam for a specific Adobe software product. Adobe Certified Experts are eligible to promote themselves to clients or employers as highly skilled, expert-level users of Adobe software. ACE certification is a recognized worldwide standard for excellence in Adobe software knowledge.

An Adobe Certified Training Provider (ACTP) is a certified teacher or trainer who has passed an Adobe Product Proficiency Exam. Training organizations that use ACTPs can become certified as well. Adobe promotes ACTPs to customers who need training.

ACE Benefits

When you become an ACE, you enjoy these special benefits:
• Professional recognition
• An ACE program certificate
• Use of the Adobe Certified Expert program logo

Additional benefits for ACTPs:

• Listing on the Adobe Web site
• Access to beta software releases when available
• *Classroom in a Book* in PDF

For information on the ACE and ACTP programs, go to partners.adobe.com, and look for Certified Training Programs under the Support section.